# KEYWORDS OF MOBILITY

## Worlds in Motion

Edited by Noel B. Salazar, University of Leuven, in collaboration with AnthroMob, the Anthropology and Mobility Network of the European Association of Social Anthropologists (EASA).

This transdisciplinary book series features empirically grounded studies from around the world that disentangle how people, objects, and ideas move across the planet. With a special focus on advancing theory as well as methodology, the series considers movement as both an object and a method of study.

Volume 1
KEYWORDS OF MOBILITY
Critical Engagements
Edited by Noel B. Salazar and Kiran Jayaram

# Keywords
# of Mobility
## Critical Engagements

Edited by

*Noel B. Salazar and Kiran Jayaram*

berghahn
NEW YORK • OXFORD
www.berghahnbooks.com

Published in 2016 by
Berghahn Books
www.berghahnbooks.com

**Library of Congress Cataloging-in-Publication Data**

Names: Salazar, Noel B., 1973– editor. | Jayaram, Kiran, editor.
Title: Keywords of mobility : critical engagements / edited by Noel B. Salazar & Kiran
    Jayaram.
Description: New York : Berghahn Books, 2016. | Series: Worlds in motion ;
    volume 1 | Includes bibliographical references and index.
Identifiers: LCCN 2015046288| ISBN 9781785331466 (hardback : alk. paper) |
    ISBN 9781785331473 (ebook)
Subjects: LCSH: Population geography.
Classification: LCC HB1951 .K48 2016 | DDC 304.8—dc23
LC record available at http://lccn.loc.gov/2015046288


**British Library Cataloguing in Publication Data**

A catalogue record for this book is
available from the British Library.


ISBN 978-1-78533-146-6 (hardback)
ISBN 978-1-78533-815-1 (paperback)
ISBN 978-1-78533-147-3 (ebook)

A ship is safe in harbor, but that's not what ships are for.

William G.T. Shedd

# Contents

# Keywords of Mobility
## What's in a Name?

*Noel B. Salazar*

As a concept, mobility captures the common impression that one's life-world is in flux, with not only people, but also cultures, objects, capital, businesses, services, diseases, media, images, information, and ideas circulating across (and even beyond) the planet. While history tells the story of human mobility, the scholarly literature is replete with metaphors attempting to describe (perceived) altered spatial and temporal movements: de-territorialization, reterritorialization, and scapes; time-space compression, distantiation, or punctuation; the network society and its space of flows; the death of distance and the acceleration of modern life; and nomadology. The academic interest in mobility goes hand in hand with theoretical approaches that reject a "sedentarist metaphysics" (Malkki 1992) in favor of a "nomadic metaphysics" (Cresswell 2006) and empirical studies on the most diverse kinds of mobilities (Adey et al. 2013), questioning earlier taken-for-granted correspondences between peoples, places, and cultures. The way the term is being used, mobility entails, in its coinage, much more than mere physical motion (Marzloff 2005). Rather, it is seen as movement infused with both self-ascribed and attributed meanings (Frello 2008). Put differently, "mobility can do little on its own until it is materialized through people, objects, words, and other embodied forms" (Chu 2010, 15). Importantly, mobility means different things to different people in differing social circumstances (Adey 2010).

Mobilities are central to the structuring of many people's lives. In many parts of the world, mobility is seen as an important way of belonging to today's society. We can identify many different types of "movers": tourists and pilgrims; migrants and refugees; diplomats, businesspeople, and those working for international organizations; missionaries, NGO workers, and people belonging to the most diverse transnational networks; students, teachers, and researchers; athletes and artists; soldiers and journalists; children and partners (and service personnel) accompanying the aforementioned people; and those in the traffic and transport industries who move people (including themselves) across the globe.

Mobility studies call attention to the myriad ways in which people become part, in highly unequal ways, of multiple translocal networks and linkages. Notwithstanding the many kinds of involuntary or forced movements (mostly linked to situations of conflict, persecution, or environmental threat), the currently dominant discourse across the globe links mobility to three positively valued characteristics: (1) the ability to move; (2) the ease or freedom of movement; and (3) the tendency to change easily or quickly (Glick Schiller and Salazar 2013; Salazar 2010b; Salazar and Smart 2011). This translates into three assumptions, partly influenced by capitalist ideologies, which have been widely spread via public discourses and images about globalization: (1) there is (increasing) mobility; (2) mobility is a self-evident phenomenon; and (3) movement generates positive change, often conceived of as an improvement for oneself and one's kin (e.g., in the case of migrants) or for nonrelated others (e.g., in the case of NGO workers).

Many people link voluntary geographical mobility almost automatically to some kind of symbolic "moving up," be it economic, social, or cultural. In other words, mobility is believed to be an indicator of the variable access to and accumulation of various types of capital (see Bourdieu 1986). As this edited volume illustrates, it is important to identify not only various forms of boundary-crossing movement but also the (re)production of socially shared meanings through diverse practices of mobility. Distinctions are made, which ultimately feed back into the production of the social through culturally inflected notions of mobility (e.g., the terms "local" versus "migrant"; Salazar 2010b). Transnational mobility, for instance, is often seen as endemic to globalization and as one of the most powerful stratifying factors, leading to a global hierarchy of movements (Bauman 1998). In other words, the movement of people and the various translocal connections may, and often do, create or reinforce difference and inequality, as well as blending or erasing such differences (Salazar 2010a).

Mobility—a complex assemblage of movement, imaginaries, and experience—is not only an object of study but also an analytical lens, promoted by those who talk about a *mobility turn* in social theory and who have proposed a *new mobilities paradigm* to reorient the ways in which we think about society. This mobility turn indicates a perceived transformation of the social sciences in response to the increasing importance of various forms of movement (Urry 2000; 2007). The new mobilities paradigm incorporates new ways of theorizing how people, objects, and ideas move around by looking at social phenomena through the lens of movement (Hannam, Sheller, and Urry 2006). It can be seen as a critique of both theories of sedentism and deterritorialization.

Influential theorists such as Anthony Giddens, Arjun Appadurai, Ulrich Beck, Manuel Castells, Bruno Latour, David Harvey, Zygmunt Bauman, and John Urry all conceive contemporary capitalism and globalization in terms of increasing numbers and varieties of mobility: the fluid, continuous (and often seamless) movement of people, ideas, and goods through and across space (but see Trouillot 2003 for a critique). Mobility appears self-evidently central to modernity as a key social process, "a relationship through which the world is lived and understood" (Adey 2010). People have come to "imagine that mobility is border crossing, as though borders came first, and mobility, second. The truth is more the other way around" (Ludden 2003, 1062). Considering mobility as a natural tendency in society naturalizes it as a fact of life and as a general principle that rarely needs further justification, making cosmopolitanism and reliance on mobility capital the norm (Nowicka and Rovisco 2009). However, any discourse used to discuss questions of mobility is inevitably value-laden (Bergmann and Sager 2008; Frello 2008).

Critical analyses of mobility focus attention on the political-economic processes by which people are bounded, emplaced, allowed, or forced to move (Cunningham and Heyman 2004; De Genova and Peutz 2010). Such studies show how mobility is materially grounded. The physical movement of people entails not only a measure of economic, social, and cultural mobility, but also a corresponding evolution of institutions and well-determined "circuits of human mobility" (Lindquist 2009, 7). Importantly, the substance of such circuits is "the movement of people (and money, goods, and news, but primarily people) as well as the relative immobility of people who do not travel the circuit" (Rockefeller 2010, 222). To assess the extent or nature of movement, or, indeed, even "observe" it sometimes, one needs to spend a lot of time studying things that stand still (or change at a much slower pace).

Despite all of the attention given to it over recent decades, some are of the opinion that "there is still a general failure, especially in the social sciences, to reflect on the meaning of mobility" (Papastergiadis 2010, 347). Recognizing that the mobilities the world witnesses today are not entirely new processes, what are we really talking about when we look at the current human condition through an analytical mobility lens? Deeply grounded in anthropology's long-term engagement with issues of mobility (Salazar 2013a), this book offers an in-depth conceptual reflection by analyzing some of the most influential keywords surrounding ideas of mobility.

## Keywords as an Analytical Approach

The origin of the notion *keyword* is sometimes traced to Michel Bréal's *Semantics: Studies in the Science of Meaning* (1964). This French philologist set out to determine the laws that govern changes in the meaning of words. It was only later that scholars began to turn their attention to the synchronic study of meaning too. In his seminal work *Keywords: A Vocabulary of Culture and Society* (1976), Raymond Williams explored the changing meanings and contexts of the pivotal terms used in discussions of culture (beginning with the notion of culture itself). In his introduction, he identified keywords "in two connected senses. They are significant, binding words in certain activities and their interpretation; they are significant, indicative words in certain forms of thought. Certain uses bound together certain ways of seeing culture and society" (15). The legacy of the groundbreaking work of Williams on the meaning construction of keywords lives on in the "Keywords Project," a collaborative research initiative of Jesus College, University of Cambridge, and the University of Pittsburgh (see http://keywords.pitt.edu/) and in the publication *Key Words: Journal of the Raymond Williams Society*.

Importantly, keywords are "essentially contested concepts" (Gallie 1956); that is, they never acquire a closed or final meaning (not even within one domain or discipline). The meaning of a keyword is never settled until it truly disappears from common use or its scholarly paradigm goes into decline. As keywords acquire new meanings, they do not shed old ones. Historically, keywords accumulate meanings, sometimes contradictory ones, and even when one is dominant, others remain available and can be reaffirmed. Moreover, keywords rarely shift their meaning in isolation but rather in conjunction with others. Revising *Keywords* himself for a second edition, which included twenty-one additional concepts, Williams (1985, 27) reaffirmed his "sense of the work as necessarily unfinished and incomplete." The sharing of a word across differing domains of thought and experience was often imperfect, he noted, but this very roughness and partiality indicated that the word brought something significant to discussions of "the central processes of our common life" (1985, 27).

Various scholars have played with the concept of keywords to clarify their theoretical framework. Jean Baudrillard's *Passwords* (2003) and Gilles

Deleuze's 1988–1989 televised *Abécédaire* (2011) are but two known examples. In August 2011, the Wenner-Gren journal, *Current Anthropology*, presented a set of articles about keywords in anthropology, namely *neoliberal agency, consumption, identity,* and *flow.* In the editorial introduction to the theme, Mark Aldenderfer (2011) reminded the reader that keywords are often multilayered. While some are "commonly encountered in everyday language," others have "special, more restricted meanings, such as is often the case in their scholarly use" (Aldenderfer 2011, 487). From an academic perspective, it is important "to identify the meanings the term has taken and to show how these meanings are transformed when new intellectual perspectives and paradigms make their appearance" (Aldenderfer 2011, 487). In the reply to his own contribution in *Current Anthropology*, David Graeber (2011) sketches the history that led to the special section. According to him, it was Lauren Leve's idea "to study those theoretical terms that were not, really, being debated or often, really, defined—and why" (Graeber 2011, 508).

A related methodology was also used by Joshua Barker and Johan Lindquist (2009) in their multi-authored essay "Figures of Indonesian Modernity," published in the Cornell-based journal *Indonesia.* Inspired by the work of Williams, they propose "key figures" as "particular sites that allow access to ideological formations and their contestations" (Barker and Lindquist 2009, 36). Such an approach offers an analytical perspective rather than a decisive theory. Interestingly, many of the figures covered in their article are directly related to mobility: the *TKW* (Tenaga Kerja Wanita), or overseas female labor migrant, who embodies the contradictions of class and gender mobility; the *petugas lapangan,* or field agent, who functions as an informal labor recruiter for transnational migrants; and *Pak Haji,* or Mr. Hajj, who wears the white cap that proclaims he has made the pilgrimage to Mecca.

Inspired by these approaches, we focus in this volume on the keywords that mark our understanding of mobility, broadly defined. In other words, although grounded in anthropology, our collaborative project is not specific to a discipline (Burgett and Hendler 2007), key thinker (Baudrillard 2003; Deleuze 2011), or tradition (Safri and Ruccio 2013). Instead, it grapples with common and scholarly ideas concerning mobility. Like Williams, we trace the evolution of our keywords, adopting a genealogical approach that not only explains the meaning of a concept today, but the contestation and points of rupture in which the clusters of meaning shifted in a historical perspective (Salazar 2013b). As the various contributions taken together illustrate, there is much to be gained analytically from using keywords to examine human experiences of mobility.

## Mobility as Keyword

Is mobility itself an important keyword? Williams did not think so. However, it does appear in the *New Keywords* volume, published thirty years after the original version (Berland 2005). There, it is described as expressing "different, sometimes contradictory meanings underlying our most fundamental beliefs about progress, freedom, individuation, and power" (Berland 2005, 217). Mobility is acknowledged as a key concept in globalization studies, where it is seen as "an overarching consideration rather than any particular theory" (Mooney and Evans 2007, 166). It also appears in the 2013 edition of *Theory in Social and Cultural Anthropology* (Salazar 2013c). The journal *Cultural Studies* showcased an interesting project, entitled "New Keywords: Migration and Borders" (De Genova, Mezzadra, and Pickles 2015). The idea behind this collaborative writing endeavor is to call critical attention to the ever-increasing prominence of migration and borders as key notions for apprehending culture and society in our contemporary (global) present. The stress on "the multifarious and heterogeneous practices of mobility within a field dominated by the state, empire, and capital" (De Genova, Mezzadra, and Pickles 2015, 61) certainly inspired the editors of this volume.

Our own project starts from the premise that people have always been on the move, but that human mobilities have been variously valued and interpreted through time and within as well as across cultures and societies. In addition, the sociocultural meanings attached to (im)mobility are very often gendered (Uteng and Cresswell 2008). Even though many translocal mobilities have evolved from voluntary opportunities to almost an economic necessity, it is still a widespread idea that much of what is experienced as "freedom" lies in mobility (Bergmann and Sager 2008). Partly influenced by market-based ideologies, translocal mobilities have become a new stratifying factor, producing a global hierarchy of movements. As more people cross physical and social boundaries, authorities and institutions resort to various infrastructures and regimes of mobility to maintain control (Salazar and Glick Schiller 2014). This causes multiple frictions with people's *motility,* their agency to be mobile and to choose whether to move or to stay put (Kaufmann, Bergman, and Joye 2004). Mobility studies, with its emphasis on agency, capital, regimes, and stratification, enriches current understandings of globalization, transnationalism, political economy, the role of cities, and circulation. Certain key concepts have been used, often by scholars from various disciplines, but as of yet, a working vocabulary of these has not been fully developed.

Given this context, and inspired in part by Raymond Williams's *Keywords* (1976), this volume presents ethnographically informed conceptual contributions that critically analyze the following mobility-related keywords: capital, cosmopolitanism, freedom, gender, immobility, infrastructure, motility, and regime. Of course, this is not an all-encompassing list, and we could have included many other keywords, such as typologies, routes, time, velocity, boundaries, transnationalism, or imaginaries. However, the set we present here, more general keywords, offers a coherent critical perspective on mobility, in a constructive dialogue between empirical data and transdisciplinary mobility studies. Moreover, the various contributors illustrate how the use of these concepts in our conceptualizations of mobility may change their more general place in our intellectual universe.

The volume you have in front of you took substantial time and energy to materialize. The editors were not after a traditional review of the literature (such as in the *Annual Reviews* publications). Instead, we pushed contributors, revision after revision, to reflect on how the use of certain keywords relates to mobility, conceived both as an analytical lens and as an observable practice. As our team involved anthropologists from both sides of the North Atlantic Ocean, we soon were confronted with the fact that mobility studies seem to have very different genealogies in North America and in Europe (where we could rely on the expertise of the Anthropology and Mobility Network (AnthroMob) of the European Association of Social Anthropologists, the group of scholars behind the *Worlds in Motion* book series in which this volume is being published). This collaborative project was thus a challenging but fruitful exercise in broadening our own understanding of mobility and the keywords that shape the discourses surrounding it.

In his formative work, Williams recognized that due to certain social forces, "in certain words, tones and rhythms, meanings [were] offered, felt for, tested, confirmed, asserted, qualified, changed" (1976, 12). He sought meanings to formerly understood words through examination of general discussions and separated disciplines, a process which "posed new questions and suggested new kinds of connection" (Williams 1976, 14). By design, the book chapters on each of our mobility-related keywords form the foundation of an intellectual conversation about the complex interrelationship between empirical realities, these concepts, and their analytical value for knowledge production in the social sciences and humanities at large.

## Book Outline

This volume provides an accessible and readable introduction to some of the central terms and debates that shape the study of mobility today, insisting that those debates can be enhanced by an increased understanding of the genealogies of their structuring terms and the conflicts and disagreements embedded in differing and even contradictory uses of those concepts. While we have given the authors enough academic freedom to push their contributions in various directions, every chapter contains the same basic elements: a brief review of the genealogy of the term, an in-depth conceptual reflection on how the term is used in relation to mobility, and ethnographic examples that illustrate the issues at hand. Wherever possible and relevant, the authors also cross-reference to other keywords.

Kiran Jayaram discusses the definitions, dynamics, and deployments of the keyword *capital*. He draws on the work of Karl Marx to critique the use of the term within mobility studies, with particular attention to conceptual weaknesses and pitfalls inherent in the term *mobility capital*. For him, seeing capital as a process opens up new avenues by demanding ethnographic acuity across time and space. Jayaram asks us to specify the nature of capital and whether it is a prerequisite or consequence for flow or stasis, or for reproduction or profit.

Malasree Neepa Acharya tackles the concept of *cosmopolitanism*. After tracing the term's genealogy, she investigates the historical shifts as an experiential theoretical object, practice, and orientation as it relates to the ways in which people, objects, and capital move. Cosmopolitanism has been used as a form, means, and indicator of mobility. Translocal movement has thus engaged researchers to create multiple cosmopolitanisms. Acharya challenges the dangers of normative and elitist aspects of the term's usage in the scholarly literature by showing its potential for self-reflexivity and reclamation of power in its use in discourses surrounding mobility.

Bartholomew Dean covers *freedom,* an essential theoretical construct in mobility studies. Through reference to Georges Bataille's insights, he proposes rearticulating the multifarious articulations of freedom of mobilities in ways that foreground sovereignty as a vital force shaping humanity. He illustrates this with ethnographic examples from his own research on the dynamics and consequences of mobility, especially in contemporary Amazonia. Dean concludes by considering Étienne Balibar's notion of *equaliberty,* accompanied by a call for continued ethnographic engagement oriented to comprehending the multiplex processes underlying the freedom of mobility.

Alice Elliot illustrates how there exists an intimate relationship between different forms of movement and the appearance and strengthening, or questioning and shattering, of *gender*. She unpacks some of the ways in which gender has been used when speaking of mobility and, in the process, begins to unpack the concept of gender itself in light of the constitutive relation to mobility it has been differentially accorded in the literature. Elliot differentiates two main ways in which gender is understood and used in mobility studies, what she calls the "master difference" between gender as classification and gender and process. In sum, she maps out the ways in which the relationship between gender and mobility has been framed, and some of the questions that have been asked of this relationship, critically extricating what gender can do for the study of mobility, and vice versa.

Nichola Khan reviews some uses of the keyword *immobility* pertaining to the key areas of migration, modernity, affect, and the market. Anthropology's specific contribution to immobility, she proposes, is one that offers ethnographically grounded theorizations that can draw on classic disciplinary concepts and concerns. At the same time, anthropologists should query the ethics the exercise of immobility delivers in different contexts. In her conclusion, Khan explores the question of "what lies between," or beyond (im)mobility. She emphasizes the ways immobility encompasses mobility, but is also surpassed by the existential intensities of the departures, arrivals, attachments, detachments, dead ends, impasses, and destinations that humans encounter and imagine.

Mari Korpela discusses *infrastructure* from three different angles: the moment of becoming mobile, the time of being mobile, and the moment of stopping to be mobile, that is, becoming immobile again. Different kinds of mobilities, whether forced or voluntary, short-term or long-term, are formed and regulated differently, but they always exist within current social, political, and economic structures, and within infrastructures. The emphasis is on transnational mobility, on people crossing state borders, although Korpela also questions whether there are infrastructures of mobility that function beyond the control of the current system of nation-states.

Hege Høyer Leivestad disentangles *motility,* a keyword referring to the potential to move. Motility's relative unfamiliarity makes room for a more general exploration of the concept's transdisciplinary borrowing and its analytical value for studies of mobility. Tracing motility's trajectories, her chapter critically engages with how notions of freedom and individual agency have assumed key roles in its conceptualization. Leivestad suggests that motility can be approached as a particular methodological position directed toward situations and locations of temporality in which mobility appears as yet-to-be-realized, yet-to-be-completed, or might-never-happen.

Beth Baker focuses on *regimes* of (im)mobility. She distinguishes two main tendencies in framing the concept. Functionalist approaches seek to identify the ways that systems for the regulation of mobility work in order to design more efficient and comprehensive regimes. Discursive approaches, on the other hand, parse out the ways institutions, technologies, ideas, and identities are constructed in relation to mobility, and how this might produce, shape, and prevent different kinds of mobilities. Examples are taken primarily from her own ethnographic work with undocumented youth, which point to the importance of listening to the (im)mobilized rather than fetishizing mobility.

Finally, Brenda Chalfin and Ellen Judd offer their take on the various contributions to this volume in two engaging afterwords. According to Chalfin, one of the strengths of this volume is not only its firm grounding in ethnography (as opposed to literature and text) but also the fact that each chapter charts a course for further exploration, "tracing potential paths for sustained comparative inquiry as well as theory building." Judd notes that the choice of keywords as an organizing heuristic has proven exceptionally productive. As the chapters indicate, questions about the meaning of keywords extend beyond language, narrowly construed, and require connecting with a world that is arguably outside text. This volume confirms that the creative combination of empirical data with conceptual reflection provides a unique contribution to the scholarly investigation of keywords, whether it is applied to a particular domain (such as mobility) or in general.

**Noel B. Salazar** is Research Professor of Anthropology at the University of Leuven, Belgium. He is co-editor of *Methodologies of Mobility* (2017), *Regimes of Mobility* (2014) and *Tourism Imaginaries* (2014), and author of *Envisioning Eden* (2010) and numerous journal articles and book chapters on the anthropology of mobility and travel. He is vice-president of the International Union of Anthropological and Ethnological Sciences and founder of the EASA Anthropology and Mobility Network.

## REFERENCES

Adey, Peter. 2010. *Mobility.* London: Routledge.

Adey, Peter, David Bissell, Kevin Hannam, Peter Merriman, and Mimi Sheller, eds. 2013. *The Routledge Handbook of Mobilities.* London: Routledge.

Aldenderfer, Mark. 2011. "Editorial: Keywords." *Current Anthropology* 52(4): 487.

Barker, Joshua, and Johan Lindquist. 2009. "Figures of Indonesian Modernity." *Indonesia* 87: 35–72.

Baudrillard, Jean. 2003. *Passwords.* Translated by Chris Turner. New York: Verso.

Bauman, Zygmunt. 1998. *Globalization: The Human Consequences.* New York: Columbia University Press.

Bergmann, Sigurd, and Tore Sager, eds. 2008. *The Ethics of Mobilities: Rethinking Place, Exclusion, Freedom and Environment.* Aldershot, England: Ashgate.

Berland, Jody. 2005. "Mobility." In *New Keywords: A Revised Vocabulary of Culture and Society,* edited by Tony Bennett, Lawrence Grossberg, and Meaghan Morris, 217–19. Malden, MA: Blackwell.

Bourdieu, Pierre. 1986. "The Forms of Capital." In *Handbook of Theory and Research for the Sociology of Education,* edited by John G Richardson, 241-58. Westport, CT: Greenwood Press.

Bréal, Michel. 1964. *Semantics: Studies in the Science of Meaning.* Translated by Henry Cust. New York: Dover Publications. First published 1900 by W Heinemann.

Burgett, Bruce, and Glenn Hendler, eds. 2007. *Keywords for American Cultural Studies.* New York: New York University Press.

Chu, Julie Y. 2010. *Cosmologies of Credit: Transnational Mobility and the Politics of Destination in China.* Durham, NC: Duke University Press.

Cresswell, Tim. 2006. *On the Move: Mobility in the Modern Western World.* New York: Routledge.

Cunningham, Hilary, and Josiah Heyman. 2004. "Introduction: Mobilities and Enclosures at Borders." *Identities: Global Studies in Culture and Power* 11(3): 289-302.

De Genova, Nicholas, and Nathalie Mae Peutz, eds. 2010. *The Deportation Regime: Sovereignty, Space, and the Freedom of Movement.* Durham, NC: Duke University Press.

De Genova, Nicholas, Sandro Mezzadra, and John Pickles, eds. 2015. "New Keywords: Migration and Borders." *Cultural Studies* 29(1): 55-87.

Deleuze, Gilles. 2011. *Gilles Deleuze from A to Z.* Cambridge, MA: The MIT Press.

Frello, Birgitta. 2008. "Towards a Discursive Analytics of Movement: On the Making and Unmaking of Movement as an Object of Knowledge." *Mobilities* 3(1): 25-50.

Gallie, Walter B. 1956. "Essentially Contested Concepts." *Proceedings of the Aristotelian Society* 56: 167-98.

Glick Schiller, Nina, and Noel B Salazar. 2013. "Regimes of Mobility across the Globe." *Journal of Ethnic and Migration Studies* 39(2): 183-200.

Graeber, David. 2011. "Consumption." *Current Anthropology* 52(4): 489-511.

Hannam, Kevin, Mimi Sheller, and John Urry. 2006. "Editorial: Mobilities, Immobilities and Moorings." *Mobilities* 1(1): 1-22.

Kaufmann, Vincent, Manfred M Bergman, and Dominique Joye. 2004. "Motility: Mobility as Capital." *International Journal of Urban and Regional Research* 28(4): 745-56.

Lindquist, Johan A. 2009. *The Anxieties of Mobility: Migration and Tourism in the Indonesian Borderlands.* Honolulu: University of Hawai'i Press.

Ludden, David. 2003. "Maps in the Mind and the Mobility of Asia." *Journal of Asian Studies* 62(4): 1057-78.

Malkki, Liisa H. 1992. "National Geographic: The Rooting of Peoples and the Territorialization of National Identity among Scholars and Refugees." *Cultural Anthropology* 7(1): 24-44.

Marzloff, Bruno. 2005. *Mobilités, Trajectoires Fluides.* La Tour d'Aigues: Editions de l'Aube.

Mooney, Annabelle, and Betsy Evans, eds. 2007. *Globalization: The Key Concepts.* New York: Routledge.

Nowicka, Magdalena, and Maria Rovisco, eds. 2009. *Cosmopolitanism in Practice.* Farnham, England: Ashgate.

Papastergiadis, Nikos. 2010. "Wars of Mobility." *European Journal of Social Theory* 13(3): 343-61.

Rockefeller, Stuart A. 2010. *Starting from Quirpini: The Travels and Places of a Bolivian People.* Bloomington: Indiana University Press.

Safri, Maliha, and David F Ruccio. 2013. "Keywords: An Introduction." *Rethinking Marxism* 25(1): 7–9.

Salazar, Noel B. 2010a. *Envisioning Eden: Mobilizing Imaginaries in Tourism and Beyond.* Oxford: Berghahn Books.

———. 2010b. "Towards an Anthropology of Cultural Mobilities." *Crossings: Journal of Migration and Culture* 1(1): 53–68.

———. 2013a. "Anthropology." In *The Routledge Handbook of Mobilities,* edited by Peter Adey, David Bissell, Kevin Hannam, Peter Merriman, and Mimi Sheller, 55–63. London: Routledge.

———. 2013b. "Imagining Mobility at the 'End of the World.'" *History and Anthropology* 24(2): 233–52.

———. 2013c. "Mobility." In *Theory in Social and Cultural Anthropology,* edited by R Jon McGee and Richard L Warms, 552–53. Thousand Oaks, CA: Sage.

Salazar, Noel B, and Nina Glick Schiller, eds. 2014. *Regimes of Mobility: Imaginaries and Relationalities of Power.* London: Routledge.

Salazar, Noel B, and Alan Smart. 2011. "Anthropological Takes on (Im)Mobility: Introduction." *Identities: Global Studies in Culture and Power* 18(6): i–ix.

Trouillot, Michel-Rolph. 2003. *Global Transformations: Anthropology and the Modern World.* New York: Palgrave Macmillan.

Urry, John. 2000. *Sociology Beyond Societies: Mobilities for the Twenty-First Century.* London: Routledge.

———. 2007. *Mobilities.* Cambridge: Polity Press.

Uteng, Tanu Priya, and Tim Cresswell, eds. 2008. *Gendered Mobilities.* Aldershot, England: Ashgate.

Williams, Raymond. 1976. *Keywords: A Vocabulary of Culture and Society.* New York: Oxford University Press.

———. 1985. *Keywords: A Vocabulary of Culture and Society.* Rev. ed. New York: Oxford University Press.

# Capital

*Kiran Jayaram*

"Should I stay or should I go now? If I go there will be trouble,
and if I stay it will be double."

—The Clash

## Introduction

Though the above lyrical quandary by a British punk band may simply be a
catchy match to an unforgettable song, it also evokes the idea that movement or stagnation may have consequences. Indeed, if it can be argued that
two conceptual totems define much of the concerns of global politics in
the early twenty-first century, then I posit that they are *mobility* and *capital*.
Many defenders of free markets believe that the uninhibited flow of capital
across the entire world would benefit everyone, and those with a critical
perspective often see capital as marshaling uneven development on a global
scale. Whatever one's position, the questions surrounding the relationship
between mobility and capital remain to be definitively answered.

Within the field of mobility studies, scholars from various disciplines
have conducted research and written ethnographies on the capital associated with mobility. In the same way that *Keywords* sought to understand
a word through "the significance of its general and variable usage ... not
in separated disciplines but in general discussion" (Williams 1976), in this
chapter, I present definitions, dynamics, and deployments of the keyword
capital, briefly as used in common parlance and in the social sciences, and
then as it relates to mobility. Next, I describe aspects related to capital and
mobility within the work of Marx, which subsequently allows me to critically

discuss the capital-mobility nexus. I conclude with considerations about capital for anthropologists and others interested in mobility. I argue that scholars need to determine if capital is a precursor or product of movement or a requisite of sedentariness, and we must also come to grips with the nature of the prerequisite or resultant capital.

## Etymology and Denotations

The word capital, according to the Oxford English Dictionary (2014), comes from Latin *caput* (head) through the Old French word *chattel* (moveable property) and the Middle English word capital. Hence, from the onset, this keyword has been yoked with the concept of movement. Of interest among the several denotations of the adjectival form is the reference to a type of criminal punishment involving either death or the "loss of liberty, exile, the loss of civil rights, or the seizure of property." It follows that as a sanction, the word suggests a limit on freedom of movement, death as an ultimate form of a subject's immobility, or forced movement beyond the homeland. These also imply the existence of a regime that has the power to carry out such discipline. The nominal form of this keyword refers to the top of an architectural column and to "holders of wealth as a class," but more germane to this discussion, the term points to "real or financial assets possessing a monetary value" and to "any source of profit, advantage, power" (Oxford English Dictionary 2014). This aspect is implicit in the work that references prerequisites to movement, discussed below.

A peculiar linguistic paradox exists in contemporary parlance. On one hand, the positive aspects of the word capital has been trumpeted by national and international economic policies, by university departments and scholars, and common people that hold the economic system of exchange on which it is founded as being an inherent force for good in the world, one that is isomorphic with human nature. On the other, the term is reserved for a punishment that ends a subject's mobility, that is, death, or deprives the person of property or freedom of movement. Juxtaposing these notions, capital facilitates freedom yet implies limits to life, (im)mobility, and property. The social sciences as well as mobility studies, as shown below, use the term capital in the sense of the French word *chattel*.

## Capital in the Social Sciences

Across the social sciences, various authors have used the word capital to serve their particular purposes. The work of Becker and Bourdieu deserves special mention, given how much of mobility studies have drawn upon their work. In the business and policy world, perhaps the most used capital-related term is *human capital,* championed by University of Chicago economist Becker (1964), which relates to skills and capacities that allow a person to carry out tasks related to a company within an industrialized economy. In the ensuing decades, new scholarship began questioning the rational-action explanations of human behavior advanced by economists, formalist anthropologists, and some economic sociologists.

Bourdieu, being one of Becker's critics, understood capital to mean "accumulated labor (in its materialized form or its 'incorporated,' embodied form) which, when appropriated on a private, i.e., exclusive, basis by agents or groups of agents, enables them to appropriate social energy in the form of reified or living labor" (1986, 46). He introduces various forms of capital (social and cultural) as possible transmuted forms of the "economic capital" of political economy (Bourdieu 1986).¹ Elsewhere, he introduces "political capital" (though he does not explain this), "informational capital" (which he says encompasses cultural capital), "symbolic capital" (referring to the form capital assumes when others perceive the value of the specific form of capital implemented), and linguistic capital (Bourdieu 1991). One final form of capital described by Bourdieu is his concept of the "meta-capital" of the state, which refers to the ability of it to legitimize itself through monopolizing and using physical force to control the population, different social fields, and the forms of capital that circulate among them (Bourdieu 1994). Two observations will help highlight the uses of capital in studies of mobility. First, he mentions profits gained by transmission and exchange of capital, but the lack of attention as to how profit is generated leaves the impression that capital is an object to be wielded. Second, because Bourdieu is trying to critique economistic approaches to human behavior, it is remarkable that he delineates so many different kinds of capital (and their potential exchangeability) as a way to explain human action, as if it were isomorphic with human behavior, whereas in Algeria he refers to "folk economics" and the "practical economic sense" that is linked to behavior (Bourdieu 2000).

### Other Forms of Capital

Either by agreement or by omission, other scholars have invoked capital in an increasing number of settings, echoing Harvey's (2001) idea that capital both thrives on and creates difference. Within network analysis, scholars have discussed a person's centrality as being an indicator of social capital (Borgatti, Jones, and Everett 1998). Scholars in the field of education have broken down cultural capital into even smaller categories of capital to discuss other forms of valuable knowledge that students of color bring to a classroom (Yosso 2005). Some sociologists have furthered a utilitarian approach to human behavior by detailing how valuable social relationships (i.e., social capital) can facilitate obligations, information channels, and fora for the establishment of social norms, all toward fostering profitable behavior (Coleman 1988). Hilgers identifies autochthony as a relational form of capital that "becomes a resource that allows discrimination against competitors in their access to resources" (2011, 44), yet one that requires association with economic, social, or symbolic capital. Other invocations of the keyword relate to intellectual capital (Nahapiet and Ghoshal 1998), linguistic capital, political capital (Booth and Bayer Richard 1998), professional capital (Hargreaves and Fullan 2011), beauty capital (Hua 2013; Pfann et al. 2000; Price 2008), and biological capital (Warman 2003). Almost all of these forms of so-called capital are derivatives of either human capital (á la Becker) or cultural capital (á la Bourdieu).[2] Furthermore, one infers that forms of capital can be linked to an increasing number of human behaviors in industrialized societies, an idea easily refuted by the ethnographic record. I revisit this critique in the discussion of mobility-related capital. While the above discussion does not strictly relate to movement, some of the same understandings of capital-as-object are reproduced in mobility studies.

## The Mobility of Capital

In the past two decades, a new group of scholars has taken up social research on political economy, and capitalism specifically.[3] Sadly, only a few of these works have covered the mobility of capital. Authors have defended or critiqued the unencumbered flight of money, have identified how vilified capital mobility legitimates global corporate transactions, or have linked foreign investment to migratory flows.

Since the late twentieth century, many economists and politicians have declared the need to unleash the market so that everyone would benefit. Perhaps Friedman (1999) explained it best when he explained that governments needed to, among other things, make the private sector the engine of economic growth, shrink the size of the government's budget and activities, eliminate taxes on imports, and encourage foreign investment. Essentially, once capital, as direct investments, can move freely about the planet, unhindered by any regimes, wealth will be created, eventually benefiting all people. However, even at the time Friedman was making such claims, economists and others had taken issue with such an idea.

Critics of the completely free global movement of capital point to the importance of crises in capitalism. Bhagwati (1998) cites the Asian economic crisis of the 1990s as reason to question the absolute good of complete capital mobility. There is no reason, he claims, to confuse free trade with free movement of capital. In fact, these countries often lose the political independence to enact policies that would protect a country's workers if it goes against multilateral lending institution guidelines. Thus, he advocates for some control on the mobility of capital. Harvey (1981), who also believes that crisis is inherent to capitalism, contributed the idea of a "spatial fix" to an internal contradiction in this system of exchange. According to Harvey, a crisis occurs when there is an overaccumulation of labor and value and devaluation of commodities. This demands that capitalists find markets in new locations in which to invest. He concludes that given the limited geographic area in which humans live, capital will eventually reach a material limit to its mobility.

In the era of the so-called War on Terror, de Goede (2007) writes on the way in which informal money transfer networks became a target of scrutiny. He describes how the U.S. government worked under the model of a false binary between legitimate global money flows and terrorist financing. Intelligence networks target *hawala* (informal money remittances based upon trust) in the Middle East and South Asia because these exchanges circumvent the formal financial regulatory systems via intermediaries. De Goede argues that *hawala,* as "the figure of the terrorist underground[,] is a discursive condition for the post-9/11 maintenance of the legitimate world of global finance" (2007, 157).

In an important work on the relationship between mobility, labor, and capital, Sassen seeks to connect the "the articulation of the new labor migrations with the recomposition of capital as it takes its place in the new industrial zones in Third World countries" (1988, 187). Using data from various countries from the 1960s to the 1980s, she argues that the type of U.S. activity abroad, such as direct investment as a part of an internationalization of production, shapes migratory flows. Sassen sees the U.S. military intervention and later foreign investment in the Dominican Republic as creating a framework for middle-class and subsequently lower-class Dominican migration to the United States. Similarly, she argues that the United States-based capital investment in factories and export-agricultural production zones in Haiti under Jean-Claude Duvalier contributed to migration.

## Capital within Mobility Studies

Writings on capital within mobility studies can be placed into two categories: those that consider various forms of capital related to movement, and those that explicitly refer to mobility capital.

## Versions of Capital in Mobility Studies

Robert Putnam sees movement as contributing to the demise of *social capital* in the United States, understood as "networks, norms, and social trust that facilitate coordination and cooperation for mutual benefit" (67, 1995). Urry (2002) critiques this idea, answering that mobility actually contributes to social capital. Whereas Putnam sees driving alone as a solitary act, Urry posits that in rural areas, this driving alone is what is required to maintain social relations. This debate attests to the ability of movement to maintain or destroy social relations.

Salazar (2011), in his article on the tourism industry, analyzes the role of interpretations of movement as capital, if only as a straw man, by invoking the term *cosmobility capital*. However, Salazar uses the term to critique any approach that would perpetuate a binary understanding that depicts mobile tourists as holders of cosmobility capital, defined as "resources, knowledge, and abilities that facilitate social as well as geographical mobility" (2011, 582), and immobile locals as those with "cultural capital." His contribution, then, is to show that research on the imaginations, that is, understandings, of mobility and capital is important, so as to belie any generalized tropes of mobility based upon binary extremes.

Kaufmann, Bergman, and Joye (2004) invoke the term *movement capital* and propose motility as a way of understanding mobility as a form of capital. "Movement capital" is "the potentiality of movement" (Kaufmann, Bergman, and Joye 2004, 752), and as a part of capital associated with motility, includes the preconditions of access, competence, and appropriation. They state how one can parlay economic capital into other forms, including movement capital. Though Kaufmann and colleagues correctly describe how class may affect social mobility as seen in educational choices, or in other words, that education may contribute to social reproduction rather than emancipation or self-improvement, they suggest that focusing on this reproduction places primacy on economic capital, something they dismiss as hard to calculate and not of primary interest to social scientists. They illustrate the utility of motility through micro-, meso-, and macro-level analysis that seeks to show the relation between spatial and social movements.

Other scholars (Elliot and Urry 2010; Larsen et al. 2006; Sheller 2012) discuss network capital as important for mobility and for understanding it as a source of inequality in contemporary societies (as do Murphy-Lejeune 2002; Salazar and Smart 2011). By network capital, they refer to a mix of the competences of movement, ability to move, legal documents, contacts, communication and transportation machines, meeting places, access to information, time allotment, and people with whom one can connect. Overlapping partially with social capital and motility, this term also includes preconditions of movement. Continuing in this line, Urry states in his interview with Adey and Bissell, "it's sometimes those with more network capital who are the immobile, who can summon the mobile to wherever they are. We shouldn't assume that it is those who are powerful who move" (2010, 7). These authors point to the importance of various forms of value (i.e., of capital) as preconditions that can help or hinder social relations and suggest that these constitute another form of inequality in contemporary modernity.

Finally, scholars have discussed the relationship between mobility and capital linked to Hilgers's emphasis on the role of belonging. Tseng (2000) expands upon the important work of Sassen (1988), who describes how capital investment can lead to outmigration, by focusing on the people associated with these monetary flows. Examining Taiwanese involved in business migration programs and foreign direct investment, her data shows that "sometimes immigration serves [migrants'] interest in capital accumulation; at other times capital investment serves as the means for securing a second nationality" (Tseng 2000, 146). On one hand, some Taiwanese acquire citizenship elsewhere by meeting foreign capital requirements, as this allows them to overcome limitations on noncitizens' economic activities abroad. On the other hand, using a second nationality allows business owners to *disguise* their enterprises as foreign, and thus, protect their capital from threats by state officials. Kim (2010), like Murphy-Lejeune (2002), references Simmel's stranger as a way to show value-laden mobility as related to traveling intellectuals. She argues that in addition to certain *generic competences* linked to cosmopolitanism, outsider status affords mobile academics positively valued epistemology in the form of "transnational identity capital," as in the figures of Edward Said and Stuart Hall. Favell, in his work on what he calls "Eurostars," or highly skilled and educated migrants across Europe, interrogates the freedom to move within the European Union. Though economic and human capital facilitates movement to global cities like London or Amsterdam, Eurostars often lament their inability to belong, saying that "the issue is not that you are always free to leave, but rather that you are able to settle in ways that make sense to your own mode of living" (Favell 2008, 119).

While the above writings point to subjectivities of belonging and imagined value, another work deals specifically with autochthony, mobility, and capital. Geschiere and Nyamnjoh (2000) situate their discussion of belonging within the context of globalization in a so-called neoliberal era. Contemporary capitalism, which produces its own contradictions, allows for workers' freedom of movement yet requires a regime to control and regulate their existence. Whether in Cameroon, Gabon, or France under Le Pen, imaginaries stigmatize new migrant populations that form part of a global reserve army of labor, and simultaneously, national governments seek to categorize and limit flows of people based upon the perceived market value of their human capital. Therefore, promotion of autochthony in locations experiencing political or economic liberalization presents itself as "an almost inevitable outcome of such dialectical tensions" (Geschiere and Nyamnjoh 2000, 448). In brief, the above authors demonstrate how the movement of people can produce valuable feelings of belonging (and for Kim, not belonging).

### Mobility Capital

Within mobility studies, three points of discussion emerge from the theory-based and ethnography-based works that integrate the concept of *mobility capital*. First, what words are scholars using, and what do they mean? Some scholars invoke mobility capital or "mobility as capital" (Kaufmann, Bergman, and Joye 2004), but then proceed to operationalize the term through referencing "motility" (Moret 2011), which I describe below. Murphy-Lejeune seems to be the first person to have used the term mobility capital. In her book detailing how European educational migrants embody the role of the stranger, she defines the term as a "sub-component of human capital, enabling individuals to enhance their skills because of the richness of the international experience gained by living abroad" (Murphy-Lejeune 2002, 51). She elaborates four main aspects of this: family and personal histories of mobility, previous experience with foreign people, one's first experience in another country as an initiation, and the personal characteristics of the wanderer. Sheller provides another definition, but she does not provide sufficient detail. She sees mobility capital as "the uneven distribution of these capacities and competencies [linked to motility], in relation to the surrounding physical, social and political affordances for movement (with the legal structures regulating who or what can and cannot move being crucial)" (2011, 5). Though it is easy to see that these terms and their definitions refer to preconditions of movement, reconciling the theoretical with the context-specific is difficult, at the very least.

The second emergent point about mobility capital is that it is absolutely the purview of mobile humans. Carlson (2011) recognizes that some German students may have a disposition to travel abroad for their studies. However, her processual approach shows how such preconditions were insufficient to bring about mobility until placed within a particular timing sequence, like the schedule for university admissions, or structure of social relations, such as a romantic partner who lives abroad. Similarly, Brooks and Waters (2011) give case studies of students from East Asia, Europe, and the United Kingdom to examine differences among educational migrants. Moret (2011) describes Somali migration to Europe for family, work, leisure, or politics.

Two main weaknesses arise from an anthropocentric approach to mobility capital. First, despite the fact that mobility studies focuses on the movement of many objects (both material and immaterial), no scholar has taken on the mobility capital of, say, a mango, binary code, or cryptocurrencies. Appadurai implied how value can be gleaned by studying "things-in-motion" (1986, 5), and West looked at how the global coffee trade creates "value, and the ways it is produced today with regard to both objects and human lives" (2012, 1), but West made no reference to mobility, let alone mobility capital. Rather, analysis was based upon a methodological approach that followed the objects through exchange. A second curious inconsistency in the concept arises when given the case of those who have high mobility capital, no matter what word used, yet who do not have the freedom to move in a pronounced manner. Rather than proposing immobility capital or (im)mobility capital, scholars have avoided this lacuna by resorting to discussions of network capital (Adey and Bissell 2010; Sheller 2012).

The third aspect of mobility capital concerns links to other forms of capital and transmutability.[4] The two main approaches to mobility capital both mention the importance of exchanging it for another form of capital. Kaufmann and colleagues state, "its conceptualization as a form of capital which can be mobilized and transformed into other types of capital (i.e., economic, human and social capital) allows motility to make original contributions in the research area relating to social inequality and social change" (Kaufmann, Bergman, and Joye 2004, 754). Murphy-Lejeune goes beyond mere exchange to include the necessity of profit. She states that when students make the choice to study abroad, they do so consciously "to increase professional, cultural, linguistic, and personal capital they initially started with" (2002, 73). In her ethnography of Somali migration, Moret shows how "mobility can, under certain conditions, become a form of capital giving access to economic, social, and political resources" (2011, 2). Despite these possible benefits, however, she contends that the movements of Somali women to the United Kingdom and Switzerland maintain the existing gendered regime, simply reproducing the older order in a new location and through novel movements. Borja and colleagues have recognized the likelihood of such horizontal movement, as some "individuals are not amassing any capital. They are simply submitting themselves to these orders and—paradoxically—most of them remain in the same social, economic and spatial situation they occupied before" (Borja, Courty, and Ramadier 2012, n.p.). In short, the ethnographic record reveals contradictory positions on whether or not mobility capital produces value.

## Capital within the Work of Karl Marx

As archeologists have known and discussed for more than two decades, the practices of mobility have existed prior to or outside of the context of market-based economic exchanges (Anthony 1990; Casimir and Rao 1992; Kelly 1992). As a result, discussing capital related to these settings would be intellectually inappropriate. Therefore, to understand capital in contexts of market interactions, and as a foundation for a critique of the uses of capital in mobility literature, I mine elements from Marx's political economy.

Marx's description of capital in *Das Kapital* (1976) offers the quintessential understanding of this keyword by reference to a definition of capital and to the personality of the capitalist. Early market transactions can be represented by the formula $C \rightarrow M \rightarrow C'$, where C and C' are specific amounts of distinct commodities equated through the medium of money, M. No surplus value is created, and people exchange commodities to meet their immediate needs of consumption, that is, social reproduction. In a capitalist market exchange, the formula is $M \rightarrow C \rightarrow M'$, where C is a product of human labor imbued with additional value, meaning $M < M'$.[5] It is capital in motion, rather than a static object C, that constitutes capital. "Value," he writes, "therefore now becomes value in process, money in process, and as much, *capital*" (Marx 1976, 256, emphasis mine). Through fetishism, the process that infuses the commodity with value is hidden, and as such, the object of inquiry is understood to be inherently valuable.[6] Another corollary to this processual relationship between commodities and value is that, depending on how it is used, an object may or may not be capital. Money kept in a piggy bank is money, but when that money is thrust into the market in a conscious act to generate profit, it becomes capital. The agentive element of this determination of what is or is not capital immediately leads to a consideration of human actors.

Marx the philosopher-cum-economist focused his work on critiquing political economy, but his work offers glimpses of anthropological understandings. Though he presented a historical anthropological account of the creation of capitalist farmers (Marx 1976, Chapter 29), of more concern are his comments on the dispositions of a capitalist. In his typical elegant prose, Marx averred that "it is not because he is a leader of industry that a man is a capitalist; on the contrary, he is a leader of industry because he is a capitalist" (1976, 219). In other words, a person may have as a certain quality of being the tendency to perpetually seek profit. He highlights the intentionality of the human actor in the following:

> As the *conscious* bearer of this movement, the possessor of money becomes a capitalist. His person, or rather his pocket, is the point from

which the money starts, and to which it returns. The objective content of the *circulation* we have been discussing—the valorization of value— is *his* [sic] *subjective purpose,* and it is only in so far as the appropriation of ever more wealth in the abstract is the *sole driving force behind his operations,* that he functions as a capitalist, i.e., as capital personified and endowed with *consciousness and a will.* (Marx 1976, 254, emphasis added)

This additional explanation points to the second aspect of the human actor, namely, intentionality to generate profit. Consequently, should a person engage in a commodity exchange and only incidentally generate profit, the person would not be considered a capitalist and thus, the object should not be considered capital.

One final relevant point in Marx's oeuvre relates to movement of commodities and people. In a situation of a perfect market, which is assumed to be true in his work, Marx states that by definition, circulation (i.e., movement in the market) of equivalents cannot generate surplus value. At the same time, profit does occur through market exchange. This results in his claim that capital "cannot therefore arise from circulation, and it is equally impossible for it to arise apart from circulation. It must have its origin both in circulation and not in circulation" (Marx 1976, 268). This indicates that certain preconditions of movement must exist to consider the items as capital. Turning to the movement of people, Marx relates how migration contributes to a reserve labor army, which facilitated the low wages necessary for the growth of capitalist industry. For example, in the United States,

the enormous and ceaseless flood of humanity, driven year in, year out, onto the shores of America, leaves behind a stationary sediment in the East of the United States, since the wave of immigration from Europe throws men onto the labour-market there more rapidly than the wave of immigration westwards can wash them away.... Capitalistic production advances there with gigantic strides, even though the lowering of wages and the dependence of the wage-labourer has by no means yet proceeded so far as to reach the normal European level. (Marx 1976, 940)

Yet, Marx is discussing the movement of people as a precondition to the creation of capital, and not as capital per se.

In summary, a critique of the term capital in mobility studies requires carrying forward several points from Marx. First, capital implies the generation of surplus value. Exchanging different forms of equivalents is not a capital-based exchange. Second, capital means value in motion, necessarily processual in nature. Third, the use of a commodity as capital must be due to the wielder's explicit goals rather than an unintended consequence. Fourth, capital requires its bearer to have certain character dispositions. Finally, for something to be understood as capital, certain preconditions, or a specific social and historical context, must be present. In other words, following Marx, a commodity that may possibly be used to generate value does not make it a valuable commodity. Ascribing the word capital to something can only occur after observing and analyzing the result of the exchange where a thing is consciously entered into a process for the explicit purpose of generating a profit by internalizing surplus value.

## The Capital-Mobility Nexus

In examining the capital-mobility nexus, a principal question to consider is prepositional in nature: Is it capital *for* (im)mobility or capital *from* (im)mobility? Many authors describe how some form of capital is required to move, be it prerequisites of character, money, or any of the elements included in network capital. In the case of my research among Haitian educational migrants to the Dominican Republic, students required money and legal paperwork to cross an international border before they could even consider entering a university. Once they arrived inside the Dominican Republic, they required other monies and knowledge to find, enroll in, and attend courses at their tertiary institution. It remains to be seen as to whether after graduation, these same students, neither Haitian elite nor laborers in an ethnic enclave, will net any profit because of their move from Haiti to the Dominican Republic. We must consider the possibility that such mobility may not generate capital gains, as, to paraphrase Marx, an exchange of distinct but equal values does not generate profit and, as such, is not capital. Movement itself does not create value. However, no less than the European Union has touted the benefits that freedom of movement for labor, goods, capital, and services (Andor 2014) brings to host countries. Similarly, authors have demonstrated the value that transnational mobility affords for members of the global upper classes, reinforcing the idea of variegated benefits of mobility. Ong (1999) described how Hong Kong elite acquired and used multiple passports as a transnational practice to cross borders so they could better participate in a global economy. Tseng (2000) describes how the presence of a managerial class, created to operate overseas businesses, shows that the mobility of people helps in capital accumulation. At the same time, Moret (2011) suggested that although mobility can be valuable, it could also contribute to a condition of a changing same. Drawing upon research in Cameroon, Geschiere and Nyamnjoh (2000) discuss how being perceived as not belonging to a particular area, due to internal or international mobility, could impact who could vote, where they could vote, and where one might be buried. If we consider, as Urry suggested, that there is capital necessary for immobility, what types of heroic abilities help people stay fixed? Therefore, scholars working at the capital-mobility nexus must determine the quality and quantity of elements that are marshaled to generate profit vis-á-vis movement or stagnation, if such value is even created, as well as being sensitive to whether this diminishes, reproduces, or exacerbates existing social inequalities.

Another question to consider is the nature of the capital associated with movement. If we assume that we are examining that which is required to move, what constitutes this primordial value? Murphy-Lejeune (2002) suggests that such capital is composed of social historical elements along with personality traits. Certainly, this parallels Marx's idea that certain people have a drive to amass value as a part of their character. Sheller (2012) describes how dynamics of disaster relief related to military control of space and use of Geographic Information System (GIS) technology in Haiti differentially ordered mobility along the lines of existing divisions between foreign workers and Haitian residents. Thus, she sees capital in a form of technological knowledge. Kaufmann suggests that money or other forms of capital can create the ability to be mobile, that is, movement capital. While scholars seek cultural explanations, recent scholarship in biological anthropology has examined the possibility of a genetic predisposition toward novelty seeking, including migration (Campbell and Barone 2012), raising the question of whether specific genetic codes could be seen as capital. Specifically, they argue that the D4 dopamine receptor 7R+ allele, associated with risk-taking, could be a factor that leads someone to migrate to new lands.

If our concern is the capital gained (or lost) from movement, then we must immediately return to the issue of whether capital is a good to exchange or, following Marx, whether capital is a process involving motion. I argue that viewing capital as a process rather than an object exchanged at a point in time will enrich our understanding of the capital-mobility nexus by demanding ethnographic acuity. My work among Haitian laborers in urban Dominican Republic, those who carry out various trades within the informal economy, demonstrates Marx's idea that circulation is necessary but not sufficient for something to be considered capital. Several ambulant shoe shiners and vendors from a *bak paletèl* (snack cart) would regularly talk about the need to *sikile* (circulate) to either avoid police harassment or to reposition themselves at a place and time to encounter more customers. They moved not only to find customers and *fè lajan mache* (make their money work for them), but also to ensure that the police would not detain them, and thus preventing them from generating profits. Despite their mobility in the city, at the end of the day, many of them lamented their inability to take in money beyond their *manmanlajan* (capital). Only a processual approach to capital could reveal such an insight. Murphy-Lejeune, following an interpretation of Bourdieu, uses a more fixed notion of capital. She explains that mobile European students harbor a desire for improvement, but her work fails to show that an increase in other forms of capital actually occurs. As readers, however important it is to understand the motivations for and expected outcomes of movement, we are apparently invited to engage in a Coleridgean suspension of disbelief due to lack of presented data. If we seek to claim that mobility has created capital, as a new global outlook described by Kim, Favell, and Acharya, or in some transmuted form, only a processual approach will provide the empirical basis for such a contention. Additionally, if we are to consider capital as gained from movement, we need to consider the social and political conditions under which such accumulation can occur.

When thinking about the mobility of capital, scholars must consider the role of imaginations of the mobility and the effects of such flows. As de Goede shows, so-called underground flows may be perceived as threatening due to who is sending and receiving, whereas other money transfers are sanitized through accountability practices. This raises one of the key issues of mobility: how capital's movement is imagined. Second, the impact of large-scale money flows across international boundaries should be examined for their impact not only on economies, but also on migratory patterns, and even on what new knowledge and subjects are created (see Fisher and Downey 2006).

Other considerations of the capital-mobility nexus link specifically to the term mobility capital. First, the various implicit and explicit definitions of mobility capital along with the range of forms of capital in social science are dispositional in nature (Borja et al. 2012), yet having these traits does not absolutely mean that the person will move accordingly. As Murphy-Lejeune (2002) implies, some people will be necessarily unable to study abroad, presumably because of limited means. Second, mobility capital, even if we allow for it, only makes sense within the general context of a capitalist system. While scholars have discussed mobility based upon the archeological record, the concept of mobility capital does not and cannot apply to foraging populations or the large-scale human movement out of Africa and across the globe. Third, I am troubled by the fact that increasing numbers of factors in our industrialized world are being linked to capital, as if this economic system were isomorphic with human nature.[7] It seems that anything that can be considered as valuable or helpful in certain situations runs the risk of being immediately assumed to be capital, as it may have been in an apparently (though not necessarily) similar situation. However, traditional rites of passage, outside of a capitalist system, have existed through-out time across the planet. By definition, such rites are valuable, yet linking them to mobility capital would transmogrify them and belie their cultural meaning. To wit, borrowing from Adey's discussion (2006) of the omni-presence of mobility, if capital is everything, then it is nothing. Allowing such facile attribution of the term capital means doing a *tendu derrière en face* (from ballet, stepping backwards while facing forwards) into the idea that in the industrialized world, the logic of capitalism is singular, omnipresent, and omnipotent, a premise that does not match what I have seen in my re-search across the Caribbean or in my life in the United States. Fourth, I raise the issue of verbiage within a new field of social science inquiry. Within mo-bility studies, Marzloff (2005) coined the terms altermobility, infomobility, and chronomobility. Now, we are wrestling with motility, mobility capital, movement capital, and cosmobility capital. From my research, the case of cryptocurrencies, like Bitcoin, could raise the possibility of the "capital of capital" (perhaps a type of meta-capital distinct from that described by Bourdieu). To mine (i.e., generate and subsequently own) these currencies, a person needs technological infrastructure, knowledge of the specific cryp-tocurrency, and computer literacies, all which require some other form of money. As scholars, we need to be more conservative in coining new terms before acting as if we have exhausted the value of existing material. New ver-biage might not be worth the time and energy required to vet new concepts. If conceptual terms come from outside of academia, to close this discus-sion with an appeal to the original *Keywords,* we need to study the processes by which they are generated, circulated, and implemented.

## Conclusion

Mobility, either imagined or experienced, has played an important role for humans across the globe for tens of thousands of years. In the past two centuries, the concept of capital has shifted from the product of an exchange at a market to a principle that endeavors to organize business, governments, and human behavior. These two concepts are increasingly fig-uring into social scientists' analysis. Rather than a static form based upon the work of Bourdieu, capital should be understood as the process whereby a person or thing moves with the intention of generating profit. Scholars need to determine if capital is a precursor or product of movement, or if it is a requisite of sedentariness, and we must also come to grips with the nature of the prerequisite or resultant capital. While I believe that mobility capital as understood by Sheller and Murphy-Lejeune does not provide adequate purchase, given several related dispositional forms of capital extant in the literature (e.g., cultural, social, symbolic), the importance lies how the term challenges us to see the variegated distribution of elements in our cultural and biological worlds that contribute to our condition of being stuck or of being global movers.

Much work at the mobility-capital nexus remains incomplete. As I write, many more Europeans and Canadians are carrying out mobility scholarship than their colleagues in the United States are.[8] The promotion and politics of mobility in the European Union and the rise of China and other countries in Southeast Asia as global economic players makes obvious the need to study students, professionals, tourists, and business leaders. However, given the large role that women intermediaries play in Caribbean economies, it is surprising that not more publications have dealt with the value linked to their movement (but see Ulysse 2007). Similarly, attention should also be paid to cases of south-south migration (see Bartlett and Ghaffar-Kucher 2013), internal migration, urban dwellers, and of course, the movement of nonhuman entities (animals, currencies, binary code, etc.), as each of these play an important role in the world today.

Finally, as the inequality between the richest and the poorest on our planet continues to grow, the role of regimes of mobility (Glick Schiller and Salazar 2013) cannot be underestimated, whether considering either the mobility of capital or the capital of mobility. As (im)mobility increasingly becomes a marker of difference, ethnography attuned to the values, subjectivities, processes, imaginaries, and prepositions of capital may hold the key for a clearer vision of the trouble of those who stay or go throughout our world.

**Kiran Jayaram** is Assistant Professor of Anthropology at the University of South Florida. He is co-editor of *Transnational Hispaniola* (2018) and author of several articles, a book chapter, and professional reports on mobility, political economy, and education. He was formerly Program Chair for the Society of Latin American and Caribbean Anthropology (AAA) and Co-Chair for the Haiti-Dominican Republic Section (LASA).

## NOTES

1. For genealogical purposes, it deserves that Marx (1976) used the term *social capital,* but more in the sense of what might be understood as average capital

investment across all productive industries, and Jacobs (1961) also used the term *social capital*.

2. Warman's notion of *biological capital* is curious because the possessor of capital is a plant rather than an animal, that is, human. Still, as Warman describes, specific biological traits of the cereal crop allowed it to generate other forms of value.

3. This includes many works on so-called late capitalism. The year 2012 alone saw the launch of the *Journal of Business Anthropology*, a critical set of exchanges on neoliberalism in *Social Anthropology*. See also Blim (2000), Callon (1998), Comaroff and Comaroff (2000), Fisher and Downey (2006), and Swedberg (2005).

4. Salazar (2011) discusses how some people in Tanzania exchange one form of capital (e.g., social capital or autochthonous capital) based upon imaginaries of immobility or cosmopolitanism, yet he does not use the term mobility capital.

5. Specifically, Marx contrasts "the simple circulation of commodities ... [which] is a means to a final goal which lies outside circulation, namely the appropriation of use-values, the satisfaction of needs" with "the circulation of money as capital [as] an end in itself, for the valorization of value takes place only within this constantly renewed movement" (Marx 1976, 253).

6. The value-added process leads the commodity to appear to have the "occult ability of value to itself. It brings forth living offspring, or at least lays golden eggs" (Marx 1976, 256).

7. I will readily admit that conditions of capitalism at a specific location may lead people to teach themselves a particular way of self-making, but such an observation cannot be removed from discussions of how such an education contributes to an existing social and political order.

8. The lack of inclusion of anthropologies of mobility from beyond the North Atlantic, rather than being an oversight, reflects the canonization of theory, with all the implied hierarchical power relations.

## REFERENCES

Adey, Peter. 2006. "If Mobility Is Everything Then It Is Nothing: Towards a Relational Politics of (Im)mobilities." *Mobilities* 1(1): 75–94.

Adey, Peter, and David Bissell. 2010. "Mobilities, Meetings, and Futures: An Interview with John Urry." *Environment and Planning D: Society and Space* 28: 1–16.

Andor, László. 2014. "Labour Mobility in the European Union: The Inconvenient Truth." Available at http://europa.eu/rapidpress-release_SPEECH-14-115_en.htm

Anthony, David W. 1990. "Migration in Archaeology: The Baby and the Bathwater." *American Anthropologist* 92: 895–914.

Appadurai, Arjun. 1986. *The Social Life of Things: Commodities in Cultural Perspective.* New York: Cambridge University Press.

Bartlett, Lesley, and Ameena Ghaffar-Kucher. 2013. *Refugees, Immigrants, and Education in the Global South: Lives in Motion.* New York: Routledge.

Becker, Gary. 1964. *Human Capital: A Theoretical and Empirical Analysis, with Special Reference to Education.* Chicago: University of Chicago Press.

Bhagwati, Jagdish. 1998. "The Capital Myth: The Difference between Trade in Widgets and Dollars." *Foreign Affairs* 77(3): 7–12.

Blim, Michael. 2000. "Capitalisms in Late Modernity." *Annual Review of Anthropology* 29: 25–38.

Booth, John A, and Patricia Bayer Richard. 1998. "Civil Society, Political Capital, and Democratization in Central America." *The Journal of Politics* 60(3): 780–800.

Borgatti, Stephen P, Candace Jones, and Martin G Everett. 1998. "Network Measures of Social Capital." *Connections* 21(2): 27–36.

Borja, Simon, Guillaume Courty, and Thierry Ramadier. 2012. "'Mobility as Capital': Sketching the Arguments." Available at http://en.forumviesmobiles.org/arguing/2012/12/11/mobility-capital-sketching-arguments-533

Bourdieu, Pierre. 1986. "The Forms of Capital." In *Handbook of Theory and Research for the Sociology of Education,* edited by JG Richardson, 46–58. New York: Greenwood Press.

———. 1991. *Language and Symbolic Power.* Cambridge: Polity Press.

———. 1994. "Rethinking the State: Genesis and Structure of the Bureaucratic Field." *Sociological Theory* 12(1): 1–18.

———. 2000. "Making the Economic Habitus: Algerian Workers Revisisted." *Ethnography* 1(1): 17–41.

Brooks, Rachel, and Johanna Waters. 2011. *Migration and the Internationalization of Higher Education.* New York: Palgrave Macmillan.

Callon, Michel. 1998. *Laws of the Markets.* Malden, MA: Blackwell.

Campbell, Benjamin C, and Lindsay Barone. 2012. "Evolutionary Basis of Human Migration." In *Causes and Consequences of Human Migration,* edited by Michael H Crawford and Benjamin C Campbell, 45–64. New York: Cambridge University Press.

Carlson, Sören. 2011. "Just a Matter of Choice? Student Mobility as a Social and Biographical Process." Working Paper no. 68, Sussex Centre for Migration Research.

Casimir, Michael J, and Aparnu Rao. 1992. *Mobility and Territoriality: Social and Spatial Boundaries among Foragers, Fishers, Pastoralists and Peripatetics.* New York: Berg.

Coleman, James S. 1988. "Social Capital in the Creation of Human Capital." *American Journal of Sociology* 94: S95–S120.

Comaroff, Jean, and John L Comaroff. 2000. "Millenial Capitalism: First Thoughts on a Second Coming." *Public Culture* 12(2): 291–343.

de Goede, Marieke. 2007. "Underground Money." *Cultural Critique* 65: 140–63.

Elliot, Anthony, and John Urry. 2010. *Mobile Lives: Self, Excess, and Nature.* New York: Routledge.

Favell, Adrian. 2008. *Eurostars and Eurocities: Free Movement and Mobility in an Integrating Europe.* Malden, MA: Blackwell.

Fisher, Melissa S, and Greg Downey. 2006. *Frontiers of Capital: Ethnographic Reflections on the New Economy.* Durham, NC: Duke University Press.

Friedman, Thomas L. 1999. *The Lexus and the Olive Tree.* New York: Farrar, Straus, and Giroux.

Geschiere, Peter, and Francis Nyamnjoh. 2000. "Capitalism and Autochthony: The Seesaw of Mobility and Belonging." *Public Culture* 12(2): 423–452.

Glick Schiller, Nina, and Noel B Salazar. 2013. "Regimes of Mobility Across the Globe." *Journal of Ethnic and Migration Studies* 39(2): 1–12.

Hargreaves, Andy, and Michael Fullan. 2011. *Professional Capital: Transforming Teaching in Every School.* New York: Teachers College Press.

Harvey, David. 1981. "The Spatial Fix-Hegel, Von Thunen, and Marx." *Antipode* 13(3): 1–12.

———. 2001. *Spaces of Capital.* New York: Routledge.

Hilgers, Mathieu. 2011. "Autochthony as Capital in a Global Age." *Theory Culture Society* 28(1): 34–54.

Hua, Wen. 2013. *Buying Beauty: Cosmetic Surgery in China.* New York: Columbia University Press.

Jacobs, Jane. 1961. *The Death and Life of Great American Cities.* New York: Random House.

Kaufmann, Vincent, Manfred Max Bergman, and Dominique Joye. 2004. "Motility: Mobility as Capital." *International Journal of Urban and Regional Research* 28(4): 745–56.

Kelly, Robert L. 1992. "Mobility/Sedentism: Concepts, Archaeological Measures, and Effects." *Annual Review of Anthropology* 21: 43–66.

Kim, Terri. 2010. "Transnational Academic Mobility, Knowledge, and Identity Capital." *Discourse: Studies in the Cultural Politics of Education* 31(5): 577–91.

Marx, Karl. 1976. *Capital.* Vol. 1. Middlesex, England: Penguin Books.

Marzloff, Bruno. 2005. *Mobilités, trajectoires fluides.* France: Editions de l'Aube.

Moret, Jöelle. 2011. "Mobility Capital: Challenging the Gender Order in a Transnational Space?" Paper presented at Reframing Gender, Reframing Critique, University of Basel, 16–17 September.

Murphy-Lejeune, Elizabeth. 2002. *Student Mobility and Narrative in Europe.* New York: Routledge.

Nahapiet, Janine, and Sumantra Ghoshal. 1998. "Social Capital, Intellectual Capital, and the Organizational Advantage." *Academy of Management Review* 23(2): 242–66.

Ong, Aihwa. 1999. *Flexible Citizenship: The Cultural Logics of Transnationality.* Durham, NC: Duke University Press.

*Oxford English Dictionary.* 2014. "Capital, adj. and n.2." Available at http://www.oed.com.www2.lib.ku.edu:2048/view/Entry/27450?result=2&rskey=nGxMvE&.

Pfann, Gerard A, Jeff Biddle, Ciska Bosman, and Daniel Hamermesh. 2000. "Business Success and Businesses' Beauty Capital." *Economics Letters* 67: 201–7.

Price, Michael K. 2008. "Fund-raising Success and a Solicitor's Beauty Capital: Do Blondes Raise More Funds?" *Economics Letters* 100: 351–54.

Putnam, Robert. 1995. "Bowling Alone: America's Declining Social Capital." *Journal of Democracy* 6(1): 65–78.

Salazar, Noel B. 2011. "The Power of Imagination in Transnational Mobilities." *Identities: Global Studies in Culture and Power* 18(6): 576–98.

Salazar, Noel B, and Alan Smart. 2011. "Anthropological Takes on (Im)Mobility." *Identities: Global Studies in Culture and Power* 18(6): i–ix.

Sassen, Saskia. 1988. *The Mobility of Labor and Capital: A Study in International Investment and Labor Flow.* Cambridge: Cambridge University Press.

Sheller, Mimi. 2011. "Mobility." *Sociopedia.isa,* 1–12.

———. 2012. "The Islanding Effect: Post-Disaster Mobility Systems and Humanitarian Logistics in Haiti." *Cultural Geographies* 20(2): 185–204.

Swedberg, Richard. 2005. "Toward an Economic Sociology of Capitalism." *L'Année Sociologique* 55(2): 419–49.

Tseng, Yen-Fen. 2000. "The Mobility of Entrepreneurs and Capital: Taiwanese Capital-Linked Migration." *International Migration* 38(2): 143–68.

Ulysse, Gina. 2007. *Downtown Ladies: Informal Commercial Importers, a Haitian Anthropologist and Self-Making in Jamaica.* Chicago: University of Chicago Press.

Urry, John. 2002. "Mobility and Proximity." *Sociology* 36(2): 255–74.

West, Paige. 2012. *From Modern Production to Imagined Primitive: The Social World of Coffee in Papua New Guinea.* Durham, NC: Duke University Press.

Warman, Arturo. 2003. *Corn & Capitalism: How a Botanical Bastard Grew to Global Dominance.* Translated by NL Westrate. Chapel Hill, NC: Duke University Press.

Williams, Raymond. 1976. *Keywords: A Vocabulary of Culture and Society.* New York: Oxford University Press.

Yosso, Tara J. 2005. "Whose Culture Has Capital? A Critical Race Theory Discussion of Community Cultural Wealth." *Race Ethnicity and Education* 8(1): 69–91.

# CHAPTER
# 2

# Cosmopolitanism

*Malasree Neepa Acharya*

In their edited volume on cosmopolitanism, Breckenridge, Pollock, Bhabha, and Chakrabarty (2002) define cosmopolitanism by highlighting its amorphous nature as a theoretical project with a conceptual content that is continuously moving as much as the mobile concepts and beings in its purview. In their attempts to galvanize the concept of a cosmopolitanism that is "yet to come" (Breckenridge et al. 2002, 4), its indeterminacy has made the project of utilizing cosmopolitanism as political practice near impossible—the term itself, as the authors claim, being resistant to any particularly ascriptions of categorizations, genealogies, and rules that define particular modes of action (2002, 4). In this way, cosmopolitanism, by way of its characteristic murkiness, can itself stand as a productive point of departure, lifting away from the liminal fog that surrounds it. Breckenridge and colleagues contend that in many ways, it is a concept "awaiting realization" (2002, 1), which is the only certain aspect from which we can derive a productive means of mobilizing the term for particular cases. If we can extract the ambiguity surrounding cosmopolitanism as being one of the few certain things from which to depart and engage the concept of mobility, then cosmopolitanism as a keyword within the anthropology of mobility functions as an instrument for analysis.

In this chapter, I engage with cosmopolitanism as a keyword in the ways in which it derives meanings and contexts specifically concerning mobility. Originating from the Greek word *kosmopolitês*—from *cosmos*, the "world," and *polites*, "citizen"—the term literally connotes a "citizen of the world" (Harper 2014; Liddel 1940). Throughout history, however, the definition of the world has shifted from identification with the city or *polis*, to global and universal citizenship in varying political and philosophical contexts in time and in constantly shifting or even migrating spaces. Williams describes how the social and historical context of a keyword evolves through "extension, variation, and transfer" (1976, 21). In its current iteration, cosmopolitanism as a socioideological project toward a global citizenry has been revived as a philosophical justification for the globalized world. As such, the keyword merits a historical context to concretize how meanings are shaped in varying embodiments across simultaneous moments in time and space (Levitt and Glick Schiller 2004). In the first half of this chapter, I therefore trace a genealogy of cosmopolitanisms[1] by investigating historical shifts as an experiential theoretical object, practice, and orientation as it relates to the ways in which people, objects, capital, and other actors move.

Cosmopolitanism as a keyword has become a form, means, and indicator of mobility; translocal movement has inspired researchers to create multiple cosmopolitanisms that have particular uses in grammar as a noun, who is *cosmopolitan* (Hannerz 1990); adjective, what it means to be *cosmopolitan* (Glick Schiller 2012; Salazar 2010; Werbner 2008); and verb, *cosmopolitanization* (Beck 2006). In ascribing cosmopolitanism's role in the study of mobility, in the second half of the chapter, I discuss the dynamics of these various grammatico-syntactical variants and modifications of the term as they are used in ethnographic interventions pertaining to mobility. In the introduction to this volume, Salazar defines mobility as an assemblage of movement, social imaginaries, and experiences of people on the move and their translocal linkages. Voluntary processes of geographical mobility are indicative of the desired acquisition and accumulation of capital—be it social, economic, or cultural.

Parallel to shifts in globalization and transnational practices, cosmopolitanism, when linked to forms of mobility, has often been typecast as allowing for an openness that is limited to a privileged few, while historical and empirical valuations in academic discourse demonstrate the contrary. Engaging the various lexical uses of cosmopolitanism, I challenge the pitfalls of normative and elitist aspects of the term's use within the humanities and social sciences by showing its potential for self-reflexivity and reclamation of power when mobilized in discourses surrounding mobility. Positing a variety of empirical and ethnographic cosmopolitan moments and analyzing philosophical ascriptions of their meaning, I claim that newly appropriated forms of cosmopolitanism—rooted, subaltern, ghetto, indigenous, diasporic, and vernacular—are building blocks centering upon changing aspects of globalization, nationalism, and postcolonialism in the process of movement, namely through the emergence of a Global South that functions as an axis of mobility. Cosmopolitanism is therefore the lens to explore mobility in terms of global movers—through global citizens as social actors (Acharya 2016) as both an identity and an ever-changing process of becoming.

In this way, cosmopolitanism offers productive potential within mobility studies. However, these new "modifiers on offer" (Glick Schiller 2012, 1) to further specify cosmopolitanisms, juxtapose seemingly contradictory notions of communalism and worldliness by questioning normative assumptions about how cosmopolitanism can be a lived reality and by whom, and who has the right to be open to the world (Glick Schiller and Salazar 2013; Werbner 2008). I conclude by asking whether these current theoretical interventions of cosmopolitanism further bifurcate an already murky term—relinquishing the concept as ungainly and potentially exhaustible in theorizing valuations and convergences of differing forms of movement in an ever-changing global terrain.

## Constructing a Genealogy of Cosmopolitanism

Philosophies derived from movement have developed throughout time, from sensibilities surrounding citizenship, its ethics, and the ways in which it is enacted within multilayered contexts of space, linking cosmopolitanism and mobility—though coming and going within academic theory among varying representations of value within our epoch. David Harvey famously remarked, "Cosmopolitanism is back. For some that is the good news. The bad news is that it has acquired so many nuances and meanings as to negate its putative role ... as a unifying vision for democracy and governance in a globalizing world" (2009, 529). The current resuscitation of the theory has multiplied in meanings and uses, particularly in context to mobility: cosmopolitanism as a representation of ethical value for a future of global citizenship (Appiah 2006); as a means of offering possibilities beyond transnational networks to links between social movements (Vertovec and Cohen 2002); as a political means of identifying hybrid and heterogeneous identities as a challenge to conventional notions of belonging and citizenship (Levitt and Glick Schiller 2004; Pieterse 2004); and as a descriptive means of addressing specific cultural processes and/or behaviors and values that represent new forms of multiplicity (Ong 1998; Werbner 2004). These varying embodiments of cosmopolitanism find a "middle path" (Beck 2004) within a complex social field where ethnocentric notions of nationalism, globalization, and migration are regularly compounded against translocal and particularistic social processes including multiculturalism, feminism, and postcolonialism.

Genealogy functions as a tool to derive a historicization of meaning-making. Cosmopolitanism's multiple and bifurcating definitions leaves the theory as contested as a practice that is yet to come (Breckenridge et al. 2002; Werbner 2008), where the rules of implementation remain unfamiliar and difficult to apply. Breckenridge et al. contend that specifying definite aspects of cosmopolitanism is an entirely "uncosmopolitan thing to do" (2002, 1), claiming that cosmopolitanism is not a known entity, "with a clear genealogy from the Stoics to Immanuel Kant, that simply awaits a more detailed description at the hands of scholarship" (1). Common critiques to cosmopolitanism explicate that the mobile cosmopolitan identity is a prerogative of elite groups (Bayat 2010, 203; Fechter and Walsh 2010; Nashashibi 2007)—those with the necessary means to travel, learn languages, and the ability to absorb other cultures. From elite tourists to business executives and global émigrés, the contention that cosmopolitanism can only be accessed by a select mobile few has been symbiotically equated with its elite Western dominance and origins.

Looking beyond the ideologies in question for the conditions of their existence allows for a detailed mode through which cosmopolitanism can be understood. Through genealogy as counter-memory,[2] cosmopolitanism has a more complex past than solely arising from Kant or ancient Greece in the Western world. Its provenance stems from Arab and Muslim trade routes, in the spread of Hinduism, Buddhism, Jainism, and Taoism, from the standardization of empires ranging from Ashok to the Tan Dynasty, and in the development of Chinese systems of thinking. A historical genealogy of cosmopolitanism is linked to mobility. It is through mobility and the historical genealogies of mobile subjects that cosmopolitanism gains a wide net of worldly beginnings that have come to define a sense of universal worldliness. It serves as a means of exploring the connections derived in mobility and the movement of sentient (im)mobile beings across diasporas.[3] A genealogical construction is particularly relevant because of its link to mobility throughout time through values spread within cultures in motion globally.

In attaching a global historical connection to the term with its utilization in areas of moral and political philosophy, social sciences, and rhetorical discourse over time, the link to elitist chains can be broken. While it may serve various functions in differing experiential capacities—from elite diaspora members settling into motion between multiple homelands globally (Acharya 2016), to tourists in remote villages sampling local cuisine as a representation of their own global subjectivities (Molz 2007)—cosmopolitanism is essential to the meaning-making of mobility. Though seemingly blurred at times, one must locate cosmopolitanism within the greater framework of mobility.

## Contextualizing Historical Cosmopolitanism

The first utterance of cosmopolitanism dates back to the Greek Stoics of third century BCE. Diogenes the Cynic has been apocryphalyzed in his proclamation, "I am a citizen of the whole world [*kosmopolitês*]" (Diogenes Laertius VI, 63). Prior ascriptions from Plato, Aristotle, and stories of Socrates bounded a cosmopolitan to the *polis,* the city, as normative identities were tied to community belonging or place of origin (Kleingeld and Brown 2013). Diogenes's claim of world citizenship differs significantly from contemporary arguments of cosmopolitan citizenship of a world state or supranational governance structure (Hartwiger 2010).[4] Rather, a clear link to mobility as a mark of cosmopolitanism arrived as a result of the increased movements of philosophers traveling in the Greco-Roman empire and connecting along trade routes to the Arab world.

Engseng Ho's historical ethnography of an expanding "cosmopolitan Muslim ecumene" (2006, 49) of *Alawi sayyid* traders spanning the Indian Ocean reflects the importance of diaspora societies as having "intimate, sticky, and prolonged" (xxi) relationships with locals. These diaspora traders were afforded "local cosmopolitan" status through histories of integration into diverse localities while maintaining their translocal identities where mobile migrants enacted "complex languages of cosmopolitanism in which the foreign and the local negotiate coexistence in vital ways" (Ho 2006, 189). In this way, globally and throughout history, mobility underwrites the existence of local cosmopolitans as migratory diaspora members profiting from mediatory roles as locals and cosmopolitans.

## From Enlightenment Cosmopolitanism to Cosmopolitan Ethics and Hospitality

Within the Western world, cosmopolitanism philosophically reemerged during the Enlightenment period. Increased mobility for the accumulation of capital through global trade and voyages that led to discoveries of new empires and colonies throughout the Renaissance and Baroque periods promulgated a philosophical focus on human rights and human reason (Kleingeld and Brown 2013). Cosmopolitanism in connection with mobility regained its force as an ideology within the French and American Revolutions as eighteenth-century uses of the term as "world citizenship" signified a value system of impartiality and openness in the name of new discovery and freedom. Kleingeld and Brown suggest that the 1789 declaration of "human" rights grew from this reinforced cosmopolitan mode of thinking. A cosmopolitan, at the time, was someone who "felt at home everywhere" with a lifestyle founded upon traveling and measuring "transnational value" through cultural contacts while void of cultural prejudice (2013).[5]

Tracing the paradox of these Enlightenment notions reflected in contemporary France, Derrida's short essay, *On Cosmopolitanism,* advocates for "cities of refuge"—zones that connect the "*cosmo*-[world]" and "politics" by enacting pure and absolute hospitality toward the Other (Derrida 2001, 3–23). Building from historical definitions, Derrida's cosmopolitanism functions as a utopian vision of how hospitality can be practiced within particular mobile communities. From Derrida's early 1990s example of postcolonial Algerians in flux within their nation as "unwanted guests" (Derrida 2001, 50–56), to current debates in the European Union about constructing zones for refugee and asylum in the wake of regular atrocities along Mediterranean borders, the ethical and normative dimensions of cosmopolitanism continue to purport a humanistic project as much as cosmopolitanism coexists as a social condition of mobility.

## Cosmopolitanism and Mobility as Journey

Contemporary significations of cosmopolitanism as an objective process link a desire to engage with the Other through "new types of journey" (Rosello 2001, vii) including migration, diaspora, transnational labor, business travel, global tourism, and individuals that are not physically on the move but "virtually mobilized" (Molz and Gibson 2007, 2). The keywords in this volume operationalize underlying mechanisms behind conceptualizations of journey. Mobile flows are mediated by widening categories of mobile subjects—individuals, groups, nonhuman actors, thoughts, beings, objects, ideologies, and concepts—that are iterative of changes in a transnational and globalized world where mobility as journey connects cosmopolitan instances of being and becoming to a contemporary global condition.

From the 1980s onward, globalization intensified worldwide flows, circulations (Lee and Li Puma 2002), and social relations that link distant localities.[6] As parallel "conceptual travel partners" to cosmopolitanism, globalization has signified worldwide connections through free-market economies and capital movement (Forte 2010, 3), while transnationalism reacts against national boundaries, signaling the increased interconnectivity between people through movement, social networks, and "social fields" (Levitt and Glick Schiller 2004). Salazar lists, in the introduction, several diverse and interweaving types of movers that are translocally mobile. From transitory migrants, to tourists, workers, and pilgrims—these movers engage, reinterpret, and circumscribe interdependent mobile economic, cultural, social, and spatial factors across territorially bounded nation-states and societies (Glick Schiller and Salazar 2013). Complex and fluid connections surround global flows of commodities and capital, while the various transnational movers widen the field of migration types: low-skilled labor, high-skilled labor, irregular, international travel, lifestyle, environmental, human trafficking and smuggling, asylum and refugee protection, internally displaced peoples, diaspora, remittances, and root causes (Acharya 2015; Cassarino 2004; Massey 1986). From these exemplifications of mobility that compel those of diverse backgrounds to communally work and live together, built communities and nations are "internally globalized" and "cosmopolitanized" (Bayat 2010, 203; Molz and Gibson 2007, 2). The juxtaposition of peoples affects migration and tourism flows while illuminating cosmopolitanism's engagement with cultural phenomena emerging from global circulation.

A diversity of cultural factors pertaining to cosmopolitan journeys in connection with today's mobile world—iterative of globalized and translocal mobilities—has led to a plethora of cosmopolitanisms invoked both as ethical ideals and lived experiences. *Glocalization*—as an internal globalization traversing borders, routes, and crossings within social space, fields, and communities—allows for a twofold conception of cosmopolitanism: first, as situational openness of the ethical individual within local contexts, and second, as detachment from local ties through mobility (Roudometof 2005). Such cultural indicators of cosmopolitanism as a lived reality are also symptomatic of its ethics-driven turn in relation to mobility, while empirical examples of modifiers (vernacular, rooted, ghetto, diasporic, indigenous) create multiple cosmopolitanisms that simultaneously clarify and obfuscate cosmopolitanism's productive potential.

### Being Cosmopolitan "Patriots": Rootless, Rooted, Roots

Cosmopolitanism and mobility's relationship in empirical terms engages aspects of identity, belonging, and hybridity of the mobile movers and non-movers represented throughout this volume. Through its empirical-analytic uses within the social sciences, a cosmopolitan perspective reflects the interrelatedness of individual identities of people globally, across cross-border interactions and identity formation (Beck 2006, 45–46).[7] From its historical definition as a "citizen of the world," the cosmopolitan has been connected to ethical aspects of global citizenship, and yet, since the start of the twenty-first century, the idea of the cosmopolitan as a trope of identity and/or being has taken a normative, ethics-driven turn.

Appiah's (1997) work of the seemingly contradictory title, *Cosmopolitan Patriots,* portends this relationship to contemporary ethics. The existence of "normative" cosmopolitans (Appiah 2006) add to existing debates about postcolonial states on citizenship, cultural rights, equal dignity, and the rule of law. Echoing Nussbaum's (1994) notion of a cosmopolitan "patriotism," Appiah proposes that the cosmopolitan patriot lives in a world where everyone is a "rooted cosmopolitan" that feels a connection to his or her "home" or "place of origin" without abandoning moral and emotional attachments to communities, families, diasporas, and ethnic groups, while enjoying others through an openness to the world.[8] Nussbaum and Appiah's cosmopolitan patriotisms ascribe a sense of world citizenship that emerged during the 1990s, promulgated by the end of the Cold War and reunification of Germany. At that time, a variety of academic and public discourses saw a resurgence of the Kantian conception of a world order that promoted global peace just as it had after the first and second world wars (Kleingeld and Brown 2013).

A decade later, concerns with terrorism and national security in the wake of the September 11th attacks on the United States resurrected a need for an ethos of the "rooted cosmopolitan" that stood in stark contrast to the politically propagandized abuses posed by Hitler and Stalin against "rootless cosmopolitanism," representative of 1940s German and Soviet regimes where "anti-cosmopolitanism" functioned as a euphemism for anti-Semitism (Appiah 2006, xvi). Opposition to the "rootless cosmopolitan" was borne out of a need for loyalty to a particular class or nation, rather than a "hard-core cosmopolitan" that believes in shared responsibilities toward all of humankind (Appiah 2006). The rooted cosmopolitan creates positions for partial cosmopolitanisms whereby "ethnic rootedness does not negate openness to cultural difference" (Werbner 2012, 155). For these rooted cosmopolitans, rather, a local sense of belonging stimulates universal moral and civic responsibilities. Richard Werbner's study of Kalanga elite civil servants that hold radical worldviews demonstrate the capacity for ethnic rootedness, "ethnic cosmopolitanism," to function with an openness to cultural difference beyond local ties (Werbner 2004). These rooted cosmopolitans interpret culture and ethnicity to assert a wider set of cosmopolitan values that mobilize the particularistic and universal.

The normative ethical aspects of rootedness in cosmopolitan mobility can be extended to postcolonial nations and across diasporas in discussions about citizenship, belonging, multiple homelands, identity, hybridity, and actorness of the mobile cosmopolitan subjects themselves. In this way, cosmopolitanism offers new forms of belonging and opens forms of attachment for rights claims beyond the nation-state—in instances of Muslim migrant women's activism affirming their right to wear headscarves in Europe (Yeğenoğlu 2012, 416), or by "cornershop" cosmopolitan merchants in Hackney, London, that actively manage multiple local contexts as they negotiate their home spaces (Wessendorf 2010). A sense of homeland and belonging is specific to these rooted migration experiences.

Studies on roots migration investigate second-generation migration to a homeland (see Jain 2011; Levitt 2009; Wessendorf 2007), though their engagement remains simultaneous in time and space across social fields (Levitt and Glick Schiller 2004). Jain finds that returning second-generation Indian Americans to the Indian business sector seek local relationships to multiple countries, while their norms of business practice remain part of a global ecumene (2011, 896–914). Such imaginaries of multiple locales portend a sense of global citizenship mediated by diasporic encounters of identity, as seen in Christou and King's (2015) study of "counter diasporics" of Greek American and Greek-German origin in search of their own definition of "Greekness." Interdependencies between belonging and homeland on local and global levels are indicative of hybrid identities that encompass the lived experiences of cosmopolitans in their processes of becoming.

### Cosmopolitanism, Mobility, and Agency

Concepts of hybridity, belonging, and the search for multiple homelands are all tangible cosmopolitan moments made for and by the formation of becoming cosmopolitan. Cosmopolitanism's unique contribution to mobility studies, however, rests in emphasizing cosmopolitans as social actors. Actorness serves as a catalyst for developing cosmopolitanism as a worldly ideal and an identity-in-development within the lives of the movers. Such a sensibility is often lacking in other theories governing mobility such as transnationalism, structuralism, neoliberal economic theory, and social network theory (Acharya 2016).[9] In other words, the agency of people on the move contributes to defining and regulating their connection between cosmopolitanism and mobility.

Like the cosmopolitan patriot, agency through individual growth and development of identity is tied to multiple sites or locations and the mobile journeys between them. Ethnographies on the "socio-emotional agency" of high-skilled female migrant entrepreneurs in the EU (Morokvasic 2002, Tienda and Booth 1991) suggest that social innovators create attachments at home across multiple localities while mobilizing them as assets. These female entrepreneurs locate and imagine transnational ways of life utilizing borders and mobility as integrative resources to assemble families around emotional attachments to place from a global vantage point (Morokvasic 2002, 6). Movers as "bottom-up" agents of change help define cosmopolitan's relationship to mobility beyond an engagement with the Other as mobile subjects build on their social capital and innovation as mobility gateways.

Several high-skilled entrepreneurial groups function as cosmopolitan actors to develop global opportunity through mobility. Ong's "flexible citizens" include Chinese mobile business elites working against nation-state political economic control that locate markets and homes in multiple locales (1999, 43). Ong observes the "liberating" capacity of cosmopolitanism in empowering both mobile and nonmobile subjects (11)—those who can profit from a globalized economic system set up by nation-states controlling their borders, while others become localized to respond to the flows of capital. Along similar lines, Favell's "Eurostars" moving across European multilocalities desire freedom in a "cosmopolitan (cultural)" context (2011, 7). In their process of living, these social actors aspire toward cosmopolitan ideals that are post-national and traced from normative Enlightenment concepts of worldly belonging.

Studies of "expatness" among such types of high-skilled mobile migrants demonstrate how such identities are multilayered and shaped by local and cross-border involvement through "universal, cosmopolitan orientations" globally and within local "expatriate bubbles" (van Bochove and Engbersen 2015, 3–7). My work on globally circulating diaspora entrepreneurs of Indian origin choosing to permanently settle in emerging Indian cities (Acharya 2016) examines the development and impact of a cosmopolitan identity. I contend that these entrepreneurs construct new forms of interconnectedness through their mobility patterns and built networks across international technopoles such as Silicon Valley, Bangalore, and London. Linking the motivations of mobile migrants to the fluidity of shifting and hybridized cosmopolitan identities shapes a new way of understanding mobility where its very impacts have a direct bearing on the reasons for being globally mobile (Acharya 2016). Cosmopolitan aspirations, ways of being, and the process of becoming thereby offer individuating circumstances surrounding mobility and circulation.

### Cosmopolitan Tourism and the Other

While agency through hybridity and flexibility link cosmopolitans and their mobilities—tying belonging to local and global engagements—an ethos of mobile movers and their exchanges with the Other across spaces has been the focus of tourism and circulatory migration studies that highlight cosmopolitanism's normative considerations. Hannerz argues that the basic tenet of a cosmopolitan is one who is open to and knowledgeable about other cultures, possessing "an orientation, a willingness to engage with the Other" (1990, 249). As cosmopolitans that are on the move globally, journalists, business people, tourists, and exiles require "cultural competencies" (Hannerz 1990, 103, 240) as a means of their cosmopolitan being. A "genuine" cosmopolitan maintains respect for the rights of individuals with regard for the welfare, humanity, and safety of others (Hannerz 2004, 69). Such sentiments across cultures and networked interactions create a distinction between cosmopolitan mobility versus that of a more globalized, multicultural, or transnational nature.

Cosmopolitanism's unique form of engaging the Other as the basis of a mobile subject's identity formation is not a contemporary phenomenon. Beck describes that "the (forced) mixing of cultures is nothing new," having been historically linked through the mobility of plunder, conquest, slave trade, colonization, ethnic cleansing, settlement, and expulsion (2004, 137). Breckenridge et al. frame cosmopolitanism's relationship with the Other as "look[ing] at the world across time and space [to] see how people have thought and acted beyond the local" (2002, 3). Cosmopolitanisms in this sense refer to the potentially infinite ways of "living at home abroad or abroad at home" (Rao 2007, 19) where identity formation is of primary concern. Thus, cosmopolitanism as cultural context can be observed within the encounters between cosmopolitan elite travelers and immobile locals (Glick Schiller and Salazar 2013, 4) and in its varying relationships to tourism (Clifford 1992).

Cosmopolitanism rests between universalisms and diversity constructed in mobile encounters between people. Within the dynamics of tourism and touring, a cosmopolitan must possess "attitudinal and dispositional orientations," where, in connection to mobility that allows for the experience of travel, tourism becomes "cosmopolitanism-as-practice" (Salazar 2010, 56). Cosmopolitans inform themselves of "other worlds" (Hannerz 2004; Salazar 2010; Urry 2000) while respecting cultural difference and a sense of global belonging and consciousness that is integrated into everyday norms.

Moments that occur in the practice of travel represents a dualism of cosmopolitan contact both with the tourist and the other that is being "toured." Actions, for example, represent material symbols of the global within the traveler's performances of cosmopolitanism in interactions with locals, as seen in Molz's (2007) ethnography on mobile tourists that engage with the local through dining. Salazar's ethnography on local tour guides in Tanzania and Indonesia that establish their own cosmopolitan status reflects upon cosmopolitan contact with the Other, wherein the cosmopolitan tourist consumes a build-up of cosmopolitan capital from the ways in which tour guides reveal their lifeworlds as aspirational: "dreams of becoming more cosmopolitan" (2010, 55). In these instances of tourism as both experienced and highly constructed cosmopolitanisms, tourists and tour guides as mobile cosmopolitans utilize cosmopolitanism as cultural currency that can be used, concealed, transgressed, and reinforced.

Beck operationalizes "cosmopolitanization," as the formation of multiple mobile identities through the spread of transnational lifestyles (2004, 136) rooted in global social movements of the underclass and underprivileged (Beck 2006). Each of the multiple forms of cosmopolitanism can be "cosmopolitanized" through identities, belonging, and encounters between cosmopolitan mobile subjects. The cosmopolitanization of identity politics moves cosmopolitan discourse from "principle to practice" (Werbner 2011). Multiple "new normative" cosmopolitanisms are institutionalized as an enduring reality (Werbner 2006, 7–11). Placing mobile cosmopolitans and cosmopolitanisms in conversation with one another as a tool for discovery reflected within ethnographic experiences, the points at which these various instantiations of cosmopolitanisms diverge, provide opportunities for a critical self-awareness within the field of mobility studies.

### Cosmopolitan "Modifiers on Offer"

The notion that there are many coexisting cosmopolitanisms with their own genealogies and worldviews has also led to the development of cosmopolitanisms predicated upon marginality and difference. These added "modifiers on offer" juxtapose seemingly opposite conceptions of exclusivity and openness (Glick Schiller 2012, 1). Modifiers such as vernacular, rooted, ghetto, everyday, diasporic, subaltern, indigenous (Appiah 2006; Beck 2004; Bhabha 1996; Forte 2010; Gidwani 2006; Glick Schiller 2012; Nashashibi 2007), and countless other terms-in-the-making have become part of the project of structuring a "new cosmopolitanism" (Cheah 2006; Vertovec and Cohen 2002) that dissociates the term from its universalist underpinnings and assumed Eurocentric groundings.

These often contradictory binary terms query hegemonic assumptions about how cosmopolitanism is lived, whose cosmopolitanism is being noted, and who is open to the world (Werbner 2008). Bhabha, in coining the term "vernacular cosmopolitanism," responded to extreme aspects of a 1990s normative ethical cosmopolitanism going too far—where the self resides at the center surrounded by universal liberal values privileged before more intimate connections with family, ethnic groups, diaspora, and nation (Bhabha 1994). Cosmopolitan "modifiers," known also as "marginal cosmopolitanisms" (Forte 2010, 6), or "discrepant" cosmopolitanisms (Clifford 1992, 108), respond to the inadequacies of a borderless cosmopolitan community of the world by considering the millions of refugees and irregular migrants fleeing violence and poverty and being denied entry or existence as citizens of any particular nation (Bhabha 1994).[10] For mobile diaspora and high-skilled migrant communities, Richard Werbner (2004) presents the case of minority elites in postcolonial nations that seek justice for their local cultures to question the tenuous nature of who qualifies as a vernacular cosmopolitan. These elites demonstrate a vernacular while existing as multicultural citizens that are liberal world travelers (Werbner 2004).[11] Hannerz provides useful distinctions between mobile individuals: cosmopolitans who engage with "unfamiliar cultures and places"; locals, who perpetuate culture by living solely in their locale; and transnationals as travellers who see movement as a "necessary cost" (2004, 69). Transnational migrant diasporas as vernacular cosmopolitans share forms of open closure that typify elite cultures whereby modes of travel pertain to mobility desires for mobile migrants.

The various claims to vernacular cosmopolitanism as "an oxymoron that joins contradictory notions of local specificity and universal enlightenment," (Werbner 2006, 7) rests at the epicenter of this chapter's preoccupation concerning the dominance and viability of a Western worldview of cosmopolitanism for mobility studies. Pnina Werbner observes that vernacular cosmopolitanism questions the coexistence of "local, parochial, rooted, culturally specific and demotic" with the "translocal, transnational, transcendent, elitist, enlightened, universalist and modernist" (2006, 8). Applying Werbner's reflection, a question emerges as to whether such boundary-crossing "demotic" migrations are comparable to the sophisticated cultural knowledge and moral worldview gained by entrepreneurial intellectuals bridging the Global North and South through globe-trotting travel.

The preceding section located ethnographic studies of elites and highly skilled movers as active hybrid agents creating a sense of cosmopolitan mobility within local settlements (Acharya 2016; Favell 2011; Morokvasic 2013; Ong 1999; van Bochove and Engbersen 2015; Varrel 2008). These instances of cosmopolitan "vernaculars" also reflect a project of seeking justice through multicultural citizenship (Werbner 2004) and solidarity (Hollinger 2006). Globalization, postnationalism, and postcolonialism become three central issues that are addressed throughout the development of cosmopolitanisms and the resulting individuation of cosmopolitans as social actors. Instances of mobility frame cosmopolitanism as an identity through actorness. In this way, cosmopolitan vernaculars address postnationalist and postcolonial histories that emerge as a side effect of globalization.

Such conjunctions of vernacular cosmopolitanism reflect pre- and postcolonial structures of cosmopolitan conscious within acts of mobility. Pnina Werbner questions the inclusion of particular vernaculars: "are we talking about non-elite forms of travel and trade in the postcolonial world ... or of non-European but nevertheless high cultures produced and consumed by non-Western elites, such as those of the Urdu, Persian or

Ottoman worlds?" (Werbner 2008, 496–97). Diouf presents an example of Senegalese Mouride traders who engage in social rites that maintain a homogenized culture by excluding foreign values (2002, 124). The vernacular "localizes the cosmopolitan" as part of its own self-making—even "relocalizing what the cosmopolitan borrowed from it in the first place" (Pollock 2002, 39). The framework of a vernacular within cultural formations are thereby "rooted and routed" (Forte 2010, 6) in lived, everyday practices, as in examples of "indigenous" and "ghetto" vernaculars.

Everyday lived realities, from indigenous and subaltern forms of cosmopolitanism mobilities reflect a variety of cosmopolitan encounters that are constitutive of "self knowledge" (Fog Olwig 2010). Studies conducted by Fog Olwig (2010) and Wardle (2012) in the Caribbean present a full "ethnography of cosmopolitanism" (504), where social interactions and mobilities are evoked from an intellectual history of enlightenment and pre/postcolonial engagements while (im)mobile subjects encounter inequalities of within social lives of the everyday. Lived experiences of the everyday that are representative of the culturally specific modifiers of cosmopolitanism create a contextual conundrum, since an ethnography of cosmopolitan mobilities itself within the vernacular presents strong relativistic challenges to universalizing categories of both global and local thinking. Thus, a tension between universalizing concepts, of which cosmopolitanism itself espouses as a concept-metaphor, further complicates the very field in which the term serves to clarify.

## Conclusion

In his article entitled, *Mobility and the Cosmopolitan Perspective* (2008), Beck suggests that conceptual and empirical explorations surrounding globalization lost their credibility when emerging globalization studies, concerned with definitions, asked complex questions about the term's utilization within historical contexts throughout modernity, postmodernity, and the postcolonial. As a first step to find "a way of change," the author defines various versions of cosmopolitanism in relation to mobility (25). In two pages, fourteen different definitions were noted—and Beck shares his own skepticism by remarking that conceptualizing so many cosmopolitanizations raise more questions and objections than finding a common vision (27). Cosmopolitanism, particularly in its plethora of iterations in the social sciences, has come to take on a multiplicity of meanings across phenomena that imply political, moral, and aesthetic transcendence across boundaries while representing an openness to the commonalities of humankind. Cosmopolitan being, then, functions both an idealized identity as well as the process of becoming that constructs a normative and worldly relationship to multiple places for people on the move.

The murkiness of cosmopolitanism within mobility studies offers productive possibilities that are better suited than narrowly defining concepts of ethics, and universality that could design a dangerous binary of the "good and pure cosmopolitans" and the "hostile, ignorant non-cosmopolitans" (Forte 2010, 5). Appropriations of the "cosmopolitan patriot" (Appiah 2006) to draw theoretical correlations between globalization, transnationalism, ethics, culture, and the development of vernaculars to reclaim the concept for empirical moments that clash with race, gender, and class politics, has resulted in a multiplicity of cosmopolitanisms and grammatical variants of the term. Though Rapport and Stade contend that plural definitions of cosmopolitanism demonstrate the capacity of cosmopolitans to be found all over the world (2007, 232–33), the confusion involved in approaching any standardization of the term far outweighs its potential relevance. Furthermore, when inspecting a genealogy of cosmopolitanisms, it becomes clear that there is far more evidence of cosmopolitan practices globally, than solely among Western elites. As such, one must consider what cosmopolitanisms can offer for the future of mobility studies.

Latour explains that we must bring the "cosmos" back into "cosmopolitics" (2004, 456), offering an ability to recognize a plurality of othernesses universally rather than finding patterns of a universal culture of sameness.[12] The age-old challenge within the social sciences and namely the study of anthropology has been an argument about empirical studies of specificity of universalism. Within mobility studies, rather than recognizing patterns of universal cosmopolitans, a potential productive approach involves locating cosmopolitan universals. Tsing's *Friction* (2004) challenges Spivak's warning of the social researchers' need to ere on the safe side of investigating the culturally specific at the behest of the universal because of its inscription of particularly dominant Western ideals (Spivak 1990, 271). To address the universality that is produced by its very absence in discourse, Tsing crafts a history of universal ideologies—by integrating a dialogue across difference to understand how such ideas are constructed (2004, 13). With the increase of universal models, thinking toward universalism, planetarism, and cosmopolitics, one must consider what an ethnography of the universal may reflect in its connection to mobility—and whether such notions in itself are inherently cosmopolitan.

As seen throughout this chapter and particularly within the ethnographic examples, cosmopolitanism is inextricably tied to mobility. Mobility in itself comes from an area with vastly different situations of why people move and how this movement is constructed, imagined, implemented, and valued. Scholars attempt to theorize how divergent populations operate in context to borders and bounded spaces by creating their own unbounded sensibilities regarding movement while developing relationships locally, globally, and universally. While it is seductive to honor the various "modifiers" of cosmopolitanism, a question arises as to whom and for whom it is important to justify cosmopolitan vernaculars as a reclamation of power from the term's supposed Eurocentric underpinnings that scholars reify by denying the term's global past. Rather than the grand bifurcations of terminologies, grammatical changes, wordplay, and shifting forms of the concept, it is a necessary call to action a more universalizing notion of movement in relation to the cosmopolitan. Social scientists and mobility studies scholars in particular must become comfortable with using the term, cosmopolitanism, universally for what it is—beyond the comfort of cross-referencing its worldly and global potentialities that emerge from its genealogical, ethical, and contemporary iterations. Otherwise, while specificity and reflexivity offer potentialities toward understanding the human condition, overly particularizing mobility's relationship to theoretical lenses of modernity will deepen its own gradual descent into an abyss of countless -isms while the perennial productive fog continues to lift before our eyes.

**Malasree Neepa Acharya** is a researcher in migration, diversity, and justice at the Institute for European Studies, Vrije Universiteit Brussel, in Belgium, and a member of the teaching team of the Program in Entrepreneurship and Innovation, Stanford Center for Professional Development, Stanford University. Her research explores themes of return migration and circulation in the emerging Global South, cosmopolitan identities and social actorness of diaspora elites, and entrepreneurship within interconnected global technopoles of Silicon Valley, Bangalore, and London. She serves as an advisory member of the working group on Mobilizing Diaspora Resources of the Global Knowledge Partnership on Migration and Development (KNOMAD) project, chartered by the World Bank and Migration Policy Institute.

## NOTES

1. Genealogy as a historical tool for meaning-making is essential to understanding how cosmopolitanism is linked to mobility—globally. While Breckenridge et al. (2002) and Vertovec and Cohen (2002) advise against a genealogy of cosmopolitan theory, this paper addresses genealogy's problematic pitfalls while justifying why its engagement is a necessity.

2. Genealogy as counter-memory transforms history into different forms of time. The dissolution of identity of historical subjects transfigures time using modern histori-

cal techniques in opposition to a search for "origins" (Foucault 1977, 142–60). Genealogy converges movements giving rise to new epochs, concepts, and institutions.

3    In chronicling the journey of Hadrami traders, Ho explains that genealogy is part of the stories people share in this diaspora, in moments of "clarity," and "entanglement" (2006, xxiii). As a "narrative of origins" synthesizing an arboreal metaphor (xxiii), Ho claims that genealogy does not resemble internal growth, but rather, it gains momentum from local circumstances in the diaspora interchanging with foreign places and peoples. Genealogy locates a canon of peoples as it moves through historical time by exploring a diaspora's movement through geographical space as "genealogical travel" (xxiv). Throughout its genealogy, the cosmopolitan sensibility is inextricably linked to mobility.

4.   Diogenes's self-ascription as a citizen of the world resisted limitations on identity formation. Identifying not as a citizen of Sinope but as a citizen of the world, Diogenes refused his duty to his community. His statement, "I am a citizen of the cosmos" is a negative claim toward world citizenship.

5.   Within the eighteenth-century *Encyclopédie*, "cosmopolitan" signifies "a man who is nowhere a stranger" (Diderot and Le Rond d'Alembert 1754, 297). Fougeret de Montbron declares himself cosmopolitan in his 1750 autobiography, *Le Cosmopolite*, proclaiming, "All the countries are the same to me," and "[I am] changing my places of residence according to my whim" (130). In contrast to the concept of a patriot, writers such as Montesquieu, Voltaire, Diderot, Rousseau, Hume, and Jefferson described themselves as cosmopolitans (see Kleingeld and Brown 2013).

6.   Globalization, defined as, "the intensification of worldwide social relations which link distant localities in such a way that local happenings are shaped by events occurring many miles away or vice versa" (Giddens 1990, 64), then engages mobility as an iteration of cosmopolitan thought (Beck 2006).

7.   Beck warns that such engagements should be distinct from normative philosophical engagements with the cosmopolitan (2006, 45). Beck advocates for "methodological cosmopolitanism" (2008, 12) as a lens that moves away from any nationalistic proscriptions toward movement. Empirical analytic cosmopolitanism describes cross-border realities brought into being–conquest, commerce, and free movement as examples.

8.   Mitchell Cohen coined "rooted cosmopolitanism" as a concept that speaks to pluralities of patriotisms and loyalties as "multicultural exchange" between mobile subjects (1992, 483). See Werbner (2012, 154).

9.   In mobility studies, lenses for analysis include transnationalism, structuralism, neoliberal economic theory, and social network theory (Cassarino 2004, Massey 1986). I propose a fifth "lens" of cosmopolitanism for mobility studies, emphasizing particular tenets of actorness and hybridity of the mobile subject (Acharya 2015).

10.  Werbner questions cosmopolitanism's universal values: "In what sense does cosmopolitanism need to be grounded in an open, experimental, inclusive, and normative conscious of the world, which calls for perpetual peace and the end of cul-

tural intolerance and hostility?" (2006). Such consciousness necessitates reflexivity and an awareness of cultural practices and values of the Other.

11. Cultural groups adjust differently to mobility. Ong (1998) suggests that diasporas are complex entities without a homogenous set of "equally tolerant" and "open-minded" individuals normally required of cosmopolitans (cf. Werbner 2006). Thus, cosmopolitans and locals cannot be categorized as necessarily mobile or immobile.

12. Coined by Stengers (2003), "cosmopolitics [*cosmopolitiques*]" recognizes the limitations of cosmopolitanism. Political realities of a world, human and nonhuman, necessitate "constructivist politics" and "constructivist cosmologies" (Cheah 1998; Latour 2004). Devoid of a dream of a universalist project, the *politics* is present and tied to the *cosmos* (Latour 2004; Stengers 2003).

## REFERENCES

Acharya, Malasree Neepa. 2016. "'Brain-Gain' Return of India's High-Skilled Entrepreneurs: Home, Transformation and Power Politics in the Cosmopolitan Global South." PhD dissertation, Vrije Universiteit Brussel.

Appiah, Kwame A. 1997. "Cosmopolitan Patriots." *Critical Inquiry* 23(3): 617–39.

———. 2006. *Cosmopolitanism: Ethics in a World of Strangers.* New York: Norton.

Bayat, Asef. 2010. *Life as Politics: How Ordinary People Change the Middle East.* 2nd ed. Stanford, CA: Stanford University Press.

Beck, Ulrich. 2004. "Cosmopolitical Realism: On the Distinction Between Cosmopolitanism, Philosophy and the Social Sciences." *Global Networks* 4(2): 131–56.

———. 2006. *The Cosmopolitan Vision.* Cambridge: Polity Press.

———. 2008. "Mobility and the Cosmopolitan Perspective." In *Tracing Mobilities: Towards a Cosmopolitan Perspective,* edited by Weert Canzler, Vincent Kaufmann, and Sven Kesselring, 25–35. Aldershot, England: Ashgate.

Bhabha, Homi K. 1994. *The Location of Culture.* London: Routledge.

———. 1996. "Unsatisfied: Notes on Vernacular Cosmopolitanism." In *Text and Nation: Cross-Disciplinary Essays on Cultural and National Identities,* edited by Laura Garcia-Moreno and Peter Pfeiffer, 191–207. Columbia, SC: Camden House.

Breckenridge, Carol A, Sheldon Pollock, Homi K Bhabha, and Dipesh Chakrabarty, eds. 2002. *Cosmopolitanism.* Durham, NC: Duke University Press.

Cassarino, Jean-Pierre. 2004. "Theorizing Return Migration: The Conceptual Approach to Return Migrants Revisited." *International Journal on Multicultural Societies* 6(2): 253–79.

Cheah, Pheng. 1998. "Introduction Part II: The Cosmopolitical-Today." In *Cosmopolitics: Thinking and Feeling Beyond the Nation,* edited by Pheng Cheah and Bruce Robbins, 20–44. Minneapolis: University of Minnesota Press.

———. 2006. "Cosmopolitanism." *Theory, Culture & Society* 23 (2–3): 486–96.

Christou, Anastasia, and Russell King. 2015. *Counter Diaspora: The Greek Second Generation Returns "Home."* Cambridge, MA: Harvard University Press.

Clifford, James. 1992. "Traveling Cultures." In *Cultural Studies,* edited by Lawrence Grossberg, Cary Nelson, and Paula Treichler, 96–116. London: Routledge.

Cohen, Mitchell. "Rooted Cosmopolitanism." *Dissent* 39(4): 478–83.

Derrida, Jacques. 2001. *On Cosmopolitanism and Forgiveness.* Translated by Richard Rorty. New York: Routledge.

Diderot, Denis, and Jean Le Rond d'Alembert. 1754. *Encyclopédie, ou Dictionnaire raisonné des sciences, des arts et des métiers, par une société des gens de lettres.* Vol. IV. Paris: Braisson, David, Le Breton, and Durand.

Diogenes Laertius. 1925. *Lives of the Eminent Philosophers.* Vol. 2, book VI: 63. Translated by RD Hicks. Cambridge, MA: Harvard University Press.

Diouf, Mamadou. 2002. "The Senegalese Murid Trade Diaspora and the Making of a Vernacular Cosmopolitanism." In *Cosmopolitanism,* edited by Carol A Breckenridge, Sheldon Pollock, Homi K Bhabha, and Dipesh Chakrabarty, 111–37. Durham, NC: Duke University Press.

Favell, Adrian. 2008. *Eurostars and Eurocities: Free Movement and Mobility in an Integrating Europe.* Malden, MA: Blackwell Publishing.

Fechter, Anne-Maaike, and Katie Walsh. 2010. "Examining 'Expatriate' Continuities: Postcolonial Approaches to Mobile Professionals." *Journal of Ethnic and Migration Studies* 36(8): 1197–1210.

Fog Olwig, Karen. 2010. "Cosmopolitan Traditions: Caribbean Perspectives." *Social Anthropology* 18(4): 417–24.

Forte, Maximilian C. 2010. *Indigenous Cosmopolitans. Transnational and Transcultural Indigeneity in the Twenty-First Century.* New York: Peter Lang.

Foucault, Michel. 1977. *Surveiller et punir: Naissaince de la prison.* Paris: Gallimard.

Fougeret de Montbron, Louis-Charles. 1750. *Le Cosmopolite ou le Citoyen du Monde.* London: Fougeret de Montbron.

Giddens, Anthony. 1990. *The Consequences of Modernity.* Cambridge: Polity Press.

Gidwani, Vinay. 2006. "Subaltern Cosmopolitanism as Politics." *Antipode* 38(1): 7–21.

Glick Schiller, Nina. 2012. "Diasporic Cosmopolitanism: Migrants, Sociabilities, and City-Making." Research Institute for Contemporary Cosmopolitanisms (RICC) Working Paper, Manchester University, United Kingdom.

Glick Schiller, Nina, and Noel B Salazar. 2013. "Regimes of Mobility Across the Globe." *Journal of Ethnic and Migration Studies* 39(2): 183–200.

Hannerz, Ulf. 1990. "Cosmopolitans and Locals in World Culture." *Theory, Culture, and Society* 7(2/3): 237–52.

———. 2004. "Cosmopolitanism." In *A Companion to the Anthropology of Politics,* edited by David Nugent and Joan Vincent, 69–85. Oxford: Blackwell.

Harper, Douglas. 2014. "Cosmopolite (n.)." *Online Etymology Dictionary.* Ohio University. Available at http://www.etymonline.com/index.php?term=cosmopolite

Hartwiger, Alexander. 2010. "Cosmopolitan Pedagogy: Reading Postcolonial Literature in an Age of Globalization." PhD dissertation, University of North Carolina at Greensboro.

Harvey, David. 2009. "Cosmopolitanism and the Banality of Geographical Evils." *Public Culture* 12(2): 529–64.

Ho, Engseng. 2006. *The Graves of Tarim: Genealogy and Mobility across the Indian Ocean.* Berkeley: University of California Press.

Hollinger, David. 2006. *Cosmopolitanism and Solidarity: Studies in Ethnoracial, Religious and Professional Affiliation in the United States.* Madison: University of Wisconsin Press.

Jain, Sonali. 2011. "The Rights of Return: Ethnic Identities in the Workplace among Second Generation Indian-American Professionals in the Parental Homeland." *Journal of Ethnic and Migration Studies* 37(9): 1313–30.

Kleingeld, Pauline, and Eric Brown. 2013. "Cosmopolitanism." In *The Stanford Encyclopedia of Philosophy,* edited by Edward N Zalta. Stanford, CA: Center for the Study of Language and Information, Stanford University. Available at http://plato.stanford.edu/archives/fall2013/entries/cosmopolitanism

Latour, Bruno. 2004. "Whose Cosmos? Which Cosmopolitics?" *Common Knowledge* 10(3): 450–62.

Lee, Benjamin, and Edward Li Puma. 2002. "Cultures of Circulation: The Imaginations of Modernity." *Public Culture* 14(1): 191–213.

Levitt, Peggy. 2009. "Roots and Routes: Understanding the Lives of the Second Generation Transnationally." *Journal of Ethnic and Migration Studies* 3(7): 1225–42.

Levitt, Peggy, and Nina Glick Schiller. 2004. "Conceptualizing Simultaneity: A Transnational Social Field Perspective on Society." *International Migration Review* 38(3): 1002–39.

Liddel, Henry. 1940. *A Greek-English Lexicon,* edited by Sir Henry Jones and Roderick McKenzie. Oxford: Clarendon.

Massey, Douglas. 1986. "The Social Organization of Mexican Migration to the United States." *Annals of the American Academy of Political and Social Science* 487: 102–13.

Molz, Jennie Germann. 2007. "Eating Difference: The Cosmopolitan Mobilities of Culinary Tourism." *Space and Culture* 10(1): 77–93.

Molz, Jennie Germann, and Sarah Gibson, eds. 2007. *Mobilizing Hospitality: The Ethics of Social Relations in a Mobile World.* London: Ashgate.

Morokvasic, Mirjana. 2002. "Post-Communist Migration and Gender in Europe." *Journal of Gender Studies* 5: 15–45.

———. 2013. *Paradoxes of Integration Female Migrants in Europe.* London: Springer.

Nashashibi, Rami. 2007. "Ghetto Cosmopolitanism: Making Theory at the Margins." In *Deciphering the Global: Its Scales, Spaces and Subjects,* edited by Saskia Sassen, 243–64. New York: Routledge.

Nussbaum, Martha. 1994. "Patriotism and Cosmopolitanism." *Boston Review* 19(5): 3–34.

Ong, Aihwa. 1998. "Flexible citizenship among Chinese cosmopolitans." In *Cosmopolitics: Thinking and Feeling Beyond the Nation,* edited by Pheng Cheah and Bruce Robbins, 134–62. Minneapolis: University of Minnesota Press.

———. 1999. *Flexible Citizenship: The Cultural Logics of Transnationality.* Durham, NC: Duke University Press.

Pieterse, Jan Nederveen. 2004. "Hybridity, So What?" *Theory, Culture & Society* 18(2): 219–45.

Pollock, Sheldon. 2002. "Cosmopolitanism and Vernacular in History." In *Cosmopolitanism*, edited by Carol A Breckenridge, Sheldon Pollock, Homi K Bhabha, and Dipesh Chakrabarty, 15–53. Durham, NC: Duke University Press.

Rao, Rahul. 2007. "Postcolonial Cosmopolitanism: Between the Home and the World." PhD dissertation, Oxford University.

Rapport, Nigel, and Ronald Stade. 2007. "A Cosmopolitan Turn—Or Return?" *Social Anthropology* 15(2): 223–35.

Rosello, Mireille. 2001. *Postcolonial Hospitality: The Immigrant as Guest.* Stanford, CA: Stanford University Press.

Roudometof, Victor. 2005. "Transnationalism, Cosmopolitanism and Glocalization." *Current Sociology* 53(1): 113–35.

Salazar, Noel B. 2010. "Tourism and Cosmopolitanism: A View from Below." *International Journal of Tourism Anthropology* 1(1): 55–69.

Spivak, Gayatri Chakravorty. 1990. "Can the Subaltern Speak?" In *Marxism and the Interpretation of Culture*, edited by Gary Nelson and Larry Grossberg, 271–313. Urbana: University of Illinois Press.

Stengers, Isabelle. 2003. *Cosmopolitiques I.* Paris: Éditions La Découverte.

Tienda, Marta, and Karen Booth. 1991. "Gender Migration and Social Change." *International Sociology* 6(1): 51–72.

Tsing, Anna Lowenhaupt. 2004. *Friction: An Ethnography of Global Connection.* Princeton, NJ: Princeton University Press.

Urry, John. 2000. *Sociology Beyond Societies: Mobilities for the Twenty-First Century.* London: Routledge.

van Bochove, Marianne, and Godfried Engbersen. 2015. "Beyond Cosmopolitanism and Expat Bubbles: Challenging Dominant Representations of Knowledge Workers and Trailing Spouses." *Population, Space and Place* 21(4): 295–309.

Varrel, Aurélie. 2008. "'Back to Bangalore': *étude géographique de la migration de retour des indiens très qualifiés à Bangalore (Inde).*" PhD dissertation, Université de Poitiers.

Vertovec, Steven, and Robin Cohen, eds. 2002. *Conceiving Cosmopolitanism: Theory, Context and Practice.* Oxford: Oxford University Press.

Wardle, Huon. 2012. "Cosmopolitanism in the Caribbean." In *Routledge Handbook of Cosmopolitan Studies*, edited by Gerard Delanty, 504–15. London: Routledge.

Werbner, Pnina. 2006. "Understanding Vernacular Cosmopolitanism." *Anthropology Newsletter* 47(5 May): 7–11.

Werbner, Pnina, ed. 2008. *Anthropology and the New Cosmopolitanism: Rooted, Feminist and Vernacular Perspective.* Oxford: Berg Publishers.

———. 2011. "Paradoxes of Vernacular Cosmopolitanism in South Asia and the Diaspora." In *Ashgate Handbook on Cosmopolitanism*, edited by Maria Rovisco and Magdalena Nowicka, 107–23. London: Ashgate.

Werbner, Richard. 2004. *Reasonable Radicals and Citizenship in Botswana.* Bloomington: Indiana University Press.

———. 2012. "Africa's New Public Cosmopolitans." In *Routledge Handbook of Cosmopolitan Studies*, edited by Gerard Delanty, 477–90. London: Routledge.

Wessendorf, Susan. 2007. "'Roots Migrants': Transnationalism and 'Return' Among Second-Generation Italians in Switzerland." *Journal of Ethnic and Migration Studies* 33(7): 1083–1102.

———. 2010. "Commonplace Diversity: Social Interactions in a Super-Diverse Context." MMG Working Paper 10–11, Max Planck Institute for the Study of Religious and Ethnic Diversity, Germany.

Williams, Raymond. 1976. *Keywords: A Vocabulary of Culture and Society.* New York: Oxford University Press.

Yeğenoğlu, Meyda. 2012. "Cosmopolitanism and Migrancy." In *Routledge Handbook of Cosmopolitan Studies,* edited by Gerard Delanty, 414–24. London: Routledge.

CHAPTER

# 3

# Freedom

*Bartholomew Dean*

Understanding the keyword *freedom* requires examining the nexus between the freedom of mobility and the mobility of freedom. It includes the potential and actual capacity of people to be both spatially and socioculturally mobile. The freedom of mobility—be it in terms of the freedom of movement, as well as the actual experience and or imagination of freedom—can also be viewed as what people gain from moving or from staying put.

Since World War II, social anthropologists grappled with the conceptual dynamics of freedom, animating a number of classic ethnographic monographs and collections (see for example Bidney 1963; Malinowski 1944; or Riesman's 1974 self-reflective ethnography of Fulani notions of freedom), yet freedom of mobility and the mobility of freedoms have been largely absent in the emergent mobility studies literature. As noted by Salazar's introduction to this volume, "much of what is experienced as freedom lies in mobility." Indeed, freedom of mobility is part and parcel of, "an entanglement of movement, representation, and practice" (Cresswell 2010, 17). While I make no major effort to break with what Sheller and others deem, "the new mobilities paradigm" (2008, 26; see Urry 2000, 1), I do challenge regnant theoretical constructs that link the putative "freedom gained from" mobility, and the notion that the imagined freedoms to be mobile are merely tied to free-market ideologies and rationalist, utilitarian practices and beliefs.

I underscore freedom of mobilities and mobility of freedoms in ways that foreground *sovereignty* as a *vital* force shaping humanity.[1] Humans are not simply *rational* beings—they are sooner seduced by the desires of overabundance than accommodate to the shifting socioeconomic, ecological, and geopolitical forces shaping them (Bataille 1985; 1991). My interrogation of freedom and mobility, as well as the mobilities of freedom, encourages the consideration of: rational and irrational interests; the exercise of power (symbolic and coercive); as well as the intersection of incongruous discursive practices, perceptions, and *life styles*.[2] This is followed by a critical interrogation of the ethical dynamics of Occidental regimes of situational or relational freedom of mobility and the mobilities for freedom. Accompanied by a call for continued ethnographic engagement oriented to comprehending the multiplex processes underlying the nexus of the mobilities of freedom and the freedom of mobility, I consider the utility of the notion of *equaliberty*.

## Human Freedom: From Function to Mobility Regimes

As is amply evident from the functionalist ethnographic canon dating to at least Malinowski (1926, 1944), despite their formal political or legal freedoms, people may not always be able to do what they please. In reviewing the links between freedom and law, Leach (1963) underscored the problematic relationship between social status and social prestige. This may also be because of people's deeply in-grained psychological or cultural dispositions not to take full advantage of their freedom, or their potential for "self-actualization" (Maslow 1973). Moreover, those lacking adequate resources, skills, and social networks may be structurally unfree to pursue their own choices (Marx 1852), particularly when it comes to mobility across *de jure, de facto* and imaginary borders. Overbeek (2002) contends that the twenty-first century's crisis in the "management of global migration flows" should not simply be tied to national forms of migration control, nor do they merely reflect the total, "capitulation to market-driven regulation of migration."

In Baker's contribution to this volume, the notion *regime of (im)mobility* reaffirms that mobility is only possible in terms of its inextricable relationship to immobility (see also Glick Schiller and Salazar 2013). After all, agency and freedom are the flip side of immobility. In the words of Sheller, "sovereignal freedom has often been exercised as a freedom of government which immobilizes others" (2008, 28). Likewise, emphasizing mobility alone evokes illusionary imaginaries of unfettered individual freedom, yet the concept of a regime of (im)mobility draws attention to the fact that contemporary border crossings are not the norm, but rather an inequitably distributed global privilege.

By denying or granting peoples with passports, visas, or travel documents, governments (and nonstate entities, such as the UN or paramilitaries) act as the "gatekeepers" of freedom of mobility across sovereign borders (Bærenholdt 2013). On a conceptually different front, Salazar and Smart persuasively contend that the study of human mobility should not simply emphasize it as a "brute fact," but instead determine how the socio-cultural constructs of mobilities, "are experienced and imagined" (2011). As Jayaram puts it in this volume, mobility generates, "subjectivities of belonging and imagined value." Salazar and Smart (2011) consider the pros and cons of assessing the human condition through the optic of mobility, and warn of the shortcomings of erasing diverse interpretations of mobilities. In so doing, they argue against simply emphasizing cases that support current mobilities paradigms, or extreme cases, such as (hyper)mobility or (im)mobility (Salazar and Smart 2011, i–ix.).

Recent mobilities studies have shifted attention to how the flux of global markets configures fluidity in terms of governmentalities. Following Deleuzo-Guattarian approaches to comprehending the survival of capitalism in light of the movements of territorialization (maintenance) and of deterritorialization (dissipation), recent works of cultural analysis have developed the idea of assemblage as an, "anti-structural concept that permits the researcher to speak of emergence, heterogeneity, the decentered and the ephemeral in nonetheless ordered social life" (Marcus and Saka 2006, 101). Relying on his study of civil aviation that foregrounds notions of circulation and *assemblages,* Salter, for example echoes Salazar and Smart's (2011) point by critiquing the "methodological privileging of mobile subjects, or the structures, policies, or authorities that constrain them" (2013, 7).

Mobility is linked with flows, assemblages, and freedom; but so too is it embedded in relations of power and government. This point was raised over three decades ago by the Millsian political theorist Houseman who recognized the right of mobility as a "social 'good,' a first premise, that people should possess a right of mobility" (1979, 11). Rights of mobility provide individuals with a legal framework to realize their hopes and desires, as well as a basis for those forced to move or flee because of threats to their very existence, livelihood, culture, or basic human rights.

Finding purchase in Foucault's concept of governmentality (see 1991), Bærenholdt claims that societies are increasingly governed through mobility, instead of the government of mobility (2013). The idea of interpersonal or social freedom denotes relationships of interaction between individuals or collectivities in such a way that one actor leaves another party free to act in particular ways. This understanding of freedom comes into sharp relief compared with another interaction relation—that of personal or social unfreedom—which reflects the political economy of how people and groups are restricted, emplaced, forced, or (dis)allowed spatial and social mobility and immobility. Freedom and immobility and the mobilities of freedoms can all be experienced at the same time, however ambiguous, discordant, liberating, or enslaving. In a post-Westphalian world now challenging the basis of sovereignal nation-states, this has further confounded late modernity's contradictory stance on the freedom of mobility and the mobility of freedoms.

## Theoretical Figurations: Freedom of Mobility and Freedoms of Mobilities

Inherently polythetic categories (Needham 1975), elaborations of freedom of mobility and freedoms of mobilities are cultural constructs that have many, but not all properties in common. Etymologically speaking, the word freedom is nearly a millennium old, thus tracing its intellectual genealogy is challenging. In modern English usage, the term typically denotes the lack of a specific constraint, or of constraints in general (Bidney 1963). In this sense, slavery whereby people are the chattel property of others and obliged to follow their master's commands is inimical to Occidental, liberal articulations of the freedom of mobility, despite the centrality of slavery (chattel and indentured) to Western colonial and postcolonial projects of hegemonic control (in the Gramscian sense).

In much of anthropological thought, the mobilities of freedom and the freedom of mobility have been dominated by liberal individualism, which has analytically emphasized sovereignty as denoting the possession of ultimate legal authority. Individuals may be said to be sovereign to themselves when they do not require the permission of others to exercise freedom of movement or enjoy the mobility of freedoms, including the rights to stay put or to move. Negative perspectives of freedom emphasize the "absence of restraints that one person may exercise over another, or the state may exercise over individuals" (Sager 2006, 468). In contrast, positive freedom "is not freedom *from,* but rather freedom *to.*" For Sager, this represents, "the power a person has to realise a desired state of affairs, concentrating on what he/she can chose to do or achieve" (2006, 468).

Freedom of mobility—the right to stay put, to leave, and to return— cannot be used without considering the coconstitutive experiences and practices of the mobilities of freedom. A multiaxial understanding of the interstices of freedom and mobility is embedded in one's personal commitment and imagination(s) of freedom. This in turn reflects a wide range of ethical standards and historically contingent orientations.

Human history is replete with countless conflicting views of political freedoms of mobility and the mobility of freedoms. Such contrasts are often framed in terms of the regulation of the mobilities of freedom, and the freedom of mobility (manifest, for instance, in culturally bounded legal regimes and imaginaries, border security/checkpoints, passports, shadow networks of human trafficking, infrastructure, etc.). As Korpela notes in this volume, sophisticated cross-border smuggling arrangements of undocumented migrants and systematic human trafficking are both blatant examples of sociocultural phenomena that rely on "hard and soft" infrastructures operating beyond or in complicity with existing state, trans-state, or nonstate entities and social collectivities. The mobility of freedoms is integral to the variegated experiences associated with mobility, whether across real or imagined national or sociocultural borders. Migrants (undocumented and otherwise) often exist at the ideological and cultural margins of society, in a *betwixt and between* place, "feeling stuck"—where mobility and immobility are restricted, as is deftly described in Khan's chapter in this volume.

Meaningful consensus about the *value* of the freedom of mobility presumes a shared sense, albeit partial or fragmented, of imaginary communities, the mobilities of freedom, and the flexible nature of citizenship. In the post-Fordist world of knowledge economies, the idea of political freedom has fortunately expanded to respond to multiple demands, including: economic liberty; "freedom from want"; cultural self-determination; and what Sager (2006) deems "positive freedom," including the right to be mobile or to stay put.

Sager's research assesses the relationship between the libertarian notion of freedom, "as self-determination and mobility as potential transport" (2006, 466). This is also stressed by Martin, who tackles the turbulent mobilities of what he aptly deems the "desperate passenger" as a way to situate the significance of corporeal passage within mobility studies (2011, 1046–52). Because of the limitations of choice, modes of desperate passage contrast sharply from other types of corporeal mobility. Many undocumented migrants are simply unfree to participate in legitimate networks of mobility. Hence, alternative types of human movements have emerged, as in the case described by Martin, such as the, "infiltration of non-corporeal networks," including dangerous passage on the underbellies of cargo transport vehicles (2011, 1046). The individual, collective, and state reactions to dangerous passages—be they from North Africa to Europe, or Latin America and the Caribbean to the United States—have led to desperation, and death, but have not stemmed unprecedented waves of global migratory flows.

The so-called "tracks left by people on the move open up opportunities for surveillance thus offsetting the freedom gains of being mobile" (Sager 2006, 466). For example, Zilberg's (2011) research reveals that the processes of neoliberalism, globalization, and the intersection of migratory flows and criminalization associated with transnational gangs must be comprehended in relation to the long history of US neocolonial involvement in Central America. Such forces have united to produce what Zilberg deems as volatile "neoliberal securityscapes," readily apparent in the current political and humanitarian crisis regarding undocumented migration of Mexican and Central American children to the United States, or the forced "repatriation" of impoverished Haitians from the relatively more prosperous Dominican Republic back across the imagined and legal borders dividing Hispaniola.[3]

Examining the relationships between how the practices and idioms of freedom and sovereign mobility are used within specific ethical, ritual, political, and legal framings elucidates the extent to which they have been implemented as part of normative practices pivotal to colonial and postcolonial strategies of governance (Hannoum 2010; Nugent 1997; Sanjiné 2013). Notwithstanding, I contend that the problem of *sovereignty* has not been, and is not posed entirely within rigid frames of reference merely limited to Occidental, liberal-derived models of individualized freedoms of mobility. This is a point well illustrated when considering indigenous conceptions of freedom of movement and territorial sovereignty, particularly in Peruvian Amazonia (Dean and Levi 2003). As demonstrated among the Urarina, the critical interplay between territorial integrity, political autonomy, and freedom of movement should be assessed in light of how customary patterns of land use and mobility are informed by cosmological referents, the exigencies of everyday life, and the *exuberance* of state inspired ethnocide and ecocide in the name of modernization and seamless incorporation into global markets driven by wanton consumerism—be it for mahogany, petroleum, or cocaine (Dean 2013b, 2013c).

Whether an individual or group is unfree to participate in "multiple regimes of mobility" (Glick Schiller and Salazar 2013) can only be established with certainty *ex post facto* (cf. Kaufmann 2002, 43). Instead of promoting freedom of movement, regimes of (im)mobility are hierarchies of inequality whereby the logic of statecraft and capital overrides the needs or supposed rights of people. Here it is worthy to recall that the mobility of a person or group's freedoms does not necessarily depend on their actual behavior. The collusion of race, gender, class, and ethnicity enables some individuals and collectivities to experience sovereignal mobility that many are unfree to imagine (for example, tourism or cosmopolitanism). Likewise, the mobility of freedoms, accelerated by the very forces underwriting globalization, has resulted in regimes of mobility whereby many are constrained from actions that only some are free to perform, such as complying with all the governmental formalities of internal national travel, as well as international border crossings.

McNevin (2014) holds that current forms of border security have exhausted the explanatory registers of the spatial (territorial) and subject (citizen/migrant) routinely employed to understand human mobility. In orthodox mobility studies, these paradigms restrict our understandings of contemporary techniques of migration governance. By so doing, such research obfuscates the operation of power mobilized to impose intensely inequitable hierarchies of mobility, while concurrently depicting them as politically neutral (McNevin 2014). Here Bataille exhorts us to recognize that "an immense industrial network cannot be managed in the same way that one changes a tire.... It expresses a circuit of cosmic energy on which it depends, which it cannot limit, and whose laws it cannot ignore without consequences. Woe to those who, to the very end, insist on regulating the movement that exceeds them with the narrow mind of the mechanic who changes a tire" (1991, 26).

## The Freedom of Sovereign Mobility

Influenced by analysis of the potlatch (e.g., Mauss 1925), Bataille's theory of consumption—or the "accursed share"—elucidates the opulent and nonredeemable aspects of any economy, which is expended in two modes: economic and social. This is revealed in a number of ways, including: conscious, sumptuous consumption without gain in the esthetic or performative realms; in nonprocreative eroticisms; in incredible spectacles; leisure travel; pilgrimages; and monumental infrastructures. It can also be most lavishly channeled to outrageous and catastrophic outpouring of violence, which has given rise to enormous shifts in patterns of human migration; refugees; stateless persons; and distinctive sociocultural imaginaries. The boundless yearning for unfettered freedom of movement (as prefigured by Bataille's notion of "sovereign mobility"), glocalized ethnoscapes, the contradictory impulses of transnationality, migration (Glick Schiller and Simsek-Caglar 2011; Salazar and Glick Schiller 2014), and displacement (Lavie and Swedenburg 1996) all frame my own research on the dynamics and consequences of mobility, especially in contemporary Amazonia (Dean 2013c; cf. Clastres 1987, 1998). Sovereignal mobility—the mobilities of freedom and their corollary, the freedom of mobility (imagined and otherwise)—is a characteristic of every human being. Sovereignal mobility exposes itself in the continued *vitality* of kinship and flexible citizenship in modernity.[4] The freedom of mobility is manifest in all walks of life, including: *exuberant* desires to travel; to revel in imprudent behavior; consumptive *excess*; sexual abandon; cosmopolitanism(s); and in wanton episodes of so-called nonanticipatory existence whereby "an individual experiences the miraculous sensation of having the world at his disposal" (Hansen and Sepputat 2005).

At the heart of Bataille's (1991) examination of freedom of mobility and its imaginary potency in *bourgeois* modernity is sovereignty. In his view, sovereignty is not merely an ancient mode of power, but rather manifests itself in dispositions that form multiple circuits of exchange beyond the simple "regimes of value" determined by utility and calculation. Examining the creation of cultural value through the optic of circulation illustrates that power is, as Clastres famously observed, "faithful to the law of exchange which founds and regulates society" (1987, 38; see also Rodríguez and Hill 2011). Echoing Bataille, Polanyi reminded us that: "value ensures the usefulness of the goods produced ... its source is human wants and scarcity—and how could we be expected not to desire one thing more than another? Any opinion or desire will make us participants in the creation of power and in the constituting of economic value. No freedom to do otherwise is conceivable" (1944).

Bataille contends that capitalism transforms human desires—the laborer must toil to eat, and consume to work, paving the way to the eventual loss of sovereignty. Sovereignty can only be regained when the workers abandon themselves to heed to their desires of freedom of mobility and wanton excess, such as binge drinking; gambling; dance; transgressive expression; pleasure treks or journeys; consumerism; exuberant violence; and so on. Scarcity may be a foundation of market economics, but life itself, as Bataille notes (1985, 1991), is usually lived in *excess* one way or another—and it always finds nodes of expressive, *performative* enunciation, as Graham has skillfully illustrated among the Xavante peoples of Central Brazil (1995; see also Maybury-Lewis 1967 classic ethnography). Nevertheless, the surrealist/nihilist tensions surrounding Bataille's (1985) consideration of sovereignty begs the practicality of its implementation. For Bataille, thoughts self-dissolve into nothingness and become sovereign when they cease to be (1991, 203).

Like other rights, sovereignal mobility must be considered in contrast to democratic objectives, which are themselves ideologically charged. Mobility rights pertain not only to the freedom of staying put or moving, but also to the assemblages facilitating the surveillance of travelers, as well as those who wish to not want to move, or those who are forced to be mobile (Sager 2006, 472). In the panoptic digital age, all collectivities need to show a minimum of respect for human freedom—including the right to be (im)mobile. Considering freedom as potential travel "clarifies the distinction between having rights and exercising them," while it discourages excessive policies aimed at enhancing transport in order to maximize freedom (Sager 2006, 483). Though difficult to distinguish what comprises rights of mobility, perhaps more confounding is how does one exercise or ensure the protection of such rights? Moreover, if one person has their mobility needs accepted, "as the right to be decisive over one pair of alternatives, no other individual can have any rights" (Sager 2006, 476). Inevitably, the moral, political structures and socioeconomic manifestations of the rights of movement are bound to vary—hence the apparent Gordian knot between consensus, let alone robust implementation of the freedom of sovereignal mobility, particularly in the bifurcated age of global economies predicated on knowledge or export oriented, low-skill productive and extractive activities.

## Ethnographically Engaging Freedom, Mobility, and the Mobilities of Freedom

Ethnography, anthropological theory, and ethical engagements are crucial for determining the extent to which beliefs in freedom are forged by notions, experiences, and practices of immobility, free will, conformity, and/ or resistance. While studying the unintended consequences of mobility, Freudendal-Pedersen's (2009) work underscores the tenuous relationship between freedom and unfreedom as manifest in the binary opposition between individuality and community. In a range of everyday life narratives, this tension is analyzed by Freudendal-Pedersen (2009) through the concept of "structural stories." By reviewing a spectrum of structural stories illustrating these fault lines, Freudendal-Pedersen demonstrates how mobility both generates ambiguities, while they enable individuals and collectivities to surmount these ambivalences (see also Brettell 2003; von Schnitzler 2013).

Undergirded by realist ethnographic observation, qualitative research is much needed to comprehend the continual reconfiguration(s) of freedom and sovereignty in ways that consider how trans-local epistemologies and ontologies have simultaneously exacerbated the disruptive impacts of migration, rapid urbanization, and national belonging, especially for indigenous peoples, ethnic minorities, and the impoverished (Anderson 2003). For anthropologists, this calls for an integrative approach to understanding and addressing the challenges of adapting to environmental, social, and cultural transformations associated with the frictions of freedom, mobility, and sovereignty.

While the edges of indigenous Amazonian societies have become blurred by global transformations,[5] Urarina mobility strategies are still intimately tied to the matrices of subsistence and to debt-peonage extractive "production." Their customary territory, Peru's Chambira River Basin, was a relatively unimportant geopolitical space for colonial and postcolonial frontiers of national expansion. Residential oscillation is consistent with Urarina patterns of seasonal migration, as well as the region's historical integration into capitalist markets at regional and national levels. Urarina domestic groups have developed migratory strategies for coping with economic duress, including attempts to better their conditions through resettlement aimed at participation in inequitable relations of debt peonage (Dean 2013c). As demonstrated in this volume, freedom and mobility is most commonly gendered. My own work among the Urarina of Peruvian Amazonia underscores the contradictory implications of gendered space and supra-local political and economic contexts (Dean 2003, 217–54; see also Brettell 2003; Judd 2010).

The Urarina have only recently begun formulating a hegemonic conception of the sole dominion over a bounded territory, despite the fact that they continue to practice extensive residential mobility. The upper reaches of the Chambira watershed is largely the Urarina's own territorial domain, whereas the middle to lower portions represent relatively more pluralized ethnoscapes. The Urarina are not frozen in aspic. Rather than merely rationalist conceptions of freedom, Urarina understandings of the nexus of mobility and the mobilities of freedom are expressed in their elaborate shamanic cosmology linked to sacred geographies, which find expression in their differential experiences of mobility, imagined and otherwise. Their decisions regarding freedom and mobility are driven not only by satisfying exuberant desires emanating from establishing or maintaining access to trade goods and market opportunities, but also due to Urarina cosmological referents, such as the threat of *Anekái,* the malevolent spirits of the dead (Dean 2013c).

Inequitable patterns of contemporary freedom in native Amazonia are inextricability linked to "multiple regimes of value" and complex networks of global-commodity-chains, which in turn shape durable patterns of (im) mobility. In a decidedly anti-enlightenment turn, I have pursued a line of scholarship contesting the notion that humans are universally driven to fashion increasingly more efficient technologies of mobility (see also Hornborg 2013; Hornborg, McNeill, and Martinez-Alier 2007). In Peruvian Amazonia, decades of violence and war continue to cast their penumbra, particularly in the Huallaga Valley—one of the world's epicenters for coca production. Unabated extractive economies underwritten by global interconnections and the commoditization of communal resources (Tapayuri Murayari 2012, vii), coupled with the booming illicit trade in the area's precious hardwoods and the processing and trafficking in cocaine paste (*pasta básica de cocaína*) have all taken a high human and ecological toll (Dean 2013b; Kernaghan 2009; UNODC/DEVIDA 2013). Dispossessed of their hunting, fishing resources, and farming lands—and hence their livelihoods—many rural inhabitants of Peruvian Amazonia have lost their sovereignal mobility. They have been forced to migrate to the cities and towns to flea violence and impoverishment, or lured in search of employment, educational opportunities, and social mobility. As a result, indigenous peoples in geographically isolated regions, such those in Peru's province of Alto

Amazonas are coming to terms with novel "ways-of-being free" in a liminal world, spurred in great part by massive migratory flows now refiguring quotidian life with immense rapidity and contradictory consequences (Dean 2015).

Notwithstanding the transformative potential of migration to reconfigure the Peruvian body politic, these shifts have unleashed forces that undermine sovereignal freedom. The technological developments facilitating human mobilities in Peruvian Amazonia—be they in terms of the neoliberal expansion of extractive infrastructure, media connections, or the recent completion of a trans-Andean all-weather road (IRSA Norte)—are reflective of Bataille's (1985) notion of the state's exuberant expenditure. They also represent what Hornborg (2013) has aptly described as a "zero-sum game" involving uneven global resource flows.

## Freedom, Mobility, and Morality

A resurgent interest in the anthropology of morality has emerged in conjunction with mobility studies and philosophical issues of freedom (Faubion 2011). Debate in this realm has been influenced by the distinction between the free and the constrained; as it has been shaped by the quandaries over good and evil, or the ethics of human rights and wrongs, not to mention the murky divide between justice and impunity. In contrast to what I broadly characterize as *libertarian* perspectives on freedom of mobility and the mobilities of freedom, socialists typically reject a restricted definition of freedom, which they note fails to recognize that the majority of the globe's formally free are powerless in crossing state-sanctioned borders or fully participating in opportunities for upward sociocultural mobility afforded by the multiple regimes of freedom. This has occurred in part because of the leapfrogging nature of capital, which when mobilized can be largely free of such spatial or cultural restrictions.

Relative to the fluidity of capital, human beings are no more liberated than a sequestered prisoner or hostage in the world of capitalism (Marx 1969). In contrast, many libertarians see freedom as equivalent to a status or state of being, whereas from a socialist or postcolonial vantage point it is a manifestation of agentive power (on various iterations of agency, among others see Dean 2013c; Laidlaw 2002, 2013; Mahmood 2005).

Drawing in part on Foucault, Laidlaw's research has consistently pushed for the anthropological study of ethics, focusing on the study of competing idioms of freedom (2002, 2013; cf. Bergmann and Sager 2008). Rejecting scholarship that simply underscores people's unfreedom, Laidlaw is inspired by Foucault's (1988) latter iterations on the delimitations of the technologies of self, where forms of freedom (albeit still imbricated by sequestration) are shown to have been configured by historical, and socially lived experiences, but by no means have they been fully determined by such forces.

In contrast to Laidlaw, others have claimed that freedom is continuously a normative model central to the technologies of secular governance and an Occidental (read Protestant) derived constellation of modernity (Asad 2003; Keane 2007). As is noted by Acharya in her contribution to this volume, it was a Kantian view of cosmopolitanism that after all provided the anchoring for the United Nation's Universal Declaration of Human Rights' Article 13 proclaiming that: "Everyone has the right to freedom of movement and residence within the borders of each State. Everyone has the right to leave any country, including his own, and to return to his country" (United Nations General Assembly 1948).

## Equaliberty and Mobility

The modern, global citizen is product of a tenuous balance between equality, on the one hand, and manifestations of sovereignty, freedom, and liberty, on the other hand. Balibar (1994, 2014) neologistically deems this *equaliberty*, a state marked by unknowable *excess*. In this regard, "checkpoints" (real or imagined) represent modes of subjection—including sequestration, not to mention the mobility of freedoms. Juridico-legal and cultural gatekeepers are practices and experience of excess, testing the inherent limits of contemporary freedom of movement and the mobilities of freedom (Jegananathan 2004).

Heir to both continental and analytic philosophical traditions, Balibar's (2014) elaboration of equaliberty sheds insight on the conflictual relations between humanity and modernity: namely the freedom of citizenship in a neoliberal age.[6] In Balibar's estimation, equaliberty stands for the inherent contradiction between two foundations of modern liberal democracy: equality (e.g., socioeconomic rights and representation) and liberty (e.g., the freedom citizens possess to challenge the social contract). Advancing a theory of the polity predicated on social relations, Balibar's favors a deterritorialized, mobile citizenship that could be reinvigorated anew in the digital age of global assemblages and knowledge economies.

Yet what about power and mobility? Presumably, relationships of freedom of movement must have at least two alternative responses. One is unfree to move freely; or conversely one is free to behave according to their desires. In the latter sense, freedom allows persons to act in multiple ways—

including mobility—given there is no other actor (state or otherwise) who curtails their actions and generates unfreedom. "Freedom of mobility" means freedom either to move (spatially or socially) or to stay put, but "freedom to restrict mobility" is tantamount to unfreedom. Moreover, one may be free to act or behave in one form or another with regard to a person or group, whereas in other contexts, actors, institutions, and ideologies make people or collectivities unfree to fully engage in the body politic. Simply put, mobility is predicated upon a "moral geography," whereby the rights of freedom of human movement are spatialized (Cresswell 2006). Likewise, for Sager, mobility is fashioned through surmounting "friction" in terms of the metrics of "physical distance, costs, or other variables indicating inertia or resistance" (2006, 467).

## Conclusion: Freedom and Mobility

Teasing out a theoretical construct of equality in terms of sovereignty undermines orthodox understandings of freedom and mobility posed merely in terms of functional, *purposive* actions or behavior associated with the right to stay put, leave, and return. Notwithstanding, instead of jettisoning insights yielded from functional approaches to the freedom of mobility and the multiple, culturally fluid mobile regimes of freedoms, we do well in considering the dialectic interplay between purposive action and mutuality in shaping the rights of the freedom of movement, which after all is a central girder in international human rights jurisprudence. While the purposive action approach highlights the effectual mitigation of problems and the minimization of risk, the notion of freedom of movement likewise accentuates loyalty (partial or otherwise) to a shared moral economy, the continuation of social solidarity and the perpetuation of *communitas* (Turner 1969; cf. Andrews and Roberts 2012; Esposito 2009).

Surveillance is a technique for exerting power, whereas trust is its antipode (Sager 2006). But as Caldwell (2013) points out, it is precisely because of empathetic cofeeling that strangers become intimates. In such conditions, freedom has a chance to flourish in a world of transcultural relations, albeit one marked by battles over the mobilities of freedom and the freedom of mobility (Dean 2013a). Pace Khan's contribution to this collection, agency, freedom, and immobility are entwined. Not surprisingly, ethnographic research in indigenous Amazonia has revealed competing localized and translocal imaginaries of the freedom of mobility and glocalized jurisdictions marked by social strife rather than a mere Rousseauian community of intimates.

Theoretical and pragmatic obstacles emerge when engaging with the complex relationship between mobility and freedom, particularly when it comes to how can they be imagined and implemented in ways that humanely respond to the ever increase of mobility, rapid urbanization, and a growing global gap between the rich and the poor. Paralleling theoretical shifts in anthropology challenging Kantian notions of rationalist freewill, the study of the freedom(s) of mobility and the mobilities of freedom, now emphasize the socially situated states of individual and collective being, phenomena that are culturally contingent in any given historical instance.

**Bartholomew Dean** (Oxford MPhil, Harvard PhD) is an associate professor, Department of Anthropology, University of Kansas. In addition, he is research affiliate at the Universidad Nacional de San Martín (Peru), where he directs the Anthropology Section of the Regional Museum. Dean is a contributing editor for Lowland South America, US Library of Congress's *Handbook of Latin American Studies*. His publications include the acclaimed *Urarina Society, Cosmology and History in the Peruvian Amazonia* (2009, 2013), as well as a coedited book, *At the Risk of Being Heard: Identity, Indigenous Rights and Postcolonial States* (2003), and numerous articles, chapters, and several textbooks.

## NOTES

1. In the case of Canada, "First Nations," and "First People" are used to "signal the sovereign status prior to all others who came to North America" (Ames 1994, 10). On the issue of sovereignal freedom, see among others Patterson (1991, 3–4).
2. Among others, see Jansen (2009); Fine-Dare and Rubenstein (2009); Korpela (2014), and her contribution on "lifestyle migrants" in this volume as well.
3. Bartlett, Jayaram, and Bonhomme (2011) provide an excellent comparative example of how literacy is a source of mobility and inequity among Haitian immigrants in the Dominican Republic.
4. On the vital role of kinship in state systems and their influence on the present and imagined global future, see McKinnon and Cannell (2013).
5. As demonstrated in this volume, the freedom of mobility is most commonly gendered. My own work among the Urarina of Peruvian Amazonia underscores the contradictory implications of gendered space and supra-local political and economic contexts (Dean 2003, 217–54; see also Brettell 2003; Judd 2010; and Elliot's insightful contribution on gender in this volume).
6. On Amazonian migration, see Alexiades (2009) most useful collection. Of particular relevance for my essay is Pinedo-Vasquez and Padoch's (2009) contribution to Alexiades' volume.

## REFERENCES

Alexiades, Miguel, ed. 2009. *Mobility and Migration in Indigenous Amazonia: Contemporary Ethnoecological Perspectives.* New York: Berghahn Books.

Ames, Michael. 1994. "The Politics of Difference: Other Voices in a Not Yet Post-Colonial World." *Museum Anthropology* 18(3): 9–17.

Anderson, Benedict. 2003. "Nationalism and Cultural Survival in Our Time: A Sketch." In *At the Risk of Being Heard: Identity, Indigenous Rights and Postcolonial States,* edited by Bartholomew Dean and Jerome Levi, 165–90. Ann Arbor: University of Michigan Press.

Andrews, Hazel, and Les Roberts, eds. 2012. *Liminal Landscapes: Travel, Experience and Spaces In-Between.* New York: Routledge.

Asad, Talal. 2003. *Formations of the Secular: Christianity, Islam, Modernity.* Stanford, CA: Stanford University Press.

Bærenholdt, Jørgen Ole. 2013. "Governmobility: The Powers of Mobility." *Mobilities* 8(1): 20–34.

Balibar, Étienne. 1994. *Masses, Classes, Ideas: Studies on Politics and Philosophy Before and After Marx.* New York: Routledge.

———. 2014. *Equaliberty: Political Essays.* Durham, NC: Duke University Press.

Bartlett, Lesley, Kiran Jayaram, and Gulin Bonhomme. 2011. "State Literacies and In-equality: Managing Haitian Immigrants in the Dominican Republic." *International Journal of Educational Development* 31(6): 587–95.

Bataille, Georges. 1985. *Visions of Excess: Selected Writings, 1927–1939.* Minneapolis: University of Minnesota Press.

———. 1991. *The Accursed Share, Volume 1: Consumption.* New York: Zone Books.

Bergmann, S, and T Sager, eds. 2008. *The Ethics of Mobilities: Rethinking Place, Exclusion, Freedom and Environment.* Burlington, VT: Ashgate.

Bidney, David, ed. 1963. *The Concept of Freedom in Anthropology.* The Hague: Mouton & Co.

Brettell, Caroline. 2003. *Anthropology and Migration: Essays on Transnationalism, Ethnicity, and Identity.* Walnut Creek, CA: AltaMira Press.

Caldwell, Melissa. 2013. "The Compassion of Strangers: Intimate Encounters with Assistance in Moscow." In *Ethnographies of Social Support,* edited by Markus Schlecker and Friederike Fleischer, 103–20. New York: Palgrave Macmillan.

Clastres, Pierre. 1987. *Society against the State: Essays in Political Anthropology.* New York: Zone Books.

———. 1998. *Chronicle of the Guayaki Indians.* London: Zone Books.

Cresswell, Tim. 2006. *On the Move: Mobility in the Modern Western World.* New York: Routledge Press.

———. 2010. "Towards a Politics of Mobility." *Environment and Planning D: Society and Space* 28(1): 17–31.

Dean, Bartholomew. 2003. "At the Margins of Power: Gender Hierarchy & the Politics of Ethnic Mobilization among the Urarina." In *At the Risk of Being Heard: Identity, Indigenous Rights & Postcolonial States,* edited by Bartholomew Dean and Jerome Levi, 217–54. Ann Arbor: University of Michigan Press.

———. 2013a. "Epilogue." In *Ethnography of Support Encounters,* edited by M Schlecker and F Fleischer, 195–211. New York: Palgrave Macmillan.

———. 2013b. "The Transgressive Allure of White Gold in Peruvian Amazonia." *ID: International Dialogue, A Multidisciplinary Journal of World Affairs* 3: 74–91.

———. 2013c. *Urarina Society, Cosmology and History in Peruvian Amazonia.* 2nd ed. Gainesville: University Press of Florida.

———. 2015. "Indigenous Education in Peruvian Amazonia." In *Indigenous Education: Language, Culture and Identity,* edited by W James Jacob, SY Chin, and M Porter, 429–46. Dordrecht, Netherlands: Springer.

Dean, Bartholomew, and Jerome Levi, eds. 2003. *At the Risk of Being Heard: Identity, Indigenous Rights and Postcolonial States.* Ann Arbor: University of Michigan Press.

Esposito, Roberto. 2009. *Communitas: The Origin and Destiny of Community.* Palto Alto, CA: Stanford University Press.

Faubion, James. 2011. *An Anthropology of Ethics.* Cambridge: Cambridge University Press.

Fine-Dare, Kathleen, and Steve Rubenstein, eds. 2009. *Border Crossings: Transnational Americanist Anthropology.* Lincoln: University of Nebraska Press.

Foucault, Michel. 1988. *The Archaeology of Knowledge.* London: Tavistock Publications.

———. 1991. "Governmentality." In *The Foucault Effect: Studies in Governmentality,* edited by Graham Burchell, Colin Gordon, and Peter Miller, 87–104. Chicago: University of Chicago Press.

Freudendal-Pedersen, Malene. 2009. *Mobility in Daily Life: Between Freedom and Unfreedom.* Burlington, VT: Ashgate.

Glick Schiller, Nina, and Ayse Simsek-Caglar. 2011. *Locating Migration: Rescaling Cities and Migrants.* Ithaca, NY: Cornell University Press.

Glick Schiller, Nina, and Noel B Salazar. 2013. "Regimes of Mobility Across the Globe." *Journal of Ethnic and Migration Studies* 39(2): 183–200.

Graham, Laura. 1995. *Performing Dreams: Discourses of Immortality among the Xavante of Central Brazil.* Austin: University of Texas Press.

Hannoum, Abdelmajid. 2010. *Violent Modernity: France in Algeria.* Cambridge, MA: Harvard University Press.

Hansen, Thomas, and Finn Stepputat. 2005. *Sovereign Bodies: Citizens, Migrants, and States in the Postcolonial World.* Princeton, NJ: Princeton University Press.

Hornborg, Alf. 2013. *Global Ecology and Unequal Exchange: Fetishism in a Zero-Sum World.* London: Routledge.

Hornborg, Alf, JR McNeill, and Joan Martinez-Alier, eds. 2007. *Rethinking Environmental History: World-System History and Global Environmental Change.* London: Routledge.

Houseman, Gerald. 1979. *The Right of Mobility.* Port Washington, NY: Kennikat Press.

Jansen, Stef. 2009. "After the Red Passport: Towards an Anthropology of the Everyday Geopolitics of Entrapment in the EU's 'Immediate Outside.'" *Journal of the Royal Anthropological Institute* 15: 815–32.

Jegananathan, Pradeep. 2004. "Checkpoint: Anthropology, Identity, and the State." In *Anthropology in the Margins of the State,* edited by Veena Das and Deborah Poole, 67–80. Santa Fe, NM: School of American Research.

Judd, Ellen. 2010. "Family Strategies: Fluidities of Gender, Community and Mobility in Rural West China." *The China Quarterly* 204: 921–38.

Kaufmann, Vincent. 2002. *Re-Thinking Mobility: Contemporary Sociology.* Aldershot, England: Ashgate.

Keane, Webb. 2007. *Christian Moderns: Freedom and Fetish in the Mission Encounter.* Berkeley: University of California Press.

Kernaghan, Richard. 2009. *Coca's Gone: Of Might and Right in the Huallaga Post-Boom.* Stanford, CA: Stanford University Press.

Korpela, Mari. 2014. "Lifestyle of Freedom? Individualism and Lifestyle Migration." In *Understanding Lifestyle Migration: Theoretical Approaches to Migration and the Quest for a Better Life,* edited by M Benson and N Osbaldiston, 27–46. Bassingstoke: Palgrave Macmillan.

Laidlaw, James. 2002. "For an Anthropology of Ethics and Freedom." *Journal of the Royal Anthropological Institute* 2: 311–22.

———. 2013. *The Subject of Virtue: An Anthropology of Ethics and Freedom.* Cambridge: Cambridge University Press.

Lavie, Smadar, and Ted Swedenburg. 1996. *Displacement, Diaspora, and Geographies of Identity.* Durham, NC: Duke University Press.

Leach, Edmund. 1963. "Law as a Condition of Freedom." In *The Concept of Freedom in Anthropology,* edited by David Bidney, 74–90. The Hague: Mouton & Co.

Mahmood, Saba. 2005. *Politics of Piety: The Islamic Revival and the Feminist Subject.* Princeton, NJ: Princeton University Press.

Malinowski, Bronislaw. 1926. *Crime and Custom in Savage Society.* New York: Rowman & Littlefield.

———. 1944. *Freedom and Civilization.* New York: Roy.

Marcus, George, and Erkan Saka. 2006. "Assemblage." *Theory, Culture & Society* 23(2–3): 101–6.

Martin, Craig. 2011. "Desperate Passage: Violent Mobilities and the Politics of Discomfort." *Journal of Transport Geography* 19(5): 1046–52.

Marx, Karl. 1852. "Der 18te Brumaire des Louis Napoleon." *Die Revolution.*

———. 1969. "Theories of Surplus-Value." In *Capital 2.* Vol. IV. London: Lawrence & Wishart.

Maslow, Abraham. 1973. *Dominance, Self-Esteem, Self-Actualization: Germinal Papers of AH Maslow.* Monterey, CA: Brooks & Cole.

Mauss, Marcel. 1925. "Essai sur le don. Forme et raison de l'échange dans les sociétés archaïques." *L'Année Sociologique,* nouvelle série 1 (1923–1924): 30–186.

Maybury-Lewis, David. 1967. *Akwe-Shavante Society.* Oxford: Clarendon Press.

McKinnon, Susan, and Fenella Cannell, eds. 2013. *Vital Relations: Modernity and the Persistent Life of Kinship.* Santa Fe, NM: School of American Research.

McNevin, Anne. 2014. "Beyond Territoriality: Rethinking Human Mobility, Border Security and Geopolitical Space from the Indonesian Island of Bintan." *Security Dialogue* 45(3): 295–310.

Needham, Rodney. 1975. "Polythetic Classification: Convergence and Consequences." *Man* 10(3): 349–69.

Nugent, David. 1997. *Modernity at the Edge of Empire: State, Individual, and Nation in the Peruvian Andes, 1885–1935*. Stanford, CA: Stanford University Press.

Overbeek, Henk. 2002. "Neoliberalism and the Regulation of Global Labor Mobility." *The Annals of the American Academy of Political and Social Science* 581(1): 74–90.

Patterson, Orlando. 1991. *Freedom in the Making of Western Civilization*. Vol. 1. Cambridge, MA: Harvard University Press.

Pinedo-Vasquez, M, and C Padoch. 2009. "Urban and Rural and In-Between: Multi-Sited Households, Mobility and Resource Management in the Amazon Floodplain." In *Mobility and Migration in Indigenous Amazonia: Contemporary Ethnoecological Perspectives*, edited by Miguel Alexiades, 86–96. Oxford: Berghahn Books.

Polanyi, Karl. 1944. *The Great Transformation*. New York: Farrar & Rinehart.

Riesman, Paul. 1974. *Freedom in Fulani Social Life: An Introspective Ethnography*. Chicago: University of Chicago Press.

Rodríguez, JL, and JD Hill. 2011. "Materiality, Exchange, and History in the Amazon: A Growing Field of Study." *Ethnohistory* 58(3): 525–32.

Sager, Tore. 2006. "Freedom as Mobility: Implications of the Distinction between Actual and Potential Travelling." *Mobilities* 1(3): 465–88.

Salazar, Noel B, and Nina Glick Schiller, eds. 2014. *Regimes of Mobility: Imaginaries and Relationalities of Power*. London: Routledge.

Salazar, Noel B, and Adam Smart. 2011. "Anthropological Takes on (Im)Mobility." *Identities: Global Studies in Culture and Power* 18(6): i–ix.

Salter, Mark. 2013. "To Make Move and Let Stop: Mobility and the Assemblage of Circulation." *Mobilities* 8(1): 7–19.

Sanjiné, Javier. 2013. *Embers of the Past: Essays in Times of Decolonization*. Durham, NC: Duke University Press.

Sheller, Mimi. 2008. "Mobility, Freedom and Public Space." In *The Ethics of Mobilities: Rethinking Place, Exclusion, Freedom and Environment*, edited by Sigurd Bergmann and Tore Sager, 25–38. Burlington, VT: Ashgate.

Tapayuri Murayari, B. 2012. "Preface." In *Anthropological Illuminations of the Varieties of Human Experience*, 2nd ed., edited by Bartholomew Dean and Joshua E Homan, vii. Dubuque, IA: Kendall/Hunt Publishing.

Turner, Victor. 1969. *The Ritual Process*. London: Aldine.

United Nations General Assembly. 1948. "Universal Declaration of Human Rights: Adopted the 10th December 1948 in Plenary Session by the General Assembly of the United Nations." Publication, 869. New York: UNESCO.

UNODC/DEVIDA. 2013. *Pasta Básica de Cocaína: Cuatro décadas de historia, actualidad y desafíos*. Lima: Oficina de las Naciones Unidas Contra la Droga y el Delito (UNODC).

Urry, John. 2000. *Sociology Beyond Societies: Mobilities for the Twenty-First Century*. London: Routledge.

von Schnitzler, Antina. 2013. "Travelling Technologies: Infrastructure, Ethical Regimes, and the Materiality of Politics in South Africa." *Cultural Anthropology* 28(4): 670–93.

Zilberg, Ellen. 2011. *Space of Detention: The Making of a Transnational Gang Crisis between Los Angeles and San Salvador*. Durham, NC: Duke University Press.

CHAPTER
# 4

# Gender

*Alice Elliot*

> The girl of five does not make any use of lateral space. She does not stretch her arm sideward; she does not twist her trunk; she does not move her legs, which remain side by side. All she does in preparation for throwing is to lift her right arm forward to the horizontal and to bend the forearm backward in a prone position. The ball is released without force, speed, or accurate aim. A boy of the same age, when preparing to throw, stretches his right arm sideward and backward; supinates the forearm; twists, turns and bends his trunk; and moves his right foot backward. From this stance, he can support his throwing almost with the full strength of his total motorium. The ball leaves the hand with considerable acceleration; it moves toward its goal in a long flat curve.
> — Erwin W. Straus, *The Upright Posture,* quoted in Iris Marion Young, *Throwing Like a Girl.*

Whatever scale we choose for our analysis of mobility, there exists an intimate relationship between different forms of movement and the appearance and strengthening, or questioning and unmaking, of gender. Since the eruption of the concept of gender into the social sciences in the late 1970s, scholars have systematically highlighted its fundamental role for understanding mobility in its varied forms (Bernstein 2008; Byrne Swain 1995; Frederick and McLeod 1993; Frohlick 2006; Hanson 2010; Law 1999; Mahler and Pessar 2006; Uteng Priya and Cresswell 2007; Valentine 1989). Often criticized in the past for overlooking the mutually constitutive relationship between gender and mobility (see e.g., Hondagneu-Sotelo 1999; Kofman et al. 2000; Morokvasic 1984; Pessar 1986; Pessar and Mahler 2003), mobility studies today are saturated by commentaries on it. However, what is the actual texture, and indeed the analytical purchase, of the concept of gender that is receiving increasing attention in the study of mobility—from tourism (Frohlick 2013) to urban travel (Thornbury 2014), from sex trafficking (Andrijasevic 2007) to social mobility (Higginbotham and Weber 1992)? The fact that mobility studies are increasingly sensitive to and interested in gender does not imply that scholars are speaking of the same thing, evoking the same problems, and thinking through the same complexities when they utilize the word. Rather, the keyword gender evokes a variety of different meanings in the study of mobility. These forms carry very different premises and implications, which in turn have different consequences on the ways in which gender interacts with the understanding of mobility, and vice versa.

In this chapter I wish to unpack some of the ways in which the keyword gender has been used when speaking of mobility and, in the process, begin to unpack the concept of gender itself in light of the different ways it has been related to mobility in the literature. Rather than an extensive review of the gender and mobility literature, of which an impressive number already exist, my intention here is to map out some of the ways in which *the relationship* between gender and mobility has been framed, and some of the questions that have been asked of this relationship, critically extricating what gender can do for the study of mobility, and vice versa. Instead of focusing on those works that explicitly take mobility as their object of enquiry, I tease out interesting and creative ways of juxtaposing gender and mobility from a varied body of work.

I begin the chapter by distinguishing two main ways in which gender is understood and used in mobility studies, what I call the "master difference" between gender as classification and gender and process. Taking the notion of efficacy as a lens through which to observe the ways in which gender and mobility have been related in different bodies of literature, I then trace how the two concepts are accorded different purchases and constitutive powers by different authors. I conclude with the critical proposal of taking the efficacy of mobility a step further from where most mobility studies leave it, and in this way trace how gender may be conceived, in certain instances at least, as constituted by different forms of movement.

In focusing on the keyword of gender, I have unavoidably extricated gender from the web of other keywords, some carefully analyzed by other chapters of this book, that are constitutive of what gender is, does, and means in social life. Class, race, colonialism, sexuality, political and theological imagination, together with those ethnographic specificities that define gender, have been somehow dimmed in order to bring to the fore intersections between gender and mobility. My hope is that this unavoidably selective focus will provide a fruitful perspective from which to observe the "sticky materiality of practical encounters" (Tsing 2005, 1) between different ethnographic concepts and domains that produce and reproduce specific forms of gender, specific forms of mobility, and specific relations between the two.

## Master Difference

A master difference lies at the core of the varied ways in which gender is used in mobility literature, between understanding gender as *classification* and understanding it as *process*. On the one hand, gender has been conceived of and utilized in the study of mobility as a way to classify, distinguish, and compare between two sexes and their respective mobility. This emerges perhaps most clearly in the work that has been developed since the late 1970s by, mostly, female scholars of migration (from anthropologists to historians) to shed light on female experiences of migration invisible in mainstream migration scholarship (e.g., Buijs 1993; Diner 1983; Ets 1970; Hondagneu-Sotelo and Avila 1997; Morokvasic 1984). It emerges, however, also in a variety of other fields that touch upon mobility, from studies in urban geography of the ways in which men and women move differently within urban landscapes (e.g., Grosz 1992; Law 1999; Saegert 1980), to philosophy or feminist studies that trace the different modalities and phenomenology of movement of the male and female body (e.g., Gianini Belotti 2004; Young 1980), to historical accounts of female adventurers and imperial travelers (e.g., Blunt 1994; Frederick and McLeod 1993; Wallach 2005). Gender, here, is used first and foremost—though not in all cases solely—as classification, as a useful and productive axis of distinction between human beings on the move that allows for important comparisons and insights. It is not necessarily taken in all cases as a natural given, but rather it is used as a way to divide between two groups and understand them in their specificity, a kind of divide and (intellectually) conquer use of gender, if you will.

Gender however emerges in the study of mobility also as a more nuanced, relational concept, made of fuzzy boundaries and negotiated processes, rather than as a neat division between the sexes. Drawing heavily on the 1990s constructivist and performative turn in the study of sex and gender—Butler (1990, 1993, 2004) being here one of the field's materfamilias—strands in the study of mobility have increasingly shifted in the past decades from using gender as a dichotomous tool to analyze society, to a conception of gender as a relational, political, historical process engrained in the very texture of mobility, as of life more generally (Donato et al. 2006; Frohlick 2006; Hanson 2010; Herrera 2013; Hondagneu-Sotelo 2011;

Mahler and Pessar 2006). This take on gender proposes not only to denaturalize the categories of mobile men and women, but also to trace how gendered relations are part and parcel of mobility, inflecting it, transforming it, activating it in multiple ways. Gender is not about observing how men and women move differently, but about a theoretical and methodological toolbox able to capture how socially, culturally, historically constructed relations between the sexes inflect the texture of mobility, and vice versa.

As is often the case, the master difference I set up here between two different uses of gender in the study of mobility[1] is not so unambiguously clear-cut in the literature. Studies that take a commitment to gender to mainly imply, for example, bringing to the fore the role of women in global migration, do not necessarily adopt a naturalistic conception of sexual difference (Cattaneo and dal Verme 2005), may carry Judith Butler firmly under their belt (Salih 2003), and may be sensitive to the gendered processes that have brought the women they speak of to move in the first place (Lutz 1997). Here, the classificatory use scholars make of gender is more a question of focus than of politico-theoretical positioning on the meaning of gender. Similarly, the field is ripe with papers that contain in their introduction a heartfelt declaration of subscription to the conception of gender as process, negotiation, cultural construction, just to then delve into a discussion of a specific kind of mobility and treat gender as a finished and self-evident product. Indeed, it may be argued that the "gender as process" front in our dichotomous analysis presents a more inherent risk of leaving the keyword untheorized, as it makes a theoretical (rather than classificatory) claim on gender, and is often satisfied with the claim alone.

Despite the unavoidable residues produced by imposing a neat classificatory scheme onto a sprawling social field, this master difference is an important starting point for the mapping of the kinds of uses to which gender is put in the study of mobility. From this master difference, other significant differences in the use of the keyword emerge—some can be organized according to it, some go beyond it, or even in a sense contradict it.

## Efficacy

One way to develop the master differentiation between gender as classification and gender as process in our mapping of the gender keyword is to observe the distinct ways in which the literature frames *the relation* between gender and mobility. Here, gender emerges as both process and classification, as scholars interested in this relation both tend to have an intellectual/methodological proclivity for observing generative connections between gender and social reality and, on the other hand, often posit sexual differentiation, upon which analyses of mobility are built, as a relatively unquestioned given.

In analyzing the relationship between gender and mobility, scholars have tended to focus on what could be seen as two sides of the same coin. On the one hand, scholars have focused on how gender affects mobility, and, on the other, on how mobility affects gender (see also Hanson 2010). Though this distinction may sound like a mere play on words, it has important implications for the ways in which gender is put to use in analyses of mobility.[2] It also has important implications for the purchase one element of the relation is accorded to have on the other, and thus on the very texture, and efficacy, of both. In one case, gender is the premise and mobility one of its outcomes; in the other, mobility contains transformational power in its own right, able to affect gender relations. Some of the key ideas existing in the mobility literature surrounding gender emerge by mapping out the relationship between mobility and gender through their relative efficaciousness.

### The Mobile Efficacy of Gender

One of the clearest ways to capture the relationship between mobility and gender is by tracing how gender influences, shapes, and generates specific forms of mobility. This is a methodological and theoretical move made by many scholars interested in the interplay between gender and movement at different scales of social life. It is a move that, as Hanson (2010) points out in her recent review article, is generally more concerned with unpacking the different qualities of movement generated by gender difference, rather than with unpacking the cultural construct of gender itself. In other words, it is a methodological and theoretical perspective that somehow privileges the complexity of movement over the complexity of gender, taking the latter category as a starting point to analyze the former—although it does, in some cases at least, allow then mobility to recursively illuminate conceptions of gender themselves.

The long anthropological tradition of observing the subdivision of public and private space along gender lines has generated one of the wealthiest bodies of critical literature on the ways in which gender affects mobility in different sociocultural contexts (e.g., Abu-Lughod 1985; Douglas 1970; Ghannam 2002; Göle 2002; Maher 1974; Marsden 2007; Nelson 1974; Okely 1983; Schneider 1971). These studies trace, with increasing attention to complexity and ambiguity as they move away from the structuralist paradigm, how the varying ways in which societies divide space between public and private, inside and outside, domesticity and paid labor, the known and the unknown, makes and allows men and women to move differently in different realms. Although founding works that explicitly and implicitly consider the ways in which men and women move (physically, structurally, ideally) within non-Western societies predate Bourdieu's publications on the topic—*The Elementary Structures of Kinship* by Lévi-Strauss (1969) being a case in point here—it is Bourdieu's (1977) work on the "Kabyle House" that powerfully sets on the anthropological agenda the discussion of space and (what we would term now) gendered movement. Originally written in 1972 as homage to Lévi-Strauss himself, Bourdieu's essay "The Kabyle House or the World Reversed" is a seminal analysis of the symbolic and embodied socio-spatial division between men and women in rural Algeria. In the essay, Bourdieu stresses the fundamental difference between female (internal, intimate) space and male (external, public) space, and argues how specific binary contrasts that organize space (both the space within the house and a space that includes the house and the "outside") inform and are informed by the (hierarchical) organization of gender. Women, Bourdieu argues, learn to move through their bodies and throughout their lives in a centripetal fashion with respect to the domestic, intimate sphere, while men learn to move in a centrifugal way.

Bourdieu's analysis has been discussed by anthropologists of the Middle East (e.g., vom Bruck 1997) and anthropologists of gender (e.g., Moore 1996), and the classic homologies man–woman, public–private, outside–inside have been carefully dissected, questioned, and subverted by ethnographic studies conducted, in particular, in the Middle East and North Africa (e.g., Ghannam 2002; Göle 2002; Hoodfar 1997; Kapchan 1996; Marcus 1986; Nelson 1974; Newcomb 2009; Northrop 2004). However, a strong interest in the relationship between space and gendered movement has remained both within anthropology and in the social sciences at large. As mentioned above, geography, for example, has a long tradition of tracing the ways in which men and women move differently within Western urban spaces (see e.g., Stimpson 1981). Studies range from gauging how men and women use daily transport differently (Law 1999; Polk 2004), to measuring how distances traveled between home and work vary by gender (Cristaldi 2005; Hanson and Johnston 1985), to drawing "geographies of female fear" (Valentine 1989) by tracing how the experience of fear and threat affect women's mobility in the city (Deegan 1987; Pain 1991; Valentine 1993).

Similarly, recent anthropological analyses of urban spaces, albeit complicating the homologies of Bourdieu's Kabyle House, have traced how ideal and idealized gendered divisions of space affect in complex ways the quality, quantity, and meaning of male and female mobility. Anthropologist Ghannam (2002), for example, in her study of a Cairo neighborhood that houses thousands of working class relocated families, traces how public and private spaces, familiar and unfamiliar areas, commercial and kinship arenas are organized, contested, negotiated along gender lines, making the movement of women a site of tensions and subversions. Authors like Ghannam highlight the somehow "situational" and fluid character of the relationship between gender and movement, tracing how, for example, "many factors—age, marital status, economic need, number of children, and the background of the social guardian ... shape women's access to public spheres" (Ghannam 2002, 101-2). Rather than contesting the premise of Bourdieu's argument—that is, that movement in space is shaped by (embodied) gender ideals and expectations—they work toward illuminating its ethnographic complexities. Thus, we have work tracing, for example, how ideas about women's sexual morality critically affect decisions about female labor migration in posteconomic downturn Indonesia (Silvey 2000), how negative gendered connotations of "wandering aimlessly about" historically affected colonial administration, state, and family evaluations of—and (attempted) constrictions over—women's mobility in South Africa and Lesotho (Coplan 2001), or how state conceptions of "sex trafficking" intersect with stereotypical constructions of femininity and masculinity and shape contemporary mobility of women in the European Union (Andrijasevic 2007).

While observing how gender affects movement in space, some scholars have zoomed in on the workings of the actual moving *bodies* themselves, tracing how sexual difference shapes and is enacted through the body—through its comportment, posture, and gestures. Here, the focus has been on how "mobility is embodied differentially—how the act of moving is reflected in and constructed through different bodies" (Cresswell 1999, 176). A number of scholars have focused on how gender generates specific *qualities* of bodily movement, and studies span from observing the specific forms of motility of homeless women in the United States (Cresswell 1999), to the ways in which Islamic precepts of female piousness generate specific bodily comportments in Cairo mosques (Mahmood 2005) or in Istanbul gyms (Sehlikoglu-Karakas 2012). One of the pioneering contribution to this field of enquiry is Young's work (1980, 1990) on the relation between basic modalities of "feminine body comportment, manner of movement and relation in space" (Young 1980, 139) and social constructions of the "feminine body" and hence of women *tout court*. Observing with an unforgiving phenomenological and feminist eye how women go about ordinary movements such as throwing, walking, holding, playing, sitting, Young argued in the early 1980s that the striking difference between female and male bodily movements is rooted, rather than in a natural "feminine essence," in the patriarchal system women are taught and embody.[3] In her analysis, mobility is a direct product of the efficacy of the construction of gender as we intend it today: "women in sexist society are physically handicapped," Young darkly concludes (Young 1980, 152). Bourdieu (1977) can be seen in a sense as taking Young's intuition a step further, and provides in a way the link between studies that emphasize the efficacy of gender over mobility on the one hand, and the efficacy of mobility over gender on the other, by positioning the body at the juncture between both forces, making it both internalize (the body moves according to internalized gendered norms) and reproduce (through its movement, the body actively establishes/reiterates gendered norms). This peculiar property of the body to both abide to and create specific conceptions of gender through its movement is picked up, critiqued, and intensified by theorists of gender (most notably Butler 1990) and anthropologists (most recently Mahmood 2005). I return to this below.

Gender emerges as a powerful "machine for movement" also in those studies that focus on gendered *expectations,* that is, on those culturally specific idealized practices and actions that become a normative model for men and women. The link between gendered expectations and movement emerges particularly clearly in ethnographic work on migration. Anthropologists working in a variety of contexts have carefully unpacked how migration has become a normative form of mobility for young unmarried men, an expected and in many senses mandatory way to achieve social and economic adulthood (e.g., Ali 2007; Capello 2008; Elliot 2012; Osella and Osella 2000; Vigh 2009). Here, gendered ideals become powerful determinants for whom moves and when—the fact that these movements are not always possible, hindered for example by harsh border restrictions and the perilous travels they generate, makes the gendered meaning of migration even more poignant, and the detriment to masculinity in the absence of such mobility even more dramatic (Carling 2002; Jansen 2008; Jónsson 2008; Tranberg Hansen 2005). Normative gendered expectations, however, are seated not only in sending communities, but also in the receiving ones. Thus, scholars have traced how specific global economic trends (Elmhirst 2007), pockets of labor that are intrinsically gendered in the collective imagination (e.g., the feminized "labor of care"; Anderson 2000; Colen 1995; Hochschild 2000; Moya 2007; or indeed that of sex; Agustín 2007; Andrijasevic 2010; Bernstein 2008; Long 2004; Peano 2012), and legal frameworks that are implicitly and explicitly gendered (Anderson 2007; Boyd 2006; Calvo 2000; Lutz 1997) translate directly into different patterns of local and transnational mobility of men and women.

While observing how gender affects the quality, quantity, and orientation of mobility, some scholars have also traced how the actual *experience* of mobility itself—even when of the same kind—varies across gender lines. In this category fall those studies mentioned above (e.g., Blunt 1994; Buijs 1993; Diner 1983) that consider historical and current mobility, travel, and migration from a female perspective, studies where gender emerges as a tool that allows scholars to address how women experience movement in specific ways. Another field that specifically deals with the ways in which men and women experience mobility differently is, for example, the study of gendered tourism, where scholars have traced how the experience of (and decisions about) tourism are heavily influenced by gender ideals, stereotypes, and desires (Byrne Swain 1995; Kinnaird and Hall 1994). An important section of these studies has focused in particular on how gender affects the *sexual* experience, and expectations, surrounding tourism, with a growing body of literature being produced on female sex tourism in the Caribbean (e.g., Frohlick 2013), the Middle East (e.g., Jacobs 2009), and South America (e.g., Meisch 1995). Studies of this kind add a fundamental dimension to the understanding of the relationship between gender and mobility not only by examining the sensuous, physical experience of mobility in gendered terms, but also by relating it in complex ways to other fields of classification and power: colonial and postcolonial histories, racial hierarchies, class difference, and so on. In tracing how mobility is shaped by these multiple relations of power, however, the question of what agentival capacity can and should be accorded to mobility itself unavoidably emerges. In the following section, I trace some of the ways in which authors have accorded mobility the power to shape, or at least affect, gender.

### The Gendered Efficacy of Mobility

Although focusing on the effects of gender on mobility and the effects of mobility on gender is an interconnected project—and I have mentioned above how a number of authors, while focusing on the molding powers of gender, have also made important reflections on how gender itself is in turn molded by mobility—the two perspectives do carry, at least at the heuristic level, different ideas about the purchase of mobility, and indeed different insights on the concept of gender itself.

Aptly for the present discussion, mobility's powers to shape gender can be found at the very foundations of the reformulation of the concept of gender undertaken by scholars such as Butler (1990, 1993) in the 1990s. Here, movement, performativity, repetition, bodily actions, postures, and routines become not only *results* of gender norms and expectations, but what actually makes gender—and the naturalized sexual differences it relies upon and organizes—possible, palpable, "real." This impulse to trace how movement is able to shape gender is found in a number of writings both explicitly and implicitly dealing with mobility. One just needs to refer, for example, to Wacquant's (2004) pioneering ethnography of boxing in a Chicago black neighborhood, to discover to what extent scholars have attributed to movement of specific kinds—performed in specific ways and in specific places—the power of molding gendered individuals. It is not by chance that Wacquant speaks of the boxing gym as a "masculinizing ma-chine" (2005, 458). Tauber (2008) makes a similarly microscopic analy-sis of how specific forms of bodily mobility shape gender identities in her work on Sinti women in Northern Italy, where she traces how actions and movements related to begging are conceived as defining women as both "Sinti" and "women." Osella and Osella (2000) trace this mechanism at a different scale, that of international migration, and show how it is through movement to the Gulf States that men in Kerala become recognized and recognizable as men.

Indeed, migration studies such as the Osellas's have attended closely to the ways in which migration is capable of shaping gender and, in particular, gender relations and hierarchies. Interestingly, the observations on mobili-ty's gendered efficacy have taken center stage in those studies that focus on the unflatteringly named "left behind." Studies have traced how transna-tional migration can recalibrate relations between the sexes "back home," resulting in a questioning of established roles and hierarchies. Though stud-ies on left-behind men and the complex effects this has on masculinity ex-ist (see e.g., Elmhirst 2007), it is mainly among left-behind women—wives of migrants, young women in emigrant communities and so on—that the literature has been most eager to discern mobility's powers on gender. In-deed, these women have often been considered—particularly in the field of development studies—as an effective measure of the impact of migration on gender relations more generally. A general hypothesis is often made that the absence of migrant men both requires and allows their wives and female relatives to assume new roles and responsibilities in the household and sending community, something which, in turn, positively affects women's positioning in patriarchal settings and, in the long term, the gender rela-tionships of the area (Brettell 2003; Brink 1991; Chant 1997; David 1995; Ennaji and Sadiqi 2008; Taylor, Moran-Taylor, and Rodman Ruiz 2006). Other studies of women left behind have complicated the relationship be-tween male migration and women's improved social standing by placing it within a more nuanced socio-historical context and/or considering the lon-gevity of such "achievements" (e.g., Brettell 1986; Day and Içduygu 1997; de Haas and van Rooij 2010; Elliot forthcoming; Gabaccia 2006; Mondain et al. 2012). The idea, however, that migration comes to bear on gender relations in their various cultural forms is a persistent one, one that contin-ues to inform policy and development schemes for non-Western countries.

The idea that mobility is able to (positively) transform gender relations—mainly, power relations between the sexes—or gender stereotypes—ideas about what men and women are able to make, do, and be—has often been the lens through which the relationship between gender and mobility has been viewed. Beyond migration studies, we find it in work conducted, for example, on the ways in which historical female travelers/explorers affected the ways in which women were imagined as immobile, dependent beings (e.g., Frederick and McLeod 1993; Wallach 2005). The mobility of ideas, together with actual people, has been also framed as having direct effects on conceptions of gender, as Cresswell for example argues with regards to the United States suffrage movement, where "transatlantic voyage and car rides in Massachusetts" (2005, 447) contributed to transform feminism by not only allowing feminist activists to move, but also allowing the idea of suffrage itself to become mobile.

Technologies of mobility such as boats and cars—or bicycles, as the book *A Wheel within a Wheel: A Woman's Quest for Freedom* by the suffragette Frances Willard (1997) vividly testifies—often become the fundamental medium or trigger for a change in gender relations. In his recent publication on the politics of mobility in colonial and postcolonial Tanzania, Grace (2013) traces the biographies of two famous African drivers—Vincent Njovu and Hawa Ramadhani—to show how moving bodies and technologies can unexpectedly and powerfully affect nationwide discussions about gender and race. In tracing the story of Hawa Ramadhani in particular, one of the very first female bus drivers in postcolonial Dar es Salaam, he reveals how Ramadhani's transgression of gendered ideas of propriety, domesticity, and, indeed, immobility slowly move her, within the collective imagination, from the position of suspicious meandered to something of a national symbol of gendered development in postcolonial Tanzania.

Not all accounts of gendered movements trace the *positive* reverberations these have on gender and the intricate power relations that compose it, however. Indeed, in line with the persistent call to avoid considering mobility as necessarily a positive and liberating force for individuals and societies (Gaibazzi 2015; Gilbert 1998; Hochschild 2000; Westin and Hassanen 2013), studies have highlighted how movement can also consolidate unequal gender relations and/or be a detriment to a specific gendered category. In their analysis of female seclusion and restricted mobility in Northern Pakistan, Mumtaz and Salway (2005) show for example how cultural norms, which uphold restricted movements and seclusion of women, are often at odds with the practical need of the majority of women, especially those of lower status, to move outside the house (see also Ghannam 2002, 100). Poorer women, forced to leave the house for employment and daily chores, are subject to loss of prestige and susceptible to sexual violence precisely by virtue of their mobility, in a way that higher status women, who not only have little need to leave the domestic sphere, but also possess the social resources to never leave the house unaccompanied, are not. "Freedom of movement" does not necessarily work in a positive, liberating way, on gendered power relations—and this of course becomes particularly apparent when an analysis of gender is coupled with that of class and race (see also Colen 1995; Hochschild 2000).

In looking at the gendered efficacy of mobility, scholars have tended to adopt a more performative, fluid, and relational conception of gender, one that does not solely differentiate men from women, but also captures "the culturally specific symbolic articulations elaborations of these differences" (Pine 2000, 253). Mobility has provided scholars of anthropology and beyond a powerful tool for thinking through the ways in which gender is negotiated, reformed, and changed, exposing how movement at different scales can affect socially constructed relations of power, dependence, and authority. However, particularly in studies explicitly dedicated to the study of mobility—and I am thinking here especially of migration studies—scholars have hesitated to take the insights mobility offers one step further, and thus allow these effectively to open-up the concept of gender to observe what thrives inside it. I address this issue in the following section by way of conclusion.

## Conclusion: Taking Efficacy a Step Further

Even when according a more fluid, post-structuralist character to gender, scholars of mobility have often left the category analytically untouched by mobility. Mobility can shuffle things around, but what it is actually shuffling (gender and its manifestations in people) remains unaffected. Indeed, many of the authors quoted above who work explicitly on mobility, when tracing the ways in which mobility affects gender, are actually focusing on how mobility affects *the relations* (generally of power) between genders, rather than the genders being related (cf. Strathern 1988). Addressing the difference between observing gender relations and genders being related allows us to consider *to what extent*—and depth—mobility is accorded the power to affect gendered subjects, and thus the concept of gender itself (Elliot forthcoming). It allows us to ask the following question: if mobility affects gender relations, what do these genders that are being related look like?

Here, anthropologists of mobility would benefit from taking a closer look at ethnographies that, while not dealing explicitly with mobility, accord to different kinds of movement the ability to *change* people, rather than merely to reposition them vis-à-vis others (Turner 1967). Mahmood's work comes to mind in this respect. Mahmood (2005) explores a women's mosque movement in Cairo, a piety movement part of the wider Islamic Revival that has been sweeping through the Muslim world since the 1970s. In her study of the ways in which the participants in the Mosque movement cultivate themselves as specific kinds of pious subjects, Mahmood focuses on the emphasis her interlocutors put on outward markers of religiosity (ritual practices, styles of comporting oneself, dress) and outer conduct (movement of the body, gesture, actions, speech). Mahmood argues that the women in the mosque movement regard these practices "as the necessary and ineluctable means for realizing the form of religiosity they are cultivating" (2005, 31). Making use of Foucault's concept of "technologies of the self" and of the Aristotelian notion of habituation and "the centrality of gestural capacities in certain traditions of moral cultivation" (Mahmood 2001, 215), Mahmood argues that outward performances and bodily behavior, rather than being solely a measure of religiosity, become both attributes of the pious self and "a necessary means of acquiring it" (2005, 147). In other words, through bodily movements (of specific qualities, quantities, and textures), women are not just *looking* pious, but are *becoming* pious subjects.

It is this subtle but fundamental correlation between exterior movement and interior transformation that I think can be profitably transposed to our understanding of the gender keyword in the context of the study of mobility. Framing movement as something that can change people's very subjectivity opens up the conceptual possibility of imagining mobility as a form of gender in its own right (Elliot 2012). It also allows, just as importantly, our conceptualization of gender to be redefined in light of mobility. By following how mobility can generate specific kinds of gendered people—defining and redefining the actual ways in which they are people, *sensu* Mahmood—one is also automatically in the business of redefining what gender *is* and, as category, keyword, ethnographic concept. By affecting the very way people see themselves and are recognized by others, mobility tears open gender for the analytic eye. According this analytic and ethnographic power to mobility does not imply assuming that this is how it works anywhere and everywhere. Forms of movements exist that *do not* contribute to defining the ways people conceive of themselves, and are conceived by others, as gendered subjects. Such an orientation, however, can allow mobility to interact with our conceptions of gender, generating complex and creative enquiries not only into the different forms of gender we encounter in the field, but also into the blanket term gender with which we so often pepper our analyses.

**Alice Elliot** is a Leverhulme Early Career Research Fellow at the Department of Anthropology of University College London. A social anthropologist, she has been conducting ethnographic research since 2006 between North Africa and Europe on the social and intimate dimensions of migration. She is at present preparing a book titled provisionally, *The Outside: Migration and the Imagination of Life in Morocco,* which explores how migration has come to penetrate towns, households, and people in an area of the world marked by decades of transnational movement.

## NOTES

This chapter was written thanks to the support of a Pegasus Marie Curie Fellowship and a Leverhulme Trust Early Career Fellowship.

1. The "master difference" I am developing here between the two uses of gender has been noted by a number of different authors (e.g., Donato et al. 2006; Hanson 2010; Herrera 2013; Hondagneu-Sotelo 2011; Mahler and Pessar 2006), mainly in review articles that trace the development of gender in mobility studies in terms of an evolution from one stage (what I call gender as classification) to another (what I call gender as process). I show how this evolutionary approach can be misleading for our understanding of the current use of gender in mobility studies, as not only gender is still generally used as "classification"—particularly when we enter the domain of policy analyses of mobility—but, also, often these different conceptions of gender coexist.

2. The distinction between these different ways of thinking about gender and mobility has also been made by geographer Hanson (2010) in her recent article *Gender and Mobility: New Approaches for Informing Sustainability*. In her review of the mobility literature of the past three to four decades, Hanson identifies "two disparate strands of thinking that have remained badly disconnected from each other" (2010, 5). On the one hand, she identifies studies that focus on how mobility shapes gender, and, on the other, those that focus on how gender shapes mobility. Critiquing the former for lacking a nuanced understanding and exploration of mobility and the latter for lacking a nuanced understanding and exploration of gender, Hanson highlights a need, for feminist geographers in particular, to bring together the two strands of thinking about gender and mobility and, in doing so, "synthesizing across quantitative and qualitative studies and across diverse, place-based studies" (18).

3. See also Gianini-Belotti (2004) for a similar feminist analysis of the bodily education of young girls in Italy.

## REFERENCES

Abu-Lughod, Lila. 1985. "A Community of Secrets: The Separate World of Bedouin Women." *Signs* 10(4): 637–57.

Agustín, Laura María. 2007. *Sex at the Margins: Migration, Labour Markets and the Rescue Industry.* London: Zed Books.

Ali, Syed. 2007. "'Go West Young Man': The Culture of Migration among Muslims in Hyderabad, India." *Journal of Ethnic and Migration Studies* 33(1): 37–58.

Anderson, Bridget. 2000. *Doing the Dirty Work? The Global Politics of Domestic Labour.* London: Zed Books.

——. 2007. "Motherhood, Apple Pie and Slavery: Reflections on Trafficking Debates." COMPAS Working Paper No. 48: 1–20.

Andrijasevic, Rutvica. 2007. "Beautiful Bead Bodies: Gender, Migration and Representation in Anti-Trafficking Campaigns." *Feminist Review* 86: 24–44.

——. 2010. *Migration, Agency, and Citizenship in Sex Trafficking.* London: Palgrave.

Bernstein, Elizabeth. 2008. "Introduction to Special Issue—Sexual Commerce and the Global Flow of Bodies, Desires, and Social Policies." *Sexuality Research & Social Policy* 5(4): 1–5.

Blunt, Alison. 1994. *Travel, Gender and Imperialism: Mary Kingsley and West Africa.* New York: Guilford Press.

Bourdieu, Pierre. 1977. *Outline of a Theory of Practice.* Cambridge: Cambridge University Press.

Boyd, Monica. 2006. "Women in International Migration: The Context of Exit and Entry for Empowerment and Exploitation." *UN Commission on the Status of Women 50th Session,* 27 February–10 March 2006, New York.

Brettell, Caroline. 1986. *Men Who Migrate, Women Who Wait: Population and History in a Portuguese Parish.* Princeton, NJ: Princeton University Press.

——. 2003. *Anthropology and Migration: Essays on Transnationalism, Ethnicity and Identity.* Oxford: AltaMira Press.

Brink, Judy H. 1991. "The Effect of Emigration of Husbands on the Status of their Wives: An Egyptian Case." *International Journal of Middle East Studies* 23(2): 201–11.

Buijs, Gina, ed. 1993. *Migrant Women: Crossing Boundaries and Changing Identities.* Oxford: Berg.

Butler, Judith. 1990. *Gender Trouble: Gender and the Subversion of Identity.* New York: Routledge.

——. 1993. *Bodies That Matter: On the Discursive Limits of Sex.* New York: Routledge.

——. 2004. *Undoing Gender.* New York: Routledge.

Byrne Swain, Margaret, ed. 1995. "Gender in Tourism." *Annals of Tourism Research* 22(2): 247–66.

Calvo, Janet M. 2000. "Spouse-Based Immigration Laws: The Legacy of Coverture." In *Global Critical Race Feminism: An International Reader,* edited by Adriene Katherine Wing, 380–86. New York: New York University Press.

Capello, Carlo. 2008. *Le Prigioni Invisibili: Etnografia Multisituata della Migrazione Marocchina.* Milan: Franco Angeli Edizioni.

Carling, Jørgen. 2002. "Migration in the Age of Involuntary Immobility: Theoretical Reflections and Cape Verdean Experiences." *Journal of Ethnic and Migration Studies* 28(1): 5–42.

Cattaneo, Maria Luisa, and Sabina dal Verme. 2005. *Donne e madri nella migrazione: prospettive transculturali e di genere.* Milano: Edizioni Unicopoli.

Chant, Sylvia. 1997. *Women-Headed Households: Diversity and Dynamics in the Developing World.* London: Macmillan Press.

Colen, Shellee. 1995. "'Like a Mother to Them': Stratified Reproduction and West Indian Childcare Workers and Employers in New York." In *Conceiving the New World*

*Order: The Global Politics of Reproduction,* edited by Faye Ginsburg and Rayna Rapp, 78–102. Berkeley: University of California Press.

Coplan, David B. 2001. "You Have Left Me Wandering about: Basotho Women and the Culture of Mobility." In *"Wicked" Women and the Reconfiguration of Gender in Africa,* edited by DL Hodgson and SA McCurdy, 188–211. Exeter: Heinemann.

Cresswell, Timothy. 1999. "Embodiment, Power and the Politics of Mobility: The Case of Female Tramps and Hobos." *Transactions of the Institute of British Geographers* 24(2): 175–92.

———. 2005. "Mobilizing the Movement: The Role of Mobility in the Suffrage Politics of Florence Luscomb and Margaret Foley 1911–1915." *Gender, Place and Culture* 12(4): 447–61.

Cristaldi, Flavia. 2005. "Commuting and Gender in Italy: A Methodological Issue." *The Professional Geographer* 57(2): 268–84.

David, Rosalind. 1995. *Changing Places? Women, Resource Management and Migration in the Sahel: Case Studies from Senegal, Burkina Faso, Mali and Sudan.* London: SOS Sahel International.

Day, Lincoln H, and Ahmet İçduygu. 1997. "The Consequences of International Migration for the Status of Women: A Turkish Study." *International Migration* 35: 337–71.

De Haas, Hein, and Aleida Van Rooij. 2010. "Migration as Emancipation? The Impact of Internal and International Migration on the Position of Women in Rural Morocco." *Oxford Development Studies* 38(1): 43–62.

Deegan, Michael. 1987. "The Female Pedestrian: The Dramaturgy of Structural and Experiential Barriers in the Street." *Man-Environment Systems* 17: 79–86.

Diner, Hasia R. 1983. *Erin's Daughters in America: Irish Immigrant Women in the Nineteenth Century.* Baltimore, MD: The Johns Hopkins University Press.

Donato, Katharine M, Donna Gabaccia, Jennifer Holdaway, Martin Manalansan, and Patricia Pessar. 2006. "A Glass Half Full? Gender in Migration Studies." *International Migration Review* 4(1): 3–26.

Douglas, Mary. 1970. *Natural Symbols: Explorations in Cosmology.* New York: Random House.

Elliot, Alice. 2012. "Reckoning with the Outside: Emigration and the Imagination of Life in Central Morocco." PhD dissertation, University College London.

———. Forthcoming. "Paused Subjects: Waiting for Migration in North Africa." *Time & Society.*

Elmhirst, Rebecca. 2007. "Tigers and Gangsters: Masculinities and Feminised Migration in Indonesia." *Population, Space and Place* 13: 225–38.

Ennaji, Moha, and Fatima Sadiqi. 2008. *Migration and Gender in Morocco: The Impact of Migration on the Women Left Behind.* Trenton, NJ: Red Sea Press.

Ets, Marie Hall. 1970. *Rosa: The Life of an Italian Immigrant.* Madison: University of Wisconsin Press.

Frederick, Bonnie, and Susan McLeod, eds. 1993. *Women and the Journey: The Female Travel Experience.* Pullman: Washington State University Press.

Frohlick, Susan. 2006. "Rendering and Gendering Mobile Subjects: Placing Ourselves between Local Ethnography and Global Worlds." In *Locating the Field: Metaphors of*

*Space, Place and Context in Anthropology,* edited by Simon Coleman and Peter Collins, 87–104. Oxford: Berg.

———. 2013. "Intimate Tourist Markets: Money, Gender and the Complexity of Erotic Exchange in a Costa Rican Caribbean Town." *Anthropological Quarterly* 86(1): 133–62.

Gabaccia, Donna. 2006. "When the Migrants Are Men: Italy's Women and Transnationalism as a Working-Class Way of Life." In *American Dreaming, Global Realities: Rethinking U.S. Immigration History,* edited by Donna R Gabaccia and Vicki L Ruiz, 190–206. Urbana, IL: University of Illinois Press.

Gaibazzi, Paolo. 2015. *Bush Bound: Young Men and Rural Permanence in Migrant West Africa.* New York: Berghahn.

Ghannam, Farah. 2002. *Remaking the Modern: Space Relocation and the Politics of Identity in a Global Cairo.* Berkeley: University of California Press.

Gianini Belotti, Elena. 2004. *Dalla Parte delle Bambine: L'Influenza dei Condizionamenti Sociali nella Formazione del Ruolo Femminile nei Primi Anni di Vita.* Milan: Feltrinelli.

Gilbert, Melissa R. 1998. "'Race,' Space, and Power: The Survival Strategies of Working Poor Women." *Annals of the Association of American Geographers* 88(4): 595–621.

Göle, Nilüfer. 2002. "Islam in Public: New Visibilities and New Imaginaries." *Public Culture* 14(1): 173–90.

Grace, Joshua. 2013. "Heroes of the Road. Race, Gender and the Politics of Mobility in Twentieth Century Tanzania." *Africa* 83(3): 403–25.

Grosz, Elizabeth. 1992. "Bodies-Cities." In *Sexuality and Space,* edited by Beatriz Colomina and Jennifer Bloomer, 241–53. New York: Princeton Architectural Press.

Hanson, Susan. 2010. "Gender and Mobility: New Approaches for Informing Sustainability." *Gender, Place & Culture: A Journal of Feminist Geography* 17(1): 5–23.

Hanson, Susan, and Ibipo Johnston. 1985. "Gender Differences in Work-Trip Length: Explanations and Implications." *Urban Geography* 6: 193–219.

Herrera, Gioconda. 2013. "Gender and International Migration: Contributions and Cross-Fertilizations." *The Annual Review of Sociology* 39: 471–89.

Higginbotham, Elisabeth, and Lynn Weber. 1992. "Moving Up with Kin and Community: Upward Social Mobility for Black and White Women." *Gender & Society* 6(3): 416–40.

Hochschild, Arlie Russell. 2000. "Global Care Chains and Emotional Surplus Values." In *On the Edge: Living with Global Capitalism,* edited by Will Hutton and Anthony Giddens, 130–46. London: Jonathan Cape.

Hondagneu-Sotelo, Pierrette. 1999. "Introduction: Gender and Contemporary U.S. Immigration." *American Behavioral Scientist* 42: 565–76.

———. 2011. "Gender and Migration Scholarship: An Overview from a 21st Century Perspective." *Migraciones Internacionales* 6(1): 219–33.

Hondagneu-Sotelo, Pierrette, and Ernestine Avila. 1997. "I'm Here but I'm There: The Meaning of Latina Transnational Motherhood." *Gender and Society* 11(5): 548–71.

Hoodfar, Homa. 1997. *Between Marriage and the Market. Intimate Politics and Survival in Cairo.* Berkeley, CA: University of California Press.

Jacobs, Jessica. 2009. "'Have Sex Will Travel': Romantic 'Sex Tourism' and Women Negotiating Modernity in the Sinai." *Gender, Place, and Culture* 16(1): 43–61.

Jansen, Stef. 2008. "Misplaced Masculinities. Status Loss and the Location of Gendered Subjectivities amongst 'Non-Transnational' Bosnian Refugees." *Anthropological Theory* 8(2): 181–200.

Jónsson, Gunvor. 2008. "Migration Aspirations and Immobility in a Malian Soninke Village." *International Migration Institute Working Paper 10.*

Kapchan, Deborah. 1996. *Gender on the Market: Moroccan Women and the Revoicing of Tradition.* Philadelphia: University of Pennsylvania Press.

Kinnaird, Vivian, and Derek Hall, eds. 1994. *Tourism: A Gender Analysis.* Chichester: Wiley.

Kofman, Eleonore, Annie Phizacklea, Parvati Raghuram, and Rosemary Sales. 2000. *Gender and International Migration in Europe.* London: Routledge.

Law, Robin. 1999. "Beyond 'Women and Transport': Towards New Geographies of Gender and Daily Mobility." *Progress in Human Geography* 23(4): 567–88.

Lévi-Strauss, Claude. 1969. *The Elementary Structures of Kinship.* Boston: Beacon Press.

Long, Lynellyn D. 2004. "Anthropological Perspectives on the Trafficking of Women for Sexual Exploitation." *International Migration* 42: 5–31.

Lutz, Helma. 1997. "The Limits of European-Ness: Immigrant Women in Fortress Europe." *Feminist Review* 57: 93–111.

Maher, Vanessa. 1974. *Women and Property in Morocco: Their Changing Relations to the Problem of Social Stratification in the Middle Atlas.* Cambridge: Cambridge University Press.

Mahler, Sarah, and Patricia Pessar. 2006. "Gender Matters: Ethnographers Bring Gender from the Periphery toward the Core." *International Migration Review* 40(1): 27–63.

Mahmood, Saba. 2005. *Politics of Piety. The Islamic Revival and the Feminist Subject.* Princeton, NJ: Princeton University Press.

———. 2001. "Feminist Theory, Embodiment, and the Docile Agent: Some Reflections on the Egyptian Islamic Revival." *Cultural Anthropology* 16(2): 202–236.

Marcus, Abraham. 1986. "Privacy in 18th Century Aleppo: The Limits of Cultural Ideals." *International Journal of Middle Eastern Studies* 18: 165–83.

Marsden, Magnus. 2007. "All-Male Sonic Gatherings, Islamic Reform and Masculinity in Northern Pakistan." *American Ethnologist* 34(3): 473–90.

Meisch, Lynn A. 1995. "Gringas and Otavalenos: Changing Tourist Relations." *Annals of Tourism Research* 22: 441–62.

Mondain, Nathalie, Sara Randall, Alioune Diagne, and Alice Elliot. 2012. "Les Effets de L'émigration Masculine dur les Femmes et leur Autonomie: Entre Maintien et Transformation des Rapports Sociaux de Sexe Traditionnels au Sénégal." *Autrepart* 61(2): 81–97.

Moore, Henrietta. 1996. *Space, Text, and Gender.* New York: Guilford Press.

Morokvasic, Mirjana. 1984. "Birds of Passage Are Also Women." *International Migration Review* 18(4): 886–907.

Moya, Jose C. 2007. "Domestic Service in Global Perspective: Gender, Migration and Ethnic Niches." *Journal of Ethnic and Migration Studies* 33(4): 559–79.

Mumtaz, Zubia, and Sarah Salway. 2005. "'I Never Go Anywhere': Extricating the Links between Women's Mobility and Uptake of Reproductive Health Services in Pakistan." *Social Science and Medicine* 60: 1751–65.

Nelson, Cynthia. 1974. "Public and Private Politics: Women in the Middle Eastern World." *American Ethnologist* 1(3): 551–63.

Newcomb, Rachel. 2009. *Women of Fez: Ambiguities of Urban Life in Morocco.* Philadelphia: University of Pennsylvania Press.

Northrop, Douglas. 2004. *Veiled Empire: Gender and Power in Stalinist Central Asia.* Ithaca, NY: Cornell University Press.

Okely, Judith. 1983. *The Traveller-Gypsies.* Cambridge: Cambridge University Press.

Osella, Filippo, and Caroline Osella. 2000. "Migration, Money and Masculinity in Kerala." *Journal of the Royal Anthropological Institute* 6: 117–33.

Pain, Rachel. 1991. "Space, Sexual Violence and Social Control; Integrating Geographical and Feminist Analysis of Women's Fear of Crime." *Progress in Human Geography* 15(4): 415–31.

Peano, Irene. 2012. "Excesses and Double Standards: Migrant Prostitutes, Sovereignty and Exceptions in Contemporary Italy." *Modern Italy* 17(4): 419–32.

Pessar, Patricia. 1986. "The Role of Gender in Dominican Settlement in the United States." In *Women and Change in Latin America,* edited by J Nash and H Safa, 273–94. South Hadley: Bergin and Garvey.

Pessar, Patricia, and Sarah Mahler. 2003. "Transnational Migration: Bringing Gender in." *International Migration Review* 37(3): 812–46.

Pine, Frances. 2000. "Gender." In *Encyclopaedia of Social and Cultural Anthropology,* edited by Alan Barnard and Jonathan Spencer. 385–398. London: Routledge.

Polk, Merritt. 2004. "The Influence of Gender on Daily Car Use and on Willingness to Reduce Car Use in Sweden." *Journal of Transport Geography* 12: 185–95.

Saegert, Susan. 1980. "Masculine Cities and Feminine Suburbs: Polarized Ideas, Contradictory Realities." *Signs* 5: S96–S111.

Salih, Ruba. 2003. *Gender in Transnationalism: Home, Longing and Belonging among Moroccan Migrant Women.* London: Routledge.

Schneider, Jane. 1971. "Honor, Shame and Access to Resources in Mediterranean Societies." *Ethnology* 10(1): 1–24.

Sehlikoglu-Karakas, Sertaç. 2012. "Boundaries of a Veiled Female Body: Islamic Reflections on Women's Sporting Bodies in Relation to Sexuality, Modesty and Privacy." *Anthropology News* 53(6): S1–S41.

Silvey, Rachel M. 2000. "Stigmatized Spaces: Gender and Mobility under Crisis in South Sulawesi, Indonesia." *Gender, Place & Culture: A Journal of Feminist Geography* 7(2): 143–61.

Stimpson, R Catharine, ed. 1981. *Women and the American City.* Chicago, IL: Chicago University Press.

Strathern, Marilyn. 1988. *The Gender of the Gift: Problems with Women and Problems with Society in Melanesia.* Berkeley, CA: University of California Press.

Tauber, Elisabeth. 2008. "'Do You Remember the Time We Went Begging and Selling.' The Ethnography of Transformations in Female Economic Activities and Its Narrative in the Context of Memory and Respect among the Sinti in North Italy." In *Romani/Gypsy Cultures in New Perspectives,* edited by Fabian Jacobs and Johannes Ries, 155–75. Leipzig: Leipziger Universitätsverlag.

Taylor, Matthew J, Michelle J Moran-Taylor, and Debra Rodman Ruiz. 2006. "Land, Ethnic, and Gender Change: Transnational Migration and Its Effects on Guatemalan Lives and Landscapes." *Geoforum* 37: 41–61.

Thornbury, Barbara E. 2014. "Tokyo, gender and mobility: tracking fictional characters on real monorails, trains, subways and trams." *Journal of Urban Cultural Studies* 1(1): 43–64.

Tranberg Hansen, Karen. 2005. "Getting Stuck in the Compound: Some Odds Against Social Adulthood in Lusaka, Zambia." *Africa Today* 51(4): 3–16.

Tsing, Anna. 2005. *Friction: An Ethnography of Global Connection.* Princeton, NJ: Princeton University Press.

Turner, Victor. 1967. *The Forest of Symbols: Aspects of Ndembu Ritual.* Ithaca, NY: Cornell University Press.

Uteng Priya, Tanu, and Tim Cresswell, eds. 2007. *Gendered Mobilities.* Aldershot, England: Ashgate.

Valentine, Gill. 1989. "The Geography of Women's Fear." *Area* 21(4): 385–90.

———. 1993. "(Hetero)sexing Space: Lesbian Perception and Experiences of Everyday Spaces." *Environment and Planning D: Society and Space* 11(4): 395–413.

Vigh, Henrik. 2009. "Wayward Migration: On Imagined Futures and Technological Voids." *Ethnos* 74(1): 91–109.

Vom Bruck, Gabrielle. 1997. "A House Turned Inside Out: Inhabiting Space in a Yemeni City." *Journal of Material Culture* 2(2): 139–72.

Wacquant, Löic. 2004. *Body and Soul: Notebooks of an Apprentice Boxer.* New York: Oxford.

———. 2005. "Carnal Connections: On Embodiment, Apprenticeship, and Membership." *Qualitative Sociology* 28(4): 445–74.

Wallach, Janet. 2005. *Desert Queen: The Extraordinary Life of Gertrude Bell: Adventurer, Adviser to Kings, Ally of Lawrence of Arabia.* New York: Anchor Books.

Westin, Charles, and Sadia Hassanen. 2013. *People on the Move: Experiences of Forced Migration.* Trenton, NJ: Red Sea Press.

Willard, Frances. 1997. *A Wheel Within a Wheel: A Woman's Quest for Freedom.* Bedford, MA: Applewood Books.

Young, Iris Marion. 1980. "Throwing Like a Girl: A Phenomenology of Feminine Body Comportment, Motility and Spatiality." *Human Studies* 3: 137–56.

———. 1990. *Throwing Like a Girl and Other Essays in Feminist Philosophy and Social Theory.* Bloomington: Indiana University Press.

# 5

# Immobility

*Nichola Khan*

The keyword "immobility" has developed as a cipher for assemblages of blocked, stuck, and transitional movement. These involve political, economic, cultural, geographical, and human components. Recent analyses draw continuities with classic anthropological texts that detail the ecological, social, and cultural circulation of people, knowledge, objects, materiality, and time (e.g. Bourdieu 1977; Fabian 1983; Malinowski 2010; Mauss 1990). British structural-functional anthropology was at the forefront in developing ideas about the sedentarism of bounded places as the basis of human experience. Rivers, Radcliffe-Brown, and Evans-Pritchard all reified traditional cultures as if they occurred in pure form, and had existed in isolation for centuries as static, immobile structures. While these classic disciplinary figures sought to level the fictions of racial superiority that had served ideologies of empire and conquest, non-European cultures were still viewed as ultimately *different*—a legacy evident in Europe's immigration problem deemed to originate not in politics, economy, or an obstinate colonial legacy, but the fixed irrevocable Otherness of race and culture. By contrast are the more dynamic writings by eminent subjects of colonial territories moving toward independence. For example, African anthropologist Busia who analyzed the contemporary influence of social changes on the political system of the Ashanti in Ghana—and Kumar Bose whose work on Indian societal structure, hierarchy, and cultural history was deeply imbued with support for Ghandi's nationalist struggles for freedom from British rule.

This chapter elaborates on ways anthropological takes on immobility have accorded priority to the key fields of transnational migration, diaspora, and exile. The discussion principally pertains to structures, classifications, and experiences of confinement, arrested time-consciousness, liminality, and isolation associated with neoliberal globalization, war, and transnational migration. First is the spatio-temporality that shapes the postcolonial nation, failed state, or nonstate—in racialized, anachronistic terms of underdevelopment, deficiency, deprivation, cultural primitivism, and the incapacity to *move* (at all, or fast enough) toward civilizational progress (Khan 2014a). Second are critiques of humanitarianism positioning migrants and refugees, coterminously, as "stuck" in a condition of permanent transition to peace, self-governance, historical consequence, and full humanity (Nguyen 2012). These ideas are reinforced through studies of trauma, pathology, abnormality, incapacity, and arrested development invoking immobility as a biomedical technology, and a metaphor for conceptions of the viable human. Third, other variations highlight immobility's broader positive and negative relation to the conditions at stake in social and economic life; to ways immobility is imposed, but also governs people's efforts to transform or resist teleological narratives of freedom, progress, or integration; to ways problematics of immobility are inscribed into cultural events such as travel, leisure, and tourism (Salazar 2013); and to "the simultaneity of global circulation and local lifeworlds of (im)mobility, speed, motion, friction, tensions, and journeys" in ways roads become possibilities or impediments to modern nationalisms, state-building, and economic survival (Dalakoglou and Harvey 2012, 463). Drawing on fieldwork with homeless drug addicts in San Francisco, Bourgois and Schonberg (2009) explore the final immobility of early deaths produced by chronic poverty, hunger and racism, social exclusion and ostracism, and the punitive policies of corporate neoliberalism.

The chapter also explores how immobility's genealogy in anthropology is coeval with comparative developments across the social sciences and humanities, and developments in the "mobilities turn" (Cresswell 2006; Greenblatt 2009; Harvey 2000; Kaplan 1996; Urry 2007). Here, anthropological approaches to immobility can highlight otherwise invisibilized processes in the study of other phenomena, and in the priority given to mobility in many contemporary migration or transnationalism studies (Hannam, Sheller, and Urry 2006; Salazar 2012). The emphasis given to the politics, ideologies, economic developments, and technologies of modernity that enable or prohibit variations of movement has also tended to overlook the fact that mobility was a central feature of many premodern societies (Salazar and Smart 2011).

Immobility thus links to diverse epistemologies and heterologies regarding societal struggles with managing movement and inaction, and the intensities of passion generated through new communication technologies. Bissell and Fuller (2013) emphasize the political desirability of attempts to induce stillness in place of excessive movement (e.g., in "too much" democracy), and movement in place of too much stillness (e.g., in the development of consumerism). Heidegger (1977) conceived the relationship between the individual and technology as one of standing: standing in relation to each other, new technologies move (or not) them and us. Standing is not solely an immobile disposition of technology therefore, but a function of technology as a tool of governmentality that a society can deploy to regulate (also block, arrest, or frustrate) socioeconomic and culturally defined modes of movement. Some related technologies include immobilities created by the securitization and political regulation of persons, occurring alongside the mobility of goods, information, and services (Turner 2007); the conceptual movement and physical stillness (nonhuman immobility) of futuristic architecture (Bissell and Fuller 2013); the potential and threat posed by air travel to new aerial societies, or "aerealities" (Adey 2010); even immobility's articulation as an "end of the world" national imaginary (Salazar 2012). These variegated definitions arguably surpass the boundaries of theory and subject matter in academic disciplines, better indicating the multiple shaping of constitutive power within and between assemblages of political, economic, social, and cultural immobility.

To capture the complex interrelations between shifting scales on which the governance, experience, and relations of immobility play out, anthropologists have developed methodological innovations in mobilities research. Including multi-sited ethnography, and multiple qualitative mobile approaches, these have drawn on historical, literary, poetic, artistic, and imaginative research to explore the feeling of movements (including blocked, potential, and imagined movements) pertaining to labor migration, exile, and displacement (Büscher and Urry 2009, 100).

This methodological and theoretical emphasis on feeling additionally links negative/dysphoric, and positive/euphoric assemblages of immobility to the affective turn in the social sciences, and its strong genealogy in Spinoza's critique (*Ethics* 1996) of the subject-oriented philosophy of Descartes. This pertains particularly to the relation between the world and individual, real and imagined, language and subjectivity (Brown and Stenner 2001; Deleuze and Guattari 2004; Thrift 2008). In anthropology, it bears on the central role accorded to affect in shaping phenomena such as marginal communities, diasporic and exilic subjectivities, mobile identity imaginings; cosmopolitanism, economic transformations, and postwar political landscapes (Marsden 2008; Navaro-Yashin 2009).

A complete review of anthropological permutations of immobility is not the chapter's aim. Rather it is to examine some key uses pertaining, as indicated, to the relation between immobility and mobility, in some areas of migration, international politics, affect, and the market, which have received significant attention. Anthropology's specific contribution to immobility offers ethnographically grounded theorizations that can draw on classic disciplinary concepts and concerns, and query the ethics the exercise of immobility delivers in different contexts; for example, in ways immobility may transform transnational and transcultural categories, praxis, imaginaries, and subjects. This includes some reflections on what possibilities are shaped by immobility within diverse modes of hegemony, inequality, and power. It bears on motility as the potential and capacity to move; on ways ideas about staying still (and dreaming of immobility) may empower, or forbid certain kinds of action and transformation; and on ways immobility may represent a fantasized end to the acquisition of wealth and goods, or a pathologized response to never arriving.

Anthropology brings distinct disciplinary flavor to analyze some key questions. How is immobility dispersed via different ideologies and politics through time, and across the globe? If immobility and mobility are extremes on a continuum, what lies in-between? Can we define or describe immobility without referring to mobility? What negative or positive meanings are attached to immobility? How does immobility enfold ideas of freedom, free will, and resistance? Finally, how might we rethink a political body and ontology that can transcend disciplinary divisions, and divisions between movement and immobility?

## Anthropological Immobilities

The following sections reflect on some critical usages of immobility in anthropology. These emphasize ways immobility—largely in relation to mobility—is enfolded into dimensions of migration, the international state system, and local, and delocalized conjunctions of productive labor in contemporary capitalism.

### Liminal Spaces, Transition, In-Between

In the 1950s, Turner investigated rituals among the Ndembu in Northern Rhodesia, including hunters' cults, fertility cults, curative cults, rituals of affliction, and life-crisis rituals. Taking a dynamic transformational process view to ritual, Turner developed his concept of antistructure. This contrasted with French structuralist anthropology, which deemed ritual an integral part of mythology, from which the abstract universal principles underlying all human behavior could be analyzed. Turner emphasized that ritual is performed in symbolic action, and the importance of the liminal phase in ritual. His classic concept of liminality (1974, 2011), which describes movement from one state or status to another, provides a fruitful entry point into the question of what, if immobility lies on a continuum with mobility, lies in-between?

Liminality typically assists cultural understandings of events involving the dissolution and formation of order, and conditions of uncertainty, fluidity, and malleability—that apparently dissolve structure while structures are established (Szakolczai 2009). Recent research has analyzed its incorporation into more enduring spaces, structures, and imaginings of blockage, in-betweenness and never-ending transition produced by uneven geographical development, real and imagined borders associated with the nation-state, war, and transnational migration.

First, Navaro-Yashin (2003, 114) likens being a subject of peripheral or illegal states outside international recognition—as well as normal places like Britain and the United States—as akin to inhabiting an abjected space betwixt life and death, a "no man's land" wherein the symbolic presences and eerie absences of the state circumscribe everyday experience as political liminality. Her metaphor of "no man's land" to describe existence in peripheral illegal or nowhere zones captures temporal figurations associated with the specific transnational political contexts experienced by migrants, and the idea of immobility as a negative effect of the state. In the colonial trope of the globe-as-chronometer, political liminality enfolds the spatio-temporality that casts colonized subjects as inhabiting a permanently anterior time in which representations of progress position them as living in the West's historical past, and new nations late for a race already underway (Gupta 2004, 275). Ideas of immobility similarly shape studies of refugees, invoking metaphors of blocked cultural and psychic development for communities whose pain originates geographically and temporally elsewhere. According to Freud, trauma describes the psychic compulsion to repeat past events; and a formulation of history as an endless repetition or inability to move forward from previous violence. Fassin and Rechtman (2009) explore the "politics of trauma" among survivors' of an industrial accident claims for compensation; psychologists' reports testifying to the plight of Palestinian people; and the legal credibility given to medical certificates versus the personal accounts of asylum-seekers. The latter case reveals how the refugee mind and body, classified, diagnosed, and rendered "stuck" in the trauma of another time and place, become bodily incorporated as discursive tools for governing a humanitarian gateway to European citizenship. Linking the US war in Vietnam, and US wars in the Middle East after 9/11, Nguyen (2012, 52) correspondingly emphasizes ways the refugee figure is subjectivated to the US neoliberal imperium, first in relation to war, second to the gifts of freedom and refuge, *stuck* [my italics] in "endless transition" between war's remains and the rehabilitations of peace.

Second, Turner's (1974) description of liminality suggests it has a dialectical relation to societal marginality and inferiority, and that in spatial terms liminality is positioned in-between, on the edges (marginality) and beneath (inferiority). This bears on ways liminality is inflected in the broader political-economic condition of not moving, and never arriving. For many migrants, perennial obligations of remittance mean they cannot fully build lives here, or enjoy the fruits of their labor there. This institutes stuckness, in-betweenness, and marginality as permanent features of everyday life. Their experience illustrates a criticism of Turner's overly romantic, apolitical take on liminality and its destabilizing potential: "[liminality] transgresses or dissolves the norms that govern structured and institutionalized relationships and is accompanied by experiences of unprecedented potency" (2011, 128). It highlights the social fragility, and some difficult subjective and political dimensions for many migrants who experience a sense of permanently treading water in lives, goals, and places, experienced as not (not-yet, maybe never) their own, arising from the burden of multiple configurations of political and economic marginality, racism, and war they carry on behalf of their families (Khan 2014b). In chapter 3, Dean emphasizes that the freedom of mobility capital and agentive power many people putatively enjoy may resemble imprisonment more than liberation. Following calls to study freedom ethnographically (Laidlaw 2002), and the ethics the exercise of freedom furnishes in different cultural traditions and social and historical contexts, immobility can highlight how migrants' freedom may be contradictory: equivocal insofar as it enfolds desires to *block* the work of separation from the lost homeland, while retaining ambivalence in these attachments.

Third, while it should be stressed that the valuation of immobility is by no means always negative, for migrants who either voluntarily or forcibly fled their countries during war, immobility may enfold a historical problematic wherein people idealize the freedom of another time, before the devastation of the present. Here a sense of grief and attachment to the past prevents desires for progress from being fully embraced. One engaging melancholia (Freud 2005), as a political effect, which permeates continuity into the future, in tensions between holding on and moving forward, being left behind and unable to move on. For Butler (1997), being stuck in the problem of surviving with loss is a neither particularly positive nor negative permanent condition of subjectivity, and of what she terms "melancholic existence."

Elaborating on the "melancholia of freedom," Hansen's (2012) ethnography in post-apartheid South Africa takes an Indian township as a site to examine the recasting of historical and collective memories in the process of reimagining identity, within the contours of "a contested and feeble South African nationalism" (21). He argues that the "call of history" as a framework for cultural self-making is profoundly rooted in a sense of loss and displacement: because of contradictory attachments to the oppressive past, which cannot fully be grieved or acknowledged, subjectivities fail to fully move forward into the future, or embrace what they are supposed to become (4).

### Progress, Desire, and the Market

Querying immobile organizations of productive labor can also shed light on conditions intrinsic to ways immobility—in relation to desires for social and economic mobility—might recalibrate oppressive realities more positively as spaces of hope or freedom, and reshape new communications, meanings, and forms of exchange. As Jayaram in chapter 1 argues, it is only through attending to ethnographic detail that analyses of mobility and capital can become useful.

The structures of global capitalism that propel millions to migrate from their homelands have created a "maniacal offshore dream" in which the status and confidence of all previous fixed dwellings is undermined, and "life is as indifferent as money" (Berger 2007, 114). Here contradictory meanings of immobility are implicated in the paradox of a vision of upward mobility, which results in the perpetual labor of an endless present, and hopes of movement which have become traumatic. Far from the lateral freedoms, Hardt and Negri (2004, 135–37) identify in the corrosion of security and possibilities for upward mobility under contemporary capitalism, this is the deferred realization intrinsic to hope. Harvey connects the body as an "accumulation strategy" to globalization, neocolonialism, and uneven geographical development. While global inequalities and rapid technological change have produced "spaces of hope" across the globe, at the same time dreams of making it are often lost in the soulless reality of migrant life, and "the romanticism of endlessly open projects" that never close (2000, 174). Berlant's (2011) notion of "cruel optimism" compellingly describes the fantasies people direct toward "that moral-intimate-economic thing called the good life" that enable them to cope with the pursuit of progress and liberty as an activity of being worn out by it (19): a fantasy in which life is dedicated to moving forward but is actually "stuck in survival time, the time of struggling, drowning, holding onto the ledge, treading water, the time of not stopping" (169). Relatedly, Thompson and Zizek (2013) emphasize ways the excesses and disaffections of contemporary capitalism have resulted in the "privatization of hope," and new relevance for Bloch's (1986, 11) "ontology of Not Yet Being."

Continuing with different ways of analyzing and valuing mobility, insofar as out of the nightmare of movement emerges the fantasy-dream of stasis, immobility intertwines ideas of free will and freedom. For example, twentieth-century performance artist Alfred Jarry's "Machine of Absolute Rest" describes a fictional time machine in which one could "pass with impunity through all bodies, movements, or forces"—here immobility a powerful, positive (masculine) fantasy and paradoxical aesthetic of absolute movement (Harley 2013, 38). As Elliot in chapter 4 describes, gendered power relations may circumscribe "freedom of movement" in ways that are far from positive or liberating. In a study of rituals of rest (traveling picnics) among Afghan migrant men (Khan 2014b), I locate attempts to interrupt, re-pace, re-emplace, and stop lives conceived in terms of "too much movement" in a level of political economy, wherein freedom is therapeutic, while also sustaining deceptive realities impelled by exploitation, economic necessity, and hierarchy. Migrants such as these men who apply for UK citizenship face travel restrictions for several years. The enforced immobility, or variegated mobility, imposed by ultranationalist policy makers on the transnational movement of foreigners may reflect a punishment for a perceived excess of mobility, in the context of public anxieties about uncontrolled immigration.

Studies of immobility are not exclusively associated with transnational migration. In relation to desires for upward social and economic mobility, Hage (2009, 98) proposes the conditions of permanent crisis and existential trauma that many people inhabit under neoliberal economics and contemporary capitalism have produced an intensification and normalization of a sense of "stuckedness." While "existential mobility" describes the imaginary sense one is "going somewhere," "imagined existential stuckedness" is the feeling life is going nowhere. One can be upwardly socially mobile, "moving," yet if one feels one is not moving or accumulating goods and capital as fast as others, "mobility envy" may ensue (Hage 2009, 99). The heroic ability to "stick it out," Hage argues, produces a noble assertion of one's "freedom as a human." This overrides the dehumanization implied by a situation of "stuckedness," and a pathological scenario in which the more one invests in waiting, the harder it is to stop (Hage 2009, 104).

### Pathology, Waiting, Resistance

Immobility's nongeographical or spatial components also provoke an interiorized focus on ways matters and theories of the psyche link to these discussions. In short, if (any)one lingers too long in a place of exemption, a slowing down in the body and brain may be diagnosed, wherein immobility assumes pathological aspects. Developing on the catatonia of "tension insanity" (Kahlbaum 1973) and Kraepelin's (1990) definitions of "manic stupor" and "manic-depressive insanity" are immobilities associated in the psychiatric diagnostic manual the *Diagnostic and Statistical Manual of Mental*

*Disorders* (*American Psychiatric Association* 2013) with schizophrenia, bipolar, and panic disorders; PTSD; and depression. Medical anthropologists have scrutinized the epistemic cultures and pressures shaping the proliferation of disorders in psychiatry. They have tracked temporal and global movements from explanations dominated by postcolonial, cultural, and structural ecologies to those from biomedicine and clinical science (DelVecchio Good et al. 2008). Certainly, withdrawal and the inability to move or work may be consonant with the long-term anxiety, avoidance, and trauma symptoms associated with war and displacement. Among Afghan migrants, *khapgan* (Pakhto, "feeling down") can describe a sense of depression, of being unable to move (Khan 2013). *Khapgan* offers an interesting cultural lens to explore the limits of individual autonomy and capacity for action in a transnational field of interrelated physical, political, and economic mobilities. Immobility may also be an extreme, if extremely painful, form of self-protection: a positive space for mitigating and critiquing the work of integration, the weight of the past and a life in which hope has become stuck (Khan 2013, 522). Regarding ways culture supposedly moves in contemporary globalization contexts, Moore (2011) eschews an analysis of abstract processes and flows. Rather, anthropologists should analyze still life: attending to individuals' everyday hopes, desires, and satisfactions can fruitfully reshape ways we understand culture, and form the ethical basis of social change.

Within the illnesses of our contemporary era, passivity can be a forceful site of power, or an opportunity for drugs to shift us back onto a more acceptable pace of life. Martin's (2007) ethnography of bipolar disorder draws on mental health support groups, psychiatrists' rounds, individuals' experiences with psychotropic drugs, and autobiographical insights. She highlights problematic formations of movement and immobility in late modernity in the current psychiatric criteria of bipolar disorder, in the individual who "is *too* energized, or *too* immobilized" (Martin 2007, 46). Bipolar disorder emerged amid anxieties around "simple exposure to the hectic pace and excessive stimuli of modern life," and co-occurred with symptoms of a depressive, fragmented, alienated consciousness and isolation from the social (Martin 2007, 52). In the contemporary United States, where the economic dominates the social, "experiences of mania, once considered a sign of fearful and disordered irrationality, have come to epitomize the vital energy—found in the psyche rather than the laboring body—that the market *needs* to keep expanding. This is the heart of the affinity between contemporary American culture and the characteristics of manic depression" (Martin 2007, 54).

Immobility also elides normal and pathological, negatively and positively valued, organizations of *hope*. Hope is interesting insofar as it describes, positively, a state of fantasy or sometimes totally unrealizable condition of clinging to, and coping with, the impossible (the immoveable)—a "technology of patience" that "enables a concept of later to suspend questions about the cruelty of now" (Berlant 2011, 28). In a Freudian economy of traumatic suffering, hope circumvents grief. A perverse economy that sustains suffering and masochism, hope structures a "binding cathexis," a stubborn means of denying reality that effectively *paralyses* other functions, preserves the link with what one has lost, and "guarantees lack of change [movement], lack of mourning and the least expenditure of energy" (Potamianou 1997, 3-4).

Immobility may thus arrest or create space for new hope and desire to emerge. In the psychotherapeutic setting, Mitchell (1993) explores the apparent stalemate situation between therapist and client, where words fail to move a client out of a dreadful sense there is no way out. By fully immersing into the senselessness of pain, immobility may allow threatening, inchoate feelings that have not been fully felt, symbolized, or integrated into self-organization, so that richer forms of experience may emerge (Mitchell 1993, 227-28). Thus, hope and optimistic longings may underline even the most stubborn, disturbing symptomatology of psychotics. In his poetry volume *Knots,* the antipsychiatrist Laing (1969) described the "knots, tangles, fankles, impasses, disjunctions, whirligogs, binds" that indenture paradoxical forms of communication in human relationships. He analyzed these in severe form in schizophrenia, wherein kindness and love in family relations become strategies to exert power and control (e.g., I love you, but it will be impossible for you to earn that love). Drawn from his era of Cold War hostility, Laing linked pathological immobility to societal struggles for power and control.

In the sense one either cannot, or will not move, immobility's passivity is ambivalent and as emphasized, may have positive, negative, as well as ambiguous valuations. Immobility may encompass positive strategies of active resistance, or a response to shame, and an active mode of refusing to move toward assimilationist social processes (Lakha 2009, 122). Through adopting "collective immobility" in relation to formal organization, first-generation UK Afghans strategically avoid divisive conflicts based on ethnic, regional, or political identity (Khan 2013, 529). Immobility in their case may describe an emergent form of class-consciousness—and reflect the transnational mobility of an older adaptation for coping with political and economic instability in multiple hierarchies, allegiances, and divisions. In Afghanistan, Coburn's (2011) ethnography of everyday political life centers on the road between the village Istalif and the capital Kabul. Despite high political feuding and factionalism, strategies of immobility create not Hobbesian war and violence, but temporary peace and stability (Coburn 2011, 6). Coburn analyzes ways social behaviors explicitly avoid overt disputes, but also undermine opponents' political plans, social capital, and the social reputation necessary to execute these plans. He terms these as "politics of stagnation" and strategies of "masterly inaction." Rather than wealthy traders, local commanders, and politicians who travel the road, the village chiefs who stay behind wield the most power.

The Taliban movement's radical refusal to move away from traditional precepts of culture is, additionally, widely interpreted as a response to historical encounters with foreign imperial powers and the dominance of an ethnic minority elite in Kabul, which has imposed variations of Western-style modernity on Afghanistan's rural, Pashtun majority. What curious correspondence may lie between the Taliban, and *The Stuckists,* an antimodern, antiprogressive art movement established to resist the hegemony of conceptual "ego"-art? Of course (in the world according to Cartesian dualism), Latour (1993) reminds us we are neither post- nor antimodern but, quite simply, have never been modern.

Less obvious formations of immobility's social, political, and personal relation to resistance appear in studies of waiting (Hage 2009). Waiting's analytic value lies not in revealing the obvious; that waiting is inherent to gift exchange, honor, riposte, or the calendar (Bourdieu 1977); that waiting links psychodynamically, to the infant's capacity to master desire (for the breast, love, the satisfaction of desire) in the unbearable affective state of waiting for the mother. Rather, waiting's value lies in what kind of waiting is exhibited in the phenomena under examination; in waiting as a unique object of politics around who waits, what waiting entails, and who provides what one waits for (Hage 2009, 1). Waiting, like immobility, may be an exercise or lack of agency, a "passive activity" or "active passivity" (Crapanzano 1985). Within waiting is appetite. Hunger strikes organized by illegal migrants in detention centers embody challenges to states' regulative power, migration policies, and regimes (Mountz 2010). Oppositely, the religious fast or feast day marks a condition in which the cessation of work or food describes not resistance to negatively valued conditions, but the positive, ritual sanctification of a particular modality of action and belief. Dwyer (2009) distinguishes between existential waiting as a disposition toward life captured in the question "What next?," and situational waiting which is social, relational, and engaged—not least because situations implicate a political economy of waiting, and awaited movement, in which time is money and waiting a waste of time.

Then there is boredom: a precarious, existential state of not going anywhere, of both waiting and looking for something, where nothing is moving, and hope is secretly being negotiated. Psychoanalyst Phillips (1993) sees in boredom the lure of escape from desire, a solution to the problem of desire—but also the lure of a desire that will end one's boredom (the desire for a desire). In Heidegger's philosophy, boredom is, similarly, a zone of emptiness, a privileged fundamental state that leads directly into the problem of being and time (Svendsen 2005). Boredom then, moves us toward and protects us from what we wait and hope for—which may not necessarily be happiness as the desire for *exemption,* from the condition of being too foreign or Other to oneself; the desire to feel *normal.* Here immobility begs questions concerning how much pain, waiting, or hopelessness of a continual falling short can be tolerated before symptoms cannot reasonably be regarded as normal?

### The Immobile Heart

These various feeling states of immobility are shaped in relation to mobility and systematically, transiently, and symbolically present in the division and provision of power, space, and privilege in society. They implicate not *emotion* (an aspect of individual interiority connected to essentialized sociocultural, or psychological categories) but affect, as constitutive of politics, society, and economies that impinge on self and subjectivity. Correspondingly, ways immobility links ethnographically with the "affective turn," and to critiques of the dominance of Spinoza's critique of the subject-oriented philosophy of Descartes, particularly in relation to movement, language, and subjectivity. More precisely, to ways anthropologists have theorized affect as a central social, historical, and intersubjective medium of mutual constitution, which *moves* politics, economics and global flows of people, and the subjects of politics, economics, migration, and global transformations (Navaro-Yashin 2009).

On a related note, the emphasis on movement and immobility as inseparate, but intrinsic to one another is also exemplified in the paradox of the "primus movens": the primary "mover" of all motion in the universe who remains perfectly detached from what he moves. Aristotle (*Metaphysics,* Book 12) links the Unmoved Mover to the intellect, which he described as being perfectly beautiful, indivisible, and contemplating only perfect contemplation itself; the concept became widely drawn upon in theology, for example in the philosophy of St. Thomas Aquinas.

Briefly, for Descartes and Spinoza, emotions are profoundly entangled with matters such as ethics, politics, governance, God, and Nature. Spinoza (*Ethics* 1996), however, attacks Descartes's idea that the body is simply a vehicle for the mind, and passions are entirely passive perceptions of the active desires of the will and mind that exerts domination over them. In sum, the mind governs the body and passions. For Spinoza, mind and body are not separate entities but the *same* substance. Brown and Stenner argue the consequent link between being affected, and the capacity to affect, links to action and inaction in the ways that humans, things, and Nature *move,* or do not move, in response to the tenor of more or less agreeable— real and imagined—encounters with each other (2001, 97). While pleasant (euphoric) encounters increase the ability to move toward powerful, ethical forms of action, unpleasant (dysphoric) encounters have the inverse effect: thus, Spinoza establishes connections through which relations are established through affect to things, a critique of Cartesian dualism and the psychological individualism of much thinking about emotion (1996, 97).

Theorists of affect have variegatedly engaged Spinoza's critique of the fully rational, conscious subject as the unit of analysis in the subject-oriented philosophy of Descartes, enlivening several debates relevant to immobility. First is the privileging of discursivity, linguistics, and subjectivity in the social sciences associated with post-structuralism, deconstructionism, and social constructionism (Thrift 2008). Ahmed's (2004) cultural politics of emotion proposes affects circulate (separate from discourse and materiality), surfacing and sticking in historically, ideologically meaningful ways to bodies, signs, and objects to create social and national collectivities, and the material and discursive structures of the nation-state. Second, the synonymity drawn between affect, interiority, and subjectivity privileges the impact of psycho*dynamic* relations in core notion of the unconscious, and of the conflicted, stuck or split psyche on consciousness and subjective experience. Third, Deleuze and Guattari offer a rereading of Spinoza and its non- or postsubjective possibilities for theorizing affect. They propose affect as a free-floating sensation or space that is outside language, antipathetic to discourse, and dissociated with any structure, genealogical "root" or hierarchy, but nomadic and "rhizomatic" (2004, 5–9). Inimically ironic, Zizek notes, within the contemporary global order, the Deleuzian liberationist image of nomadic desubjectified flows presents quite a neat ideological fit with the deterritorializing fluxes intrinsic to global capitalism (2004, 185).

Deleuze's concept of "immobile intensities" (*A Thousand Plateaus*) addresses affect's less dysphoric relation to immobility. For Deleuze, the opposition of movement and rest create images of "immobile movement," akin to "spiritual voyages" effected without relative movement, but in intensity, in one place (2004, 381). Immobile intensities are not necessarily located in exterior space but, poised between other specific immobilities and mobilities, describe passing into states or emotions unavailable in travel—for example the "profound countries" of geo-music, or geo-philosophy (Deleuze 2004, 381). Harley (2013) examines ways airport structures impose specific patterns of movement, and transform travelers into immobile figures-in-waiting. He argues "immobile intensities" can inhabit a zone of supposed "emptiness," positively; the body registers differential elements of immobility as intensity, in order to feel them (Harley 2013, 38–40).

In its radical retreat from the power dimensions shaping subjectivity, and its incorporation of (im)mobility, Deleuze's "desubjectified subjectivity" is distinct from Foucault's "episteme," Gramsci's "hegemony," Bourdieu's "habitus," or Williams's "structures of feeling," and the attention given in these conscious and unconscious discourses, images, and modes of feeling and thinking to the (trans)formation of political subjects and cultures within hegemonic systems of power and difference. Williams suggests locating a structure of feeling can unstick alternate or suppressed narratives and rescue unrealized possibilities from dead ends in which they were stranded. Yet being inevitably articulated in language means—in his own critique—it still cannot really emerge other than as a mediation of hegemonic pressures and formalized perceptions.

A deeper examination of immobility's relation to mobility through a discussion of affect and language must await another discussion. Nonetheless, there are some interesting conceptualizations on what happens when experience or words become unhooked from their affective origins. Das's (2007) ethnography in Delhi neighborhoods with families who fled Partition, and with survivors of the 1984 Delhi riots, prioritizes a "descent into the ordinary." Inquiring into the frozen relation of violence and language, and how the memory of events become enfolded into the weave of everyday life, she uncovers ways violence is shown rather than narrated, sometimes in words, or gestures, or molded into silences. "Sometimes these were words imbued with a spectral quality. . . . I felt they were animated by some other voice. . . . What I find useful is the possibility that words might become untethered from their origin" (Das 2007, 8). "It is not that if asked people could not tell you a story, but simply that the words had a frozen slide quality to them, which showed their burned and numbed relation to life" (Das 2007, 11).

## Conclusion: Beyond Immobility?

> Everything changes and nothing remains still . . . and . . . you cannot step twice into the same stream. (Heraclitus, in Plato's *Cratylus,* 402a)

> We need immobility, and the more we succeed in imagining movement as coinciding with the immobilities of the points of space through which it passes, the better we think we understand it. To tell the truth, there never is real immobility, if we understand by that an absence of movement. Movement is reality itself." (Bergson 2002, 119)

As in Williams's *Keywords,* this conclusion will not, as is customary, elaborate further the above discussions. Rather, it returns to the question of "what lies between," or beyond (im)mobility? How we can rethink—in other words, bypass or surpass—bipolarized divisions between movement and stasis? How can we slow down enough, not just in relation to capitalism, but to give a *chance* to our encounters of feeling and thinking, to disentangle progress from mobilization and quietly destroy what are defined as obstacles to progress? (Zournazi and Stengers 2002, 252).

Bergson's epistemology of inseparable (im)mobility recalls Massumi's point that a focus on "relative immobility" may obscure a different or even increased intensity in transactions between mobilities. Massumi questions the possibilities for a transduced energy that repotentializes mobility elsewhere so that movement continues in immobility—in what he calls space, but not quite cardinal space (Massumi 2002, 178). These ideas reiterate immobility's coimbrication in mobility (this seems obvious), largely as a solution to the problem of dichotomy. It is not clear that immobility exists without real or imagined mobility, that is, that we are talking about immobility and not (im)mobility. For the moment, definitions are open, so to speak mobilized which, perhaps, is the point.

Anthropology offers key reflections on the possibilities of life (and life for anthropology) beyond the intensities of contrary or contrapuntal movement, *beyond* (im)mobility as different components on a continuum altogether. Drawing together this chapter's concerns, by way of conclusion I turn to Ingold's (2011) distinction between transport and wayfaring, theorized in respect of the ways movement is intrinsic to production, cultural knowledge, and to being alive. Ingold describes transport as the preconceived movement of a preconstituted entity from location A to B, a lateral, illusory, ultimately lifeless "movement toward terminal closure: a filling up of capacities and shutting down of possibilities" (2011, 3). By contrast, wayfaring captures being alive as an experience of continuous becoming, a fluid journey toward and beyond ends. Things are instantiated as their paths of movement, not objects located in space. The movement is all-important, not the destination. Wayfaring encapsulates the theoretical move from the problem and limits of perpetual time, to the opening-up of time passing. It works metaphorically to explain limitations in established Cartesian dualisms of mind and body, nature and society, dwelling and place, production, and its ends.

Briefly, in wayfaring the end is not a condition for production. Production is the intentionality that adheres in action itself, by which people do not impose designs upon the environment, but grow into the world as it grows in them (Ingold 2011, 6). Second, knowledge is not culturally transmitted, inherited, "passed down" to the organism, that is, "transported" through linking locations laterally or transitively. Rather, knowledge is alongly integrated; movement *is* knowing (Ingold 2011, 160). Third, dwelling is not the occupation of structures (buildings, culture, categories, etc.) already built. Rather, dwelling signifies the immersion of humans in all the real and imaginary currents of involved activity (without which designing, building or occupation could not occur; Ingold 2011, 10). Drawing on Deleuze and Guattari's (2004, 223) ideas of life being composed of lines of "flight," or "becoming," in which every being is the line or lines of its own movement, Ingold likens life to a river, which does not connect anything but flows without beginning or end (2011, 14). The metaphor of life as a river can help us to recapture the sense of being launched in the current of time, in intertwined ever-extending trajectories of becoming: "our task," Ingold writes, "is not to take stock of the world's contents but to *follow what is going on*, tracing the multiple trails of becoming, wherever they lead. To trace these paths is to bring anthropology back to life" (2011, 14).

Ingold compellingly draws together this chapter's emphasis on the ways immobility encompasses or relates to mobility, but is also surpassed by the existential intensities of the departures, arrivals, attachments, detachments, dead ends, impasses, and destinations that humans encounter and imagine, whether or not they are attained. His ideas are not the end though, or without criticism. Cochrane (2008) takes issue with Ingold's depictions of "transported travelers" existing between destination points as "nowhere at all" and rendered immobile with respect to experience; he points out that buildings do not remain static (as in "transport"), but are continually being altered and repaired by unseen/unsensed activities; and calls for fresh theoretical models to think through journeys and movement.

Wayfaring is nonetheless a useful starting point for discussions that might move us beyond Ingold's beyond. While Ingold is decisive in his incision, cutting through where theory has bifurcated, and lost the dream to classification, wayfaring as a kind of positive, antigenealogical mover beyond *all* referent seems over-optimistic. Less romantically, Navaro-Yashin (2009, 15) rejects Deleuze and Guattari's antigenealogical challenge to "modernity's vertical imagery." She insists on including history *and* politics in approach to affect as a limitless, creative, multiplicitous, horizontal mapping dynamic that can keep "all scopes of the imagination" on board.

It may be entirely accurate to claim that *every* form of movement has immobile repercussions that produce effects at different sites and in different manifestations. However, to frame all these incredibly distinct variations in metaphorical terms leads real differences in lived-experience to be effaced from Ingold's analysis. Theoretical sequelae are not necessarily reducible to ontological ones, or real feeling. Despite Ingold's precision with his readings of movement and affect, his endeavor remains constrained to the fixed theoretical positions of such analytics—where the conflation of theory with life reveals an analytical indifference or limitation with regard to life outside theory.

Ingold may be wholly correct in declaring that maps for life deaden new possibilities for living. Yet he misses opportunities for relating to the silent suffering of the disaffected, lives that *are* experienced as stuck, immobilized by their losses, or an inability to transcend their confines. What can wayfaring say about ways the distribution of immobility among social networks envisions and encourages possibilities of continuity? We might follow the question ethnographically and ask how immobility and its ramifications operate or terminate *in* particular moments of change. How exactly are we stopped? What story do we give those who appear without life? What sort of ethics, or politics of recognition position, the immobile as a form of death in life in the first place?

This chapter has shown how valuations of immobility may be positive, negative, and somewhere in-between. Anthropology's very endeavor is in thinking through theory ethnographically: through the question of what might happen in these immobile "spaces": what they enable or offer individuals in terms of the synthesizing of experiences of movement and inaction that are often held, or imagined to be held, in tension. The notion of freedom implicated in much writing on immobility so often seems to imply a model of reality, or ontological position, where movement (as freedom) or its opposite are seen as either foreground or background in different contexts. Perhaps we might think about holding both together and prioritize a reality condition over a liberationist reading, that would push us to choose between an either-or, or a positive-negative, valuation. This would be one way to allow two positions to be experienced at the same time, even if ambivalently, and that could contribute to alternative readings of the study of immobility *both* anthropologically and ethnographically. Rose's (1992) notion of the "broken middle" posits such an effort as an ethical endeavor. One way, then, to extend Ingold's invitation to continue beyond the journey's end, will be to work toward unearthing the social lines, dynamics, and networked connections that do produce real transformative forms of immobility for people in terms of belonging, a sense of self, global citizenship, and mental health.

**Nichola Khan** is a chartered psychologist and senior lecturer in the School of Applied Social Sciences at the University of Brighton. Her research and writing interests in social and psychological anthropology have developed around conflict, violence, transnational migration, and mental disorder—via a regional focus on Pakistan, Afghanistan, and Afghan diasporas.

## REFERENCES

American Psychiatric Association. 2013. *Diagnostic and Statistical Manual of Mental Disorders,* 5th ed. Arlington, VA: American Psychiatric Association.
Adey, Peter. 2010. *Aerial Life: Spaces, Mobilities, Affects.* Oxford: Wiley-Blackwell.
Ahmed, Sara. 2004. *The Cultural Politics of Emotion.* New York: Routledge.

Berger, John. 2007. *Hold Everything Dear.* London: Verso.

Bergson, Henri. 2002. *The Creative Mind: An Introduction to Metaphysics 1946.* New York: Citadel Press.

Berlant, Lauren. 2011. *Cruel Optimism.* Chicago: Chicago University Press.

Bissell, David, and Gillian Fuller. 2013. *Stillness in a Mobile World.* New York: Routledge.

Bloch, Ernst. 1986. *The Principle of Hope.* Cambridge, MA: MIT Press.

Bourdieu, Pierre. 1977. *Outline of a Theory of Practice.* Cambridge: Cambridge University Press.

Bourgois, Philippe, and Jeff Schonberg. 2009. *Righteous Dopefiend.* Berkeley: University of California Press.

Brown, Steven, and Paul Stenner. 2001. "Being Affected: Spinoza and the Psychology of Emotion." *International Journal of Group Tensions* 30(1): 81–105.

Büscher, Monika, and John Urry. 2009. "Mobile Methods and the Empirical." *European Journal of Social Theory* 12(1): 99–116.

Butler, Judith. 1997. *The Psychic Life of Power.* Stanford, CA: Stanford University Press.

Coburn, Noah. 2011. *Bazaar Politics. Pottery and Power in an Afghan Market Town.* Stanford, CA: Stanford University Press.

Cochrane, Andrew. 2008. "Meditation in a Line. Review of Lines: A Brief History by Tim Ingold, 2007." *Cambridge Archaeological Journal* 18(3): 423–25.

Crapanzano, Vincent. 1985. *Waiting: The Whites of South Africa.* New York: Random House.

Cresswell, Timothy. 2006. *On the Move: Mobility in the Modern Western World.* London: Routledge.

Dalakoglou, Dimitris, and Penelope Harvey. 2012. "Roads and Anthropology: Ethnographic Perspectives on Space, Time and (Im)mobility." *Mobilities* 7(4): 459–65.

Das, Veena. 2007. *Life and Words. Violence and the Descent into the Ordinary.* Berkeley: University of California Press.

Deleuze, Gilles, and Felix Guattari. 2004. *A Thousand Plateaus. Capitalism and Schizophrenia.* London: Continuum.

DelVecchio Good, Mary-Jo, Sarah Hyde, Sarah Pinto, and Byron Good, eds. 2008. *Postcolonial Disorders.* Berkeley: University of California Press.

Dwyer, Peter. 2009. "Worlds of Waiting." In *Waiting,* edited by Ghassan Hage, 15–26. Melbourne: University of Melbourne Press.

Fabian, Johannes. 1983. *Time and the Other: How Anthropology Makes Its Object.* New York: Colombia University Press.

Fassin, Didier, and Richard Rechtman. 2009. *The Empire of Trauma. An Inquiry into the Condition of Victimhood.* Princeton, NJ: Princeton University Press.

Freud, Sigmund. 2005. *On Murder, Mourning and Melancholia.* London: Penguin. First published 1917.

Greenblatt, Stephen. 2009. *Cultural Mobility: A Manifesto.* Cambridge: Cambridge University Press.

Gupta, Akhil. 2004. "Imagining Nations." In *A Companion to the Anthropology of Politics,* edited by David Nugent and Joan Vincent, 267–81. Malden, MA: Blackwell.

Hage, Ghassan, ed. 2009. *Waiting.* Melbourne: Melbourne University Press.

Hannam, Kevin, Mimi Sheller, and John Urry. 2006. "Mobilities, Immobilities, and Moorings." *Mobilities* 1(1): 1–22.

Hansen, Thomas Blom. 2012. *Melancholia of Freedom: Social Life in an Indian Township in South Africa.* Princeton, NJ: Princeton University Press.

Hardt, Michael, and Antonio Negri. 2004. *Multitude: War and Democracy in the Age of Empire.* New York: Penguin Press.

Harley, Ross. 2013. "Airportals: The Functional Significance of Stillness in the Junkspace of Airports." In *Stillness in a Mobile World,* edited by David Bissell and Gillian Fuller, 38–50. New York: Routledge.

Harvey, David. 2000. *Spaces of Hope.* Berkeley: University of California Press.

Heidegger, Martin. 1977. *The Question Concerning Technology, and Other Essays.* Translated by William Lovitt. New York: Harper and Row. First published 1962.

Ingold, Tim. 2011. *Being Alive. Essays on Movement, Knowledge and Description.* New York: Routledge.

Kaplan, Caren. 1996. *Questions of Travel: Postmodern Discourses of Displacement.* Durham, NC: Duke University Press.

Kahlbaum, Karl. 1973. *Catatonia.* Translated by Y Levis and T Pridon. Baltimore, MD: John Hopkins University Press. First published 1874.

Khan, Nichola. 2013. "A Moving Heart: Querying a Singular Problem of 'Immobility' in Afghan Migration to the UK." *Medical Anthropology: Cross-Cultural Studies in Health and Illness* 32(6): 518–34.

———. 2014a. "From Refugees to the World Stage: Sport, Civilisation and Modernity in Out of the Ashes and the UK Afghan Diaspora." In *Sport and South Asian Diasporas: Playing through Time and Space,* edited by Stanley Thangaraj, Daniel Burdsey, and Rajinder Dudrah, 271–85. New York: Routledge.

———. 2014b. "The Taste of Freedom: Commensality, Liminality and Return amongst Afghan Transnational Migrants in the UK and Pakistan." *Journal of the Royal Anthropological Institute* 20(3): 466–85.

Kraepelin, Emil. 1990. "Lehrbuch der Psychiatrie." In *Psychiatry: A Textbook for Students and Physicians,* edited by Jacques Quen, and translated by Helga Metoui, and Sabine Ayed. Canton: Science History Publications. First published 1895 by A. Abel.

Laidlaw, James. 2002. "For an Anthropology of Ethics and Freedom." *Journal of the Royal Anthropological Institute* 8(2): 311–332.

Laing, Ronald D. 1969. *Knots.* London: Penguin.

Lakha, Salim. 2009. "Waiting to Return Home: Modes of Immigrant Waiting." In *Waiting,* edited by Ghassan Hage, 121–35. Melbourne: University of Melbourne Press.

Latour, Bruno. 1993. *We Have Never Been Modern.* Cambridge, MA: Harvard University Press.

Malinowski, Bronisław. 2010. *Argonauts of the Western Pacific.* Oxford: Benediction Classics. First published 1922 by EP Dutton.

Marsden, Magnus. 2008. "Muslim Cosmopolitanisms? Transnational Life in Northern Pakistan." *The Journal of Asian Studies* 67(1): 213–47.

Martin, Emily. 2007. *Bipolar Expeditions.* Princeton, NJ: Princeton University Press.

Massumi, Brian. 2002. *Parables for the Virtual. Movement, Affect, Sensation.* Durham, NC: Duke University Press.

Mauss, Marcel. 1990. *The Gift: The Form and Reason for Exchange in Archaic Societies.* London: Routledge. First published 1925 by Librairie Félix Alcan.

Mitchell, Stephen A. 1993. *Hope and Dread in Psychoanalysis.* New York: Basic Books.

Moore, Henrietta. 2011. *Still Life: Hopes, Desires and Satisfactions.* Cambridge: Polity Press.

Mountz, Alison. 2010. *Seeking Asylum: Human Smuggling and Bureaucracy at the Border.* Minneapolis: University of Minnesota Press.

Navaro-Yashin, Yael. 2003. "Life Is Dead Here: Sensing the Political in 'No Man's Land.'" *Anthropological Theory* 3(1): 107–25.

———. 2009. "Affective Spaces, Melancholic Objects: Ruination and the Production of Anthropological Knowledge." *Journal of the Royal Anthropological Institute* 15(1): 1–19.

Nguyen, Mimi. 2012. *The Gift of Freedom. War, Debt and Other Refugee Passages.* Durham, NC: Duke University Press.

Phillips, Adam. 1993. *On Kissing, Tickling and Being Bored.* Cambridge, MA: Harvard University Press.

Potamianou, Anna. 1997. *Hope. A Shield in the Economy of Borderline States.* Oxon: Routledge.

Rose, Gillian. 1992. *The Broken Middle.* Oxford: Blackwell.

Salazar, Noel. 2012. "Imagining (Im)mobility at the 'End of the World.'" In *Technologies of Mobility in the Americas,* edited by Phillip Vannini, Paola Jiron, Ole Jensen, Lucy Budd, and Christian Fisker, 233–52. New York: Peter Lang.

Salazar, Noel. 2013. "Anthropology." In *The Routledge Handbook of Mobilities,* edited by Peter Adey, David Bissell, Kevin Hannam, Peter Merriman, and Mimi Sheller, 55–63. London: Routledge.

Salazar, Noel, and Alan Smart. 2011 "Anthropological Takes on (Im)mobility." *Identities: Global Studies in Culture and Power* 18(6): i–ix.

Spinoza, Benedict. 1996. *Ethics.* London: Penguin. First published 1677.

Svendsen, Lars. 2005. *Philosophy of Boredom.* Edinburgh: Reaktion Books.

Szakolczai, Arpad. 2009. "Liminality and Experience: Structuring Transitory Situations and Transformative Events." *International Political Anthropology* 2: 141–72.

Thompson, Peter, and Slavoj Zizek. 2013. *The Privatisation of Hope.* Durham, NC: Duke University Press.

Thrift, Nigel. 2008. *Non-Representational Theory: Space/Politics/Affect.* London: Routledge.

Turner, Bryan S. 2007. "The Enclave Society: Toward a Sociology of Immobility." *European Journal of Social Theory* 10(2): 287–303.

Turner, Victor. 2011. *The Ritual Process.* London: AldineTransaction. First published 1969.

Turner, Victor, ed. 1974. *Dramas, Fields, and Metaphors: Symbolic Action in Human Society.* Ithaca, NY: Cornell University Press.

Urry, John. 2007. *Mobilities.* Cambridge: Polity Press.

Zizek, Slavoj. 2004. *Organs Without Bodies: On Deleuze and Consequences.* New York: Routledge.

Zournazi, Mary, and Isabelle Stengers. 2002. "A 'Cosmo-Politics'—Risk, Hope, Change." In *Hope: New Philosophies for Change,* edited by Mary Zournazi, 244–73. Sydney: Pluto Press.

# CHAPTER 6

# Infrastructure

*Mari Korpela*

In the introduction to this volume, Salazar writes that mobility is often characterized as the ability or tendency to move. I argue that this ability and tendency to move depends, among other things, on infrastructural circumstances.[1] Moving is not simply a choice and the action of an individual: infrastructures provide the framework within which people can, or cannot, move.

Recently, infrastructures have become a popular research field among anthropologists (see e.g., Harvey 2012; Harvey and Knox 2012).[2] Rather than considering their technological characteristics, however, anthropologists focus on how people use, understand, view, and experience infrastructures and the effects they have on people's lives. There have been many studies on infrastructures of mobility in urban settings (see e.g., de Boeck 2012), and in the *Routledge Handbook of Mobilities* (2014), many examples in the section on infrastructures are from urban contexts too. It is, however, also important to look at infrastructures of mobility beyond such settings. The emphasis in this chapter is on transnational mobility, that is, on people crossing state borders. Surprisingly little attention has been paid to the infrastructures in this setting, in spite of the fact that people's transnational mobility has increased significantly in the past decades.

A key distinction in social theory is whether individuals have free agency or whether, or to what extent, structures determine what happens or can happen (see Bakewell 2010; O'Reilly 2012, 4). Social scientists often focus on social and institutional structures. Ironically, although infrastructures are often concrete and material, they tend to be treated as an invisible background. In this chapter, I argue that not only social structures but various material and institutional infrastructures are crucial when people are involved in transnational mobility.

I argue that infrastructures of transnational mobility need to be looked at from three different angles, because this brings out the processual nature of people's mobility. First, there is the moment of becoming mobile; second, there is the time of being mobile (including moments of immobility, e.g., waiting or queuing), and eventually there is the moment of stopping being mobile, that is, of becoming immobile again (in a new place).[3] I begin by briefly discussing the various definitions of the term. I then elaborate on significant infrastructures that affect people's actions, both before they become mobile and while they are on the move. I discuss informational and mediating infrastructures, along with the role of transportation, and this is followed by a section on the powerful infrastructure of passports and visas. I then argue that certain institutional infrastructures that facilitate the lives of immobile people may prevent mobile people from becoming (legally) immobile in particular locations, even if they wished to do so. I elaborate on how certain kinds of mobilities are not recognized by states and how people involved with them may end up outside, or at the margins, of particular infrastructures. At the end of the chapter, I examine whether there are infrastructures of transnational mobility that function beyond the control of the current system of nation-states and to what extent states are willing to outsource their infrastructural tasks. I also elaborate on whether people can be transnationally mobile without infrastructures. Throughout the chapter, I contend that on the one hand mobile subjects need infrastructures in order to realize their mobilities, but on the other hand, these infrastructures control and constrain people's mobilities. I also show that states are key actors that exercise power through a variety of infrastructures related to people's transnational mobility.

## Defining Infrastructures: Hard, Soft, and Critical

Infrastructures, in general, refer to the basic structures, facilities, and services that are needed for the (smooth) functioning of a country or organization (*Macmillan Dictionary*; *Oxford Advanced Learner's Dictionary*). They include transportation and communication systems, water and power systems, and public institutions such as schools and hospitals. Historically, infrastructures meant, first and foremost, roads and irrigation systems, but with the rise of modern transportation and communication systems, as well as new technologies, new infrastructures have been introduced. Infrastructures grow when locally constructed systems are linked, adapted, and standardized into coordinated networks (Jackson et al. 2007). At any given moment, most technology discourse is about new or rapidly changing technologies—currently cyberinfrastructures—and although societies also need the old technologies, these excite little interest except when they break or need expensive repairs (Edwards 2003).

Engineers and developers often distinguish between hard and soft infrastructures. By hard infrastructures, they mean large physical networks, with the soft ones being the institutions that are required to maintain the functioning of societies and organizations.[4] This distinction between hard and soft infrastructures derives, however, from a technological perspective and is not always useful in the social sciences. In my view, a better term might sometimes be that of critical infrastructures: particular infrastructures that are institutional, and thus "soft," are nonetheless crucial for a certain action. I later illustrate how the contemporary passport system is one such critical infrastructure of transnational mobility.

Infrastructures are usually understood as enabling and sustaining certain functions. Not all mobility-related infrastructures, however, facilitate movements; some, in fact, do the opposite, with a strong aspect of control and prevention exercised, above all, by states. In fact, people are in very different and unequal positions with regard to infrastructures of mobility. Glick Schiller and Salazar (2013, 189) argue that "there are several different intersecting regimes of mobility that normalize the movement of some travelers while criminalizing and entrapping the ventures of others." Infrastructures are an important part of such unequalizing regimes, and it is important to disentangle who sets up and controls the infrastructures and why. Not everyone can benefit from the same infrastructures. Some people's mobility is prevented by certain infrastructures, while others are welcomed and even encouraged to move within the same structures, and some people are in a position to bypass certain ill-functioning infrastructures while others are not. An excellent example of how some people are able to negotiate overburdened transportation infrastructures is the use of helicopters to avoid traffic jams in Sao Paolo (Cwerner 2006) and Istanbul (Yazici 2013). The majority of these cities' inhabitants cannot afford helicopter rides and must put up with the overcrowded traffic system, while some of them might not be able to afford any mode of transportation at all.

Anthropologists have pointed out that, contrary to the common understanding, infrastructures are often anything but invisible. Infrastructures are connected with modernity (Edwards 2003, 185), and many infrastructural projects are in fact copies of others, as they aim to participate in the modernization process (Larkin 2013). When infrastructures are understood as representing modernity and progress, it is important to make them visible and known. Sometimes, however, these infrastructural signs of modernity are not very useful in practice. Dalakoglou (2010) describes how an extensive road network was built in Albania in the Socialist era, even though there were very few cars on the roads. Similarly, Khan (2006) describes how the modernity of a multilane motorway in Pakistan outstrips the modernity of the country in general.

In addition to their sometimes being signs of modernity, infrastructures can also be used by states to produce modern subjects. Von Schnitzler (2013) illustrates how the use of prepaid water and electricity meters is not only a question of regulating water or electricity use but of the government aiming to produce responsible, self-monitoring, and calculating citizens. In other words, being modern is often related to the use of infrastructures (Edwards 2003). However, later in this chapter, I argue that infrastructures related to people's transnational mobility seem to accord some people the position of an immobile (nonmodern) subject.

## Becoming Mobile: Access to Information, Arrangements, and Mediators

In order to become transnationally mobile, one needs information, including information on the various infrastructures that can enable or prevent one's mobility. Information can be acquired in oral or written form—the latter either in print or online. Access to such information is, however, not equal, and access in itself does not guarantee that the information is correct. Moreover, not everyone is able to read, and even if they can, the information may not be available in their language/s. People may also choose to ignore certain information, or do not have the option to decide otherwise. For example, the European Union runs information campaigns in Africa to discourage undocumented migration, but it remains to be seen how successful such campaigns really are (Feldman 2012). It seems that many people become undocumented migrants even when they know about the risks.

The distribution of information is, to a great extent, an infrastructural issue. It is not managed by states, but states may play a role in trying to prevent their citizens from gaining access to particular information. China (Liang and Lu 2010) and Turkey (see e.g., Tattersall 2014) are current examples of this, in how they limit their citizens' access to the Internet. In addition to the Internet, telephone systems play a central role as mediators of information, and mobile phones in particular have become significant in this respect. However, in addition to enabling communication, mobile phones enable new kinds of control measures, and consequently, many undocumented migrants do not carry phones or even phone numbers with them in order to avoid being identified via their phone contacts (Sørensen and Gammeltoft-Hansen 2013).

Becoming transnationally mobile is obviously not only a matter of gaining the necessary information. When preparing to become transnationally mobile, people utilize various institutional and commercial infrastructures, without which mobility would be difficult. If one is a tourist, one may request services from travel agents and tour operators. Thomas Cook Tours were the first to offer these services in the nineteenth century (Urry 1990), and since then, tourism has become a multibillion dollar business with a multilayered infrastructure. If one is a career expatriate, one's employer usually assists with the practical arrangements of mobility. Career expatriates and tourists thus move within existing soft infrastructures that facilitate their mobility. Student exchange programs (Murphy-Lejeune 2002), au pair programs (Burikova and Miller 2010), and volunteer aid programs (Lyons and Wearing 2008) provide vast infrastructures to facilitate international mobility for their specific purposes. Similarly, refugees depend on various intermediaries and then eventually on refugee organizations that try to administer and organize their mobilities (see Bariagaber 1999). People may, of course, also use these institutional infrastructures in ways that were not intended by the administrators. For example, the au pair system is used by some Filipino women as a way of migrating to Europe: au pairs are allowed to stay in a country for only one year, but many women work in Europe for several years, changing their country of residence every twelve months. Thus, a program that was intended as a learning and cultural exchange is actually used as a migration channel and as an employment arrangement without worker protection (Asis and Battistella 2014, 274).

Labor migrations are a form of transnational mobility that involves a number of infrastructures. Xiang and Lindquist have written about "migration infrastructures," defining them as "the systematically interlinked technologies, institutions, and actors that facilitate and control mobility." They include five dimensions: "the commercial (recruitment intermediaries), the regulatory (state apparatus and procedures for documentation, licensing, training and other purposes), the technological (communication and transport), the humanitarian (NGOs and international organizations), and the social (migrant networks)" (Xiang and Lindquist 2014, 124). In other words, Xiang and Lindquist argue that migrants do not move on their own but are actually moved by others and that the migration infrastructures are in fact much more stable and durable than any particular migratory flows. On one hand, the migration infrastructures enable and facilitate people's transnational mobilities, but on the other hand, they constrain them. Above all, migration infrastructures make migration much more expensive than it would be otherwise (Xiang and Lindquist 2014, 131–33). Migration infrastructures have, in fact, become critical in many places: it is often very difficult, or even impossible, to become a labor migrant without them, as states may not grant a visa to a labor migrant unless he or she has completed certain actions, which cannot be performed without the services of intermediary agencies. Such agencies thus serve the interests of migrant-receiving states, as they take care of recruitment, preemployment checks and preparations. This suits the states and employers well because the costs are transferred to the migrants themselves.

Even undocumented mobility has its own, often illegal and thus invisible, infrastructures (Lindquist 2010; Triandafyllidou and Maroukis 2012). These infrastructures typically work beyond or regardless of states, but nevertheless must take into account the existing state-defined institutional infrastructures; they try to circumvent them, but they cannot ignore them. In addition to the illegal infrastructures, in many places the nongovernmental charity sector plays a crucial role in providing services for undocumented migrants. For example, Vogt (2012, 74) describes how undocumented Central American migrants in transit in southern Mexico utilize *migrant houses,* which have been established along the way by various religious organizations and NGOs to acquire food, shelter, transportation, safety, medical attention, and legal advice.

Migration and other forms of human mobility are thus intensively mediated, which means that people's individual agency is guided and controlled by infrastructures. In addition, infrastructures create particular subject positions of mobile and immobile people. In her study on undocumented Chinese migrants, Chu (2010) describes how her informant has had her bag ready for years, waiting for the human smuggler to call; a call that never comes. A migration infrastructure—including boat smuggling and counterfeit travel documents—thus places her in a very particular subject position: she is not concretely mobile, but she is in the mentality of mobility as she is constantly waiting for the call that would tell her to start the journey.

## Being Mobile: Transportation and (Im)mobile Subject Positions

In addition to mediating infrastructures, material ones are also crucial when people move across borders. Without the various transportation infrastructures, mobility would be extremely difficult, if not impossible. At the same time, the transportation infrastructures define to a great extent where it is possible to go, and when (Edwards 2003, 191), and one experiences mobility differently depending on which infrastructures one uses. Air travel experiences can be very different depending on the particular aviation infrastructure used, and one's experiences on a fancy cruise ship are very different from those on a cargo ship or a sailing boat. Car travel is often described as an insular movement, whereby people move within the bubble or cocoon of the vehicle (Urry 2004), whereas those traveling on foot (Ingold

2010) or by bicycle (Jungnickel and Aldred 2014) are exposed to myriad sensory experiences: they see, smell, hear, and feel the environments. Laviolette has described how hitchhikers are able to "physically and emotionally engage with places which many people only glimpse at" (Laviolette 2014, 16). Undocumented migrants may also squeeze into boats that are not meant for long-distance sea travel or hide in containers or vehicles meant for transporting goods. Yet, all the abovementioned means of mobility utilize infrastructures, some of which are mobile themselves—airplanes, for example—whereas others—including airports—are much less so,[5] although Schabacher (2013) has argued that infrastructure systems themselves are in fact mobile, since they are developed and maintained.

Access to transportation infrastructures is, however, not equal, and the quality of such infrastructures varies significantly across locations. There may also be seasonal variations, with a particular road being inaccessible in the rainy season or, as in the archipelago of Finland, roads made on ice not existing in the summer. Growing populations can also pose severe challenges to transportation infrastructures. For example, in India one must make train reservations several weeks in advance in order to secure a seat. Moreover, even if a particular infrastructure exists, not everyone necessarily has access to it. First of all, people may not have the financial means to use such systems, or if they manage to pay the fare they may end up in serious debt, as is often the case with the Thai wild berry-pickers who are brought to Finland as short-term labor. The idea is that they will be able to pay for their flight tickets and other travel costs with what they earn berry-picking, but sometimes the income from their hard work in the Finnish forests is not enough to cover these costs (Korpela et al. 2014, 104). Second, women and certain stigmatized groups may have restricted, or even denied, access to particular mobility infrastructures. An extreme example of this is in Saudi Arabia, where women are required to obtain permission from their male guardians if they want to travel abroad (Human Rights Watch 2012). Winner (1986) provides an illustrative anecdote about how those in power may purposefully direct infrastructural projects so that particular people are denied mobility to certain places: a city planner made a behind-the-scenes policy decision to make the automobile bridges in a particular area of New York too low for buses to pass underneath. Consequently, poor people were effectively barred from the area. In other words, an infrastructure played a central role in the process of creating mobile and immobile subject positions, with certain individuals' agency restricted. According to Edwards (2003, 186) "to be modern is to live within and by means of infrastructures." This raises the question of whether certain people are denied modernity when they are not allowed to use particular infrastructures, including many of those related to transnational mobility.

People's agency with regard to transnational mobility thus depends, to a large extent, on their access to particular infrastructures. Infrastructures related to transnational mobility, however, do not affect only those who move. They may be important also for people who are not mobile themselves, either because they do not want to be or because they cannot move. Abranches (2013) investigates migrants sending and receiving objects at Lisbon and Guinea-Bissau airports. She shows how people who do not travel anywhere themselves are still very much involved with mobility (of people, and of goods that people carry for them) and how this activity takes place at airports. This is also an example of how individuals try to circumvent state policies, in this case customs regulations. It is, however, also important to note that being privileged and having access to particular infrastructures of mobility does not necessarily mean that one is willing to move; it may be that those without money have to move whereas the better-off can afford to stay where they are.

## Being Mobile: The National Order of Things— Passports and Visas

In the contemporary world, people, mobile or not, act within the existing national order of things (Malkki 1995), which means that the world is divided into nation-states, and in principle, each person belongs to one such entity (or in some cases to two or three).[6] If one wants to be transnationally mobile, this mobility necessarily takes place within the system of nation-states. In spite of the increasing global mobility, people (or goods for that matter) are not free to move. Rather, their movements are controlled by various actors—states in particular—and this control culminates in the passport and visa system.[7] This system is an institutional infrastructure that every transnationally mobile person must deal with, in one way or another, either conforming to the rules and obtaining the necessary documents or finding ways to bypass the system altogether. Passports and visas are important parts of the institutional infrastructure that administers and controls people's cross-border movement. Some people try to maximize their benefits within the system by acquiring and utilizing several passports (Ong 1999), some of which are more useful than others to gain entry to particular countries. Nevertheless, a mobile person (or one wishing to become mobile) cannot ignore the existence of this infrastructure. There are ways to bypass the need for a national passport, for example, the United Nations issues a laissez-passer travel document to staff members of certain international organizations, but such documents are supplied to a very limited number of people, and their existence reinforces the rule that particular documents are needed in order to operate within the system.

Although the current passport system is a rather recent phenomenon—standardized passports were introduced at the beginning of the twentieth century—it has deep historical roots in Europe (O'Byrne 2001, 400). Starting in the sixteenth century, authorities issued travelers with "passport letters" to grant them safe passage during times of war.[8] Such single-purpose letters have since been transformed into more permanent (although still fixed-term) documents (Jansen 2009, 824), and once they became available to (almost) anyone, they also became "a requirement for legitimate movement across territorial spaces" (Torpey 1998, 242). This happened in spite of the fact that after World War I, many League of Nations delegates wanted to abandon the passport regime during peacetime (Salter 2006, 78).

When a person wishes to cross international borders, his or her movement is under state surveillance because states want to prevent mobilities of those noncitizens they have defined as unwanted. Passports enable states to identify a person and then to "distinguish members of particular nation-states from non-members" (Torpey 1998, 246–49). Nowadays, without a passport one does not have the right to cross international borders except in cases where a group of states (e.g., the Nordic countries,[9] the Schengen area,[10] or the Central America-4[11]) have formed pacts dispensing with the need for passports. Yet, even in these cases, people are requested to carry some proof of identity. In some areas, pastoral nomads cross state borders without passports because the borders arbitrarily cut through lands they traditionally use, but this type of nomadic mobility is relatively local; these people cannot get very far without passports. In other words, in most cases, a passport is needed as a proof of identification. It is not, however, always sufficient: very often a visa is required as the document that authorizes entry to a particular nation-state (Torpey 1998, 253). Moreover, one's place of birth may be an issue when crossing borders in cases where one holds a passport of a particular nation where one was not born but attained citizenship later (Cho 2013).

State monopolization of the legitimate means of movement has, in fact, led to people speaking of illegal migration when they actually mean undocumented transborder mobility (Torpey 1998, 243). Jansen has pointed out that nowadays certain passports do not secure any entry or passage at all and can instead prevent cross-border movement (Jansen 2009, 821). Therefore, although it has a facilitating function, the passport infrastructure works, perhaps above all, as a prevention mechanism. In his ethnographic study of the European Union's migration management apparatus among policy makers and administrators, Feldman argues that, with the rise of the registered traveler programs, access to the European Union is increasingly becoming a matter of income and education rather than of nationality (Feldman 2012, 116). Nevertheless, the passport is still the document that enables the administrators to distinguish those who are welcome and those who are not. Nowadays, measures taken by states to identify individuals have become increasingly powerful, with technological identification methods based on biopower (Maguire 2010, 2012). Feldman notes that the system works by considering everyone as suspect until the database declares them innocent (Feldman 2012, 118). Bigo (2010) has pointed out that, increasingly, the checking happens before one reaches the border; unwanted and desired travelers are separated out and categorized by checks against databases. Sadiq (2012) calls this the "global documentary regime," highlighting that the system requires a strong state (to maintain the databases), and that such a state does not exist in many developing nations. All in all, it seems that passports and visas or, more recently, databases based on biopower, have become critical infrastructures of people's transnational mobility, with states as key actors in defining the rules and maintaining the infrastructures necessary to implement them.

From a technological point of view, a significant characteristic of a well-functioning technical infrastructure is often stated to be its invisibility. The infrastructure of passports and visas is, however, very tangible to most people who wish to cross borders. At the same time, this critical infrastructure is not necessary in actual terms: one cannot light a bulb without electricity, but one could, de facto, move without a passport if this was institutionally allowed. The significance of documents is, thus, their controlling nature (Hull 2012), and very often, it is the state that creates such mechanisms of control. Documents, including passports, also make people visible (Sadiq 2012), but some people cannot acquire such documents at all because of their invisible status. When belonging to the globalized world comes to be defined by one's ability to move in the global arena, certain documents and certain content in databases become critical for individuals: if the databases contain the wrong kind of information or no information at all of a particular individual, he or she is defined as suspicious and high risk (Feldman 2012, 121). Not being able to get a passport, or being able to get one that does not guarantee entry to many countries, accords one a subject position that is not that of a global modern citizen. For example, Finnish embassies do not issue visas to citizens of particular countries for the stated purpose of sitting Finnish university entrance exams due to fears of visa misuse (Korpela et al. 2014, 96). Passport and visa systems thus form a critical infrastructure that effectively restricts individuals' agency in terms of transnational mobility, and information about current passport and visa policies may indeed dissuade people from trying to become transnationally mobile at all, which is obviously one of the goals of such policies.

## After Mobility: Rights to Immobility
## When There Is No Wish or Possibility to Return

Mobility and immobility cannot always be analytically separated (Salazar and Smart 2011), even with regard to infrastructures. Constant mobility is not very common. There are very few people who choose a nomadic life-style (Kannisto 2014), and circular migration is often a temporary necessity dictated by circumstances (Morokvasic 2004). Even highly mobile people may want to settle down when they are older or when their life situation changes.

Having once chosen (or been forced into) transnational mobility may, however, make it difficult to choose immobility at a later stage, at least if one wants to settle down somewhere other than where one originally came from. This can also be seen as an infrastructural issue. Very often, policies that enable, facilitate, and control transnational mobility assume that the mobile person returns to his or her place of origin after a certain period. Tourists return relatively quickly when their vacations are over, students return when their courses finish,[12] refugees are expected to return when the situation in their country of origin improves, and labor migrants are expected to return once they have earned enough money, or their work contract ends. The expectation of return becomes manifest in the various institutional infrastructures that states use to prevent nonnationals from settling down permanently within their borders. In practice, of course, not everyone who has moved to another country is able or willing to return.

Certain institutional infrastructures may, thus, prevent a person from staying in a particular place. Becoming legally immobile requires some sort of integration into the institutional structures of the destination. But even if one is allowed to enter a country, this does not necessarily mean that one is integrated into its official structures. Tourists and other short-term visitors do not need this kind of integration since they are (expected to be) integrated into their societies of origin, to which they return. In contrast, those staying abroad for longer periods may need certain structures that facilitate their state of immobility—even if this is not necessarily eternal. Many (previously) mobile people are, however, excluded from the infrastructures of immobility in their destinations, which can lead to challenging situations.

Millions of undocumented migrants sojourn in their destination countries without legal permission, thus living in an unrecognized liminal situation, in which they may not have access to health care, work (or at least legal protection at work), education, housing, and so on. In a way, they live outside of societal structures, including several institutional infrastructures, in a liminal stage, with both their mobility and immobility strongly constrained.

Living outside of certain institutional infrastructures applies not only to undocumented migrants who are forced to live as outsiders; for some people this situation is, at least to some extent, a choice. Many lifestyle migrants[13] are not officially registered as residents in their destinations even though they may have lived there for years, sometimes through their own choice (e.g., because of fiscal reasons), but sometimes because they do not know how to proceed with the registration (O'Reilly 2007) or because such an option is not available to them; for example in India, lifestyle migrants are considered tourists, and consequently, registering as residents is not possible (Korpela 2013). When one is not an official resident, one does not have certain rights and recognition, and one becomes marginalized in relation to many institutional infrastructures. For example, many lifestyle migrants in Goa, India, have lived there for several years—even decades—but because of their official status as tourists, they run their businesses in the informal sector and are very vulnerable in case of disputes. They have no say in local affairs, and their children are not allowed to attend local state schools. People navigate the institutional infrastructures of mobility and immobility as best they can. Many lifestyle migrants keep renewing their tourist visas regularly (Karkabi 2013; Korpela 2013). This practice is obviously not what the visa authorities expect people to do, but the visa renewals are a tactic with which to navigate an infrastructure that does not allow certain people to become officially immobile within particular nation-states. Undocumented migrants are, however, not in a position to navigate such systems to their own benefit. For them, certain institutional infrastructures are mechanisms that prevent their agency and force them into a liminal and invisible status, or lead to expulsion. In other words, particular institutional infrastructures become critical for them, and again, states are the key actors in defining the rules.

## Visible and Invisible Mobilities and the Significance of States

In this chapter, I have shown that states are crucial actors with regard to many infrastructures related to enabling and controlling people's transnational mobility. Administrators and states want clearly defined categories of movement because only then can they effectively administer and control people on the move. Consequently, states recognize some cross-border mobilities as desired and encouraged, while others are defined as unwanted and even illegal. Between these two poles, there are forms of mobility that, although not clearly recognized and categorized, are not illegal. Lifestyle migration, and the lifestyles of the Roma people (Okely 1998; Spreizer 2013) and New Age Travelers (Hetherington 2000; Martin 2002) are forms of mobility that easily cause people to fall outside of recognized categories and consequently outside, or at least on the edge, of existing infrastructures. At times, this may suit individuals, but it may become troublesome in certain situations (Korpela 2013). People may initially be happy to escape state control, emphasizing their individual agency, but they may later need state-run infrastructures, for example education or health care systems. It seems that in order to get (infra)structural support for one's mobility, the mobility should take place within the recognized and accepted categories. When this is not the case, people strongly experience the power exercised through infrastructures, a power that is often wielded by states.

Yet, although they are undoubtedly central actors, states do not control all mobility infrastructures. There are also infrastructures that function beyond, or in spite of, states. Human trafficking and the smuggling of undocumented migrants are obvious examples of transnational phenomena that utilize infrastructures that function outside of the existing state structures. It seems to me, however, that there is always a reason for a transnationally mobile person wanting to move outside of existing infrastructures, and such a person still needs to take these infrastructures into account in order to avoid them. In practice, this refers above all to the critical infrastructures that aim to prevent particular mobilities. In general, such people utilize alternative (often illegal) infrastructures instead of moving outside of any infrastructures. An interesting question is indeed whether there can be mobility outside of all infrastructures. Mobile people may use legal or illegal infrastructures, but can they move outside of infrastructures completely? This leads to the question of whether there can be transnationally mobile agency without infrastructures. It seems to me that although infrastructures often restrict individual agency in terms of transnational mobility, transnational agency without infrastructures is difficult, or even impossible.

In general, states have traditionally played a crucial role in the creation and maintenance of a large number of infrastructures. Their role is, however, changing. Substantial financial capital is required to build new, or maintain old, infrastructures, and states do not necessarily have such funds—for example, the railway networks in many parts of the world are rapidly deteriorating due to a lack of funds. States can borrow money for their infrastructural projects, but Dalakoglou points out that when an infrastructural project, such as the Albanian motorway that he has analyzed, is built with international aid money and loans, the result is a long-term dependency by the state on its creditors, which eventually may serve the interests of the sponsors more than those of the local society (Dalakoglou 2010, 139–40). Loans are, however, not the only option. A large number of state-owned infrastructures have recently been privatized in many countries—a fundamental change, the consequences of which are yet to be seen (see e.g., Mains 2012). John Urry (2014) has pointed out that offshoring is a current phenomenon that challenges the role of states in fundamental ways. It concerns, above all, financial flows, but hard infrastructures such as energy networks and waste management increasingly function beyond the control of states too. Urry also discusses in detail how the sea literally functions as a space of offshoring, that is, states have very limited control over what happens on seas. Also, Chaflin's (2006, 2008) research of contemporary customs systems discusses the issue of diminishing state sovereignty in detail. So far, states have kept a firm hold of the power to control people's transnational mobility, although there are variations between states regarding the extent to which they are able to do this. Yet, many states have outsourced certain tasks, as in the example of migration infrastructure outlined earlier in this chapter. Another example is that, a few years ago, the Indian embassy in Finland outsourced its visa application processes to a private German company. The outsourcing did not last long, but it illustrates that states are also willing to outsource functions that are related to people's transnational mobility.

In this chapter, I have illustrated how certain infrastructures related to people's transnational mobility appear to be critical to many mobile individuals. Many of them have also been critical for the sovereignty of states, but recently, due to outsourcing, states are not necessarily the implementing actors anymore. This, in turn, leads to concerns about whose interests are served, especially in the long run. I would argue, however, that in terms of people's transnational mobility, states are still crucial actors, and therefore, instead of diminishing state sovereignty, these processes represent a reordering of sovereignty.

## Why Infrastructures of Mobility?

Infrastructure is a keyword of mobility because infrastructures play a fundamental role in enabling and controlling people's mobilities. When looking at people's transnational mobility, the infrastructures—the invisible background—often appear as critical and consequently as the opposite of Augé's (1995) non-places, even though they may initially appear as such. In this chapter, I have argued that different kinds of transnational mobility, whether forced or voluntary, short-term or long-term, are formed and regulated differently but always exist within current infrastructures. People's transnational agency is to a large extent dependent on infrastructures, but at the same time, also constrained and even prevented by them. People's agency, or lack of it, with regard to transnational mobility thus takes place within certain infrastructural circumstances, and particular options are available to certain people while others are not. Infrastructures create particular subject positions of mobile and immobile individuals, and thus have much more significance than that of merely technically enabling people's transnational mobility. Moreover, it is not always possible or useful to distinguish between infrastructures of mobility and immobility, as both can be significant for mobile, and immobile, people.

States are central actors with regard to infrastructures related to people's transnational mobility even though the outsourcing and offshoring of a variety of infrastructural functions raises fundamental questions about the reordering of state sovereignty. In fact, in the current times of outsourcing and offshoring, it is crucial to pay attention to the role of states with regard to infrastructures related to people's transnational mobility. States are not necessarily always the implementing actors, but they do hold a great deal of power to enable, control, and prevent people's transnational mobility. Some mobilities occur beyond their control, but even these must take into account state-defined rules and the (institutional) infrastructures that control people's mobilities. In this chapter, I have shown that various infrastructures enable, control, and prevent people's transnational mobility; some of them are useful, some are necessary, and others are critical, but without them, people's transnational mobility would be very difficult, and often, even impossible.

**Mari Korpela** is a senior researcher in the School of Education at the University of Tampere, Finland. She is an anthropologist who has conducted extensive ethnographic research on lifestyle migrants in India. In addition, she has worked on a large multidisciplinary and multinational project investigating temporary migration between Asia and the European Union. She has published several articles on lifestyle migration and on transnational lifestyles.

## NOTES

1. The writing of this chapter was partly funded by the Academy of Finland (Grant 2501138405) and the School of Education, University of Tampere.
2. In 2014, the annual meeting of the American Anthropological Association and the European Association of Social Anthropologists' biannual conference both hosted a number of panels on the fashionable theme of infrastructures.

3. For the purposes of this chapter, it is useful to understand mobility as a three-stage process—immobility, mobility, and reintegration into immobility—rather than merely as a distinction between mobility and immobility. The difference lies on the third stage, as I investigate the situation in which people, rather than returning to the original place, want to settle down (that is to become immobile) in a new place.

4. With regard to mobility, hard infrastructures include, for example, ports, airports, roads, bridges, and railway and aviation networks, and soft infrastructures include, for example, financial systems, the travel industry, and passport and visa systems.

5. Cidell (2013) argues that Chicago's airport has moved, first because of a change of location, and second because of its expansion.

6. The problems that stateless people face reinforce the norm of each person being defined as belonging to a nation-state.

7. Sometimes, citizens are not free to move within state borders either. For example, China has the *hukou* system, which controls people's mobility within the country (Nyiri 2010).

8. In the medieval Islamic Caliphate, a receipt of taxes paid enabled one to travel to other regions in the Caliphate.

9. Sweden, Norway, Denmark, and Finland established a pact in 1957, and Iceland joined in 1965.

10. The Schengen Area comprises 26 European countries that have abolished passport and other type of border control at their common borders.

11. El Salvador, Guatemala, Nicaragua, and Honduras established a border control agreement in 2006, allowing their citizens free movement across borders between the four signatory states.

12. Some countries, for example Finland, try to attract international degree students in the hope that they will stay on to work after graduation, thus increasing the size of the young skilled labor force in a country with an aging population (Korpela et al. 2014, 92).

13. Lifestyle migrants are people of affluent industrialized nations who move abroad in search of a better quality of life, often in places where living costs are low and the climate pleasantly warm.

## REFERENCES

Abranches, Maria. 2013. "When People Stay and Things Make Their Way: Airports, Mobilities and Materialities of a Transnational Landscape." *Mobilities* 8(4): 508–27.

Asis, Maruja MB, and Graziano Battistella. 2014. "Flows and Patterns of Temporary Transnational Migration: The Philippine Case." In *Characteristics of Temporary Transnational Migration. Collected Working Papers from the EURA-NET project,* edited by Pirkko Pitkänen and Mari Korpela, 267–96. Available at http://www.uta.fi/edu/en/rese arch/projects/eura-net/publications/Characteristics%20of%20Temporary%20Tran snational%20Migration_EURA-NET.pdf

Augé, Marc. 1995. *Non-place: Introduction to an Anthropology of Supermodernity*. London: Verso.

Bakewell, Oliver. 2010. "Some Reflections on Structure and Agency in Migration Theory." *Journal of Ethnic and Migration Studies* 36(10): 1689–1708.

Bariagaber, Assefaw. 1999. "States, International Organisations and the Refugee. Reflections on the Complexity of Managing the Refugee Crisis in the Horn of Africa." *The Journal of Modern African Studies* 37(4): 597–619.

Bigo, Didier. 2010. "Freedom and Speed in Enlarged Borderzones." In *The Contested Politics of Mobility. Borderzones and Irregularity*, edited by Vicki Squire, 31–50. Abingdon: Routledge.

Burikova Zuzana, and Daniel Miller. 2010. *Au Pair*. Cambridge: Polity Press.

Chaflin, Brenda. 2006. "Enlarging the Anthropology of the State: Global Customs Regimes and the Traffic in Sovereignty." *Current Anthropology* 47(2): 243–76.

———. 2008. "Sovereigns and Citizens in Close Encounter: Airport Anthropology and Customs Regimes in Neoliberal Ghana." *American Ethnologist* 35(4): 519–38.

Cho, Lily. 2013. "Passports." In *The Routledge Handbook of Mobilities*, edited by Peter Adey, David Bissell, Kevin Hannam, Peter Merriman, and Mimi Sheller, 335–43. Abingdon: Routledge.

Chu, Julie Y. 2010. *Cosmologies of Credit: Transnational Mobility and the Politics of Destination in China*. Durham, NC: Duke University Press.

Cidell, Julie. 2013. "When Runways Move but People Don't: The O'Hare Modernization Program and the Relative Immobilities of Air Travel." *Mobilities* 8(4): 528–41.

Cwerner, Saulo B. 2006. "Vertical Flight and Urban Mobilities: The Promise and Reality of Helicopter Travel." *Mobilities* 1(2): 191–215.

Dalakoglou, Dimitris. 2010. "The Road: An Ethnography of the Albanian-Greek Cross-Border Motorway." *American Ethnologist* 37(1): 132–49.

de Boeck, Filip. 2012. "Infrastructure: Commentary from Filip de Boeck. Contributions from Urban Africa Towards an Anthropology of Infrastructure." *Cultural Anthropology*, Curated collections.

Edwards, Paul N. 2003. "Infrastructure and Modernity: Force, Time and Social Organization in the History of Sociotechnical Systems." In *Modernity and Technology*, edited by Thomas J Misa, Philip Brey, and Andrew Feenberg, 185–225. Cambridge, MA: MIT Press.

Feldman, Gregory. 2012. *The Migration Apparatus Security, Labor, and Policymaking in the European Union*. Palo Alto, CA: Stanford University Press.

Glick Schiller, Nina, and Noel B Salazar. 2013. "Regimes of Mobility across the Globe." *Journal of Ethnic and Migration Studies* 39(2): 183–200.

Harvey, Penny. 2012. "The Topological Quality of Infrastructural Relation: An Ethnographic Approach." *Theory, Culture & Society* 29(4–5): 76–92.

Harvey, Penny, and Hannah Knox. 2012. "The Enchantments of Infrastructure." *Mobilities* 7(4): 521–36.

Hetherington, Kevin. 2000. *New Age Travellers. Vanloads of Uproarious Humanity*. London: Cassell.

Hull, Mathew S. 2012. "Documents and Bureaucracy." *The Annual Review of Anthropology* 41: 251–67.

Human Rights Watch. 2012. *World Report 2012: Saudi Arabia.* Available at http://www .hrw.org/world-report-2012/world-report-2012-saudi-arabia

Ingold, Tim. 2010. "Footprints through the Weather-World: Walking, Breathing, Knowing." *Journal of the Royal Anthropological Institute* 16: 121–39.

Jackson, Steven, Paul Edwards, Geoffrey Bowker, and Cory Knobel. 2007. "Understanding Infrastructure: History, Heuristics, and Cyberinfrastructure Policy." *First Monday* 12(6), http://firstmonday.org/ojs/index.php/fm/%20article/view/1904/1786.

Jansen, Stef. 2009. "After the Red Passport: Towards an Anthropology of the Everyday Geopolitics of Entrapment in the EU's 'Immediate Outside.'" *Journal of the Royal Anthropological Institute* 15: 815–32.

Jungnickel, Katrina, and Rachel Aldred. 2014. "Cycling's Sensory Strategies: How Cyclists Mediate Their Exposure to Urban Environment." *Mobilities* 9(2): 238–55.

Kannisto, Päivi. 2014. "Global Nomads: Challenges of Mobility in the Sedentary World." PhD dissertation, Ridderkerk.

Karkabi, Nadeem. 2013. "Lifestyle Migration in South Sinai, Egypt: Nationalization, Privileged Citizenship and Indigenous Rights." *International Review of Social Research* 3(1): 49–66.

Khan, Naveeda. 2006. "Flaws in the Flow: Roads and Their Modernity in Pakistan." *Social Text* 24(4): 87–113.

Korpela, Mari. 2013. "Marginally Mobile? The Vulnerable Lifestyle of the Westerners in Goa." *Two Homelands* 38: 63–72.

Korpela, Mari, Jaakko Hyytiä, Pekka Rantanen, Pirkko Pitkänen, and Mika Raunio. 2014. "Temporary Migration in Finland." In *Transnational Migration in Transition: State of the Art Report on Temporary Migration. Collected Working Papers from the EURA-NET project,* edited by Pirkko Pitkänen and Sergio Carrera, 81–113. Available at http:// www.uta.fi/edu/en/research/projects/eura-net/publications/State-of-the-art_EU RA-NET.pdf

Larkin, Brian. 2013. "The Politics and Poetics of Infrastructure." *Annual Review of Anthropology* 42: 327–43.

Laviolette, Patrick. 2014. "Why Did the Anthropologist Cross the Road? Hitch-Hiking as a Stochastic Modality of Travel." *Ethnos: Journal of Anthropology*: 1–23. Available at http://dx.doi.org/10.1080/00141844.2014.986149

Liang, Bin, and Lu Hong. 2010. "Internet Development, Censorship, and Cyber Crimes in China." *Journal of Contemporary Criminal Justice* 26(1): 103–20.

Lindquist, Johan. 2010. "Images and Evidence. Human Trafficking, Auditing and the Production of Illicit Markets in Southeast Asia and Beyond." *Public Culture* 22(2): 223–36.

Lyons, KD, and S Wearing, eds. 2008. *Journeys of Discover in Volunteer Tourism.* Wallingford: CABI Publishing.

*Macmillan Dictionary.* Available at http://www.macmillandictionary.com/

Maguire, Mark. 2010. "Vanishing Borders and Biometric Citizens." In *Security/Insecurity in Europe,* edited by Gabriella Laziardis, 31–51. London: Ashgate.

———. 2012. "Biopower, Racialization and New Security Technology." *Social Identities* 18(5): 593–607.

Mains, Daniel. 2012. "Blackouts and Progress: Privatization, Infrastructure, and Developmentalist State in Jimma, Ethiopia." *Cultural Anthropology* 27(1): 3–27.

Malkki, Liisa. 1995. *Purity and Exile: Violence, Memory, and National Cosmology among Hutu Refugees in Tanzania*. Chicago: University of Chicago Press.

Martin, Greg. 2002. "New Age Travelers: Uproarious or Uprooted?" *The Sociological Review* 46(3): 735–56.

Morokvasic, Mirjana. 2004. "'Settled in Mobility': Engendering Post-Wall Migration in Europe." *Feminist Review* 77: 7–25.

Murphy-Lejeune, Elizabeth. 2002. *Student Mobility and Narrative in Europe: The New Strangers*. London: Routledge.

Nyiri, Pal. 2010. *Mobility and Cultural Authority in Contemporary China*. Seattle: University of Washington Press.

O'Byrne, Darren J. 2001. "On Passports and Border Controls." *Annals of Tourism Research* 28(2): 399–416.

Okely, Judith. 1998. *The Traveller Gypsies*. Cambridge: Cambridge University Press.

Ong, Aihwa. 1999. *Flexible Citizenship. The Cultural Logics of Transnationality*. Durham, NC: Duke University Press.

O'Reilly, Karen. 2007. "Intra-European Migration and the Mobility–Enclosure Dialectic." *Sociology* 41(2): 277–93.

———. 2012. *International Migration and Social Theory*. Basingstoke: Palgrave Macmillan.

*Oxford Advanced Learner's Dictionary*. Available at http://www.oxfordlearnersdictionaries.com/

Sadiq, Kamal. 2012. "A Global Documentary Regime? Building State Capacity in the Developing World." In *Global Mobility Regimes*, edited by Rey Koslowski, 151–60. New York: Palgrave MacMillan.

Salazar, Noel B, and A Smart. 2011. "Anthropological Takes on (Im)mobility: Introduction." *Identities: Global Studies in Culture and Power* 18(6): i–ix.

Salter, Mark B. 2006. "The Global Visa Regime and the Political Technologies of the International Self: Borders, Bodies and Biopolitics." *Alternatives* 31: 167–89.

Schabacher, Gabriele. 2013. "Mobilizing Transport. Media, Actor-Worlds, and Infrastructures." *Transfers. International Journal of Mobility Studies* 3(1): 75–95.

Sørensen, Ninna Nyberg, and Thomas Gammeltoft-Hansen, eds. 2013. *The Migration Industry and the Commercialization of International Migration*. London: Routledge.

Spreizer, Alenka Janko. 2013. "Roma, Gypsy Travellers, Gens di Voyage: People Who Travel?" *Two Homelands* 38: 87–98.

Tattersall, Nick. 2014. "Turkey's Gul Approves Law Tightening Internet Controls." *Reuters*, 18 February. Available at http://www.reuters.com/article/2014/02/18/us-turkey-government-idUSBREA1H1XL20140218

Torpey, John. 1998. "Coming and Going: On the State Monopolization of the Legitimate 'Means of Movement.'" *Sociological Theory* 16: 239–59.

Triandafyllidou, Anna, and Thanos Maroukis. 2012. *Migrant Smuggling. Irregular Migration from Asia and Africa to Europe*. Hampshire: Palgrave MacMillan.

Urry, John. 1990. *The Tourist Gaze.* London: Sage.

———. 2004. "The 'System' of Automobility." *Theory, Culture and Society* 21(4–5): 25–39.

———. 2014. *Offshoring.* Cambridge: Polity Press.

Vogt, Wendy A. 2012. "Ethnography at the Depot. Conducting Fieldwork with Migrants in Transit." In *Where Is the Field? The Experience of Migration Viewed through the Prism of Ethnographic Fieldwork,* edited by Laura Hirvi and Hanna Snellman, 66–86. Helsinki: Finnish Literature Society.

von Schnitzler, Antina. 2013. "Travelling Technologies: Infrastructure, Ethical Regimes, and the Materiality of Politics in South Africa." *Cultural Anthropology* 28(4): 670–93.

Winner, Langdon. 1986. "Do Artifacts Have Politics?" In *The Social Shaping of Technology: How the Refrigerator Got Its Hum?* Edited by Donald Mackenzie and Judy Wajcman, 26–37. Milton Keynes, UK: Open University Press.

Xiang, Biao, and Johan Lindquist. 2014. "Migration Infrastructure." *International Migration Review* 48(s1): 122–48.

Yazici, Berna. 2013. "Towards an Anthropology of Traffic: A Ride Through Class Hierarchies on Istanbul's Roadways." *Ethnos: Journal of Anthropology* 78(4): 515–42.

# Motility

*Hege Høyer Leivestad*

Widely used in biology, the term *motility,* as referring to a potential to move, found its way into the social science literature more than a decade ago. Not least through the work of sociologist Kaufmann and colleagues (2002; 2004; 2008; and 2011), who use it as a means to understand human actors' "capacities to move both socially and spatially." When diving into the rapidly expanding interdisciplinary mobility literature, one finds that motility is increasingly applied in reference to human ability or potential to move, partly due to its inclusion in the "new mobilities paradigm" (Hannam, Sheller, and Urry 2006; Sheller 2011; Sheller and Urry 2006; Urry 2003, 2007; see Glick Schiller and Salazar 2013 for a critique).

Etymologically, the noun "motility," stemming from the Latin *motus,* can be traced back to the mid nineteenth century and is defined as "capacity of movement." The adjective form is motile, meaning "capable of movement."[1] Motility has mostly been used as a biological concept, for instance in zoology and botany, to explain cells' and single-celled organisms' capability to move. According to *Oxford Dictionaries,* the concept can also be found within psychology, where it relates to responses that involve muscular sensations (as opposed to audiovisual). As a biological term, it is frequently used to explain gastric or gastrointestinal motility that refers to the movement of food from the mouth, through the inner parts of the body and out.

When thinking of "movement" in the way that social scientists usually do, motility appears as a rather unfamiliar term. Because of an analytical need of finding new concepts for tackling the gap between mobility and immobility, motility emerges, I argue, as a concept able to identify the incompleteness of mobility. The keyword motility thus indicates a pinning down of one of mobility's central elements; namely potential. Motility's relative unfamiliarity makes room for, I suggest, a more general exploration of the concept's trajectories and its analytical value for studies of mobility. Tracing motility's trajectories from its origins in biological locomotion to a tool for understanding and theorizing multifaceted human (im)mobilities, this chapter critically engages with how notions of freedom and individual agency have assumed key roles in its conceptualization. Motility can nevertheless provide, I assert, a productive platform for thinking about human appropriation of both social and spatial mobility (Kaufmann 2002; Kellerman 2012).

On that account, the last part of this chapter examines the potential of motility to analytically enrich our understanding of *aspirations* in various forms of (im)mobility. More specifically, I suggest that motility can be approached as a particular methodological position directed toward situations and locations of temporality in which mobility appears as yet-to-be-realized, yet-to-be-completed, or never-to-be. Motility's analytical value for the study of mobility phenomena is nevertheless conditioned by its ability to capture facetted notions of aspiration, a prerequisite for motility's utility in exploring and illuminating the potential mobility of human beings.

## From Biology to Sociology

A concept of motility as referring to a biological capacity to move appears sporadically in the philosophical and sociological literature, such as in work that deals with the body. In *Phenomenology of Perception* (1996), Merleau-Ponty dedicates a whole chapter to "The Spatiality of One's Own Body and Motility," in which he argues that "By considering the body in movement, we can see better how it inhabits space (and, moreover, time) because movement is not limited to submitting passively to space and time" (Merleau-Ponty 1996, 102). In Merleau-Ponty's sense, motility is used to explain certain varieties in the human consciousness of place, which he illustrates with an example of a patient, suffering from psychic blindness, who has the ability to perform movements required in daily life, such as lighting a lamp or finding the exact spot of a mosquito bite on his arm (an example Merleau-Ponty refers to as one of "morbid motility").

Merleau-Ponty shows that stimulus applied to the body of a normal person arouses a "potential movement," opposed to an actual one; while in the case of the patient, his field of actuality is limited to what is met in real contact (1996, 109). He uses these complex examples to argue for a notion of the body not as separate parts performing bodily functions, but as an irreducible entity. Merleau-Ponty deals with the human bodily potential to move in a phenomenological existential understanding, where physiology and consciousness are inseparable factors in explaining human bodily movement, and where motility is referred to as "The primary sphere in which initially the meaning of all significances ... is engendered in the domain of represented space" (1996, 142).

Another example that focuses upon bodily motility is found in gender studies. In *Throwing Like a Girl* (1980), Young seeks out to fill what she identifies as a gap between existential phenomenology and feminist theory by looking closer at the bodily comportment of women (see Cresswell 1999). Young draws on Merleau-Ponty's understanding of motility as one where intentionality is located, and the possibilities in the world is dependent upon the bodily "I can," when arguing that women's' body commitment, exemplified with the activity of throwing a ball, is withheld in an "I cannot" (Young 1980, 146). The explanation for the modalities of women's body comportment is to be found, Young argues convincingly, not in physiology or anatomy, but in "sexist oppression in contemporary society" (1980, 152).

As a contrast to Merleau-Ponty's phenomenological understanding of motility in relation to human bodily movement and "being-in-the-world," and the appearance of motility in Young's feminist analysis, we find that more recent work on globalization, speed, and modernity has made irregular references to the term. Bauman (2000) speaks of a world in which high mobility prevails, where factors of fluidity and speed largely have dissolved or weakened social structures as we used to know them. In *Liquid Modernity* (2000), Bauman uses the term motility with regard to the disembodiment of labor and its dependence upon capital contrasted with capital's "hopeful travelling": "Capital can travel fast and travel light and its lightness and motility have turned into the paramount source of uncertainty for all the rest. This has become the present day basis of domination and the principal factor of social division" (Bauman 2000, 121). Motility, in Bauman's sense, is thus used to describe similar kinds of potential for movement; not only of human beings, but also of things, ideas, capital, and so on, and the danger this potential has in terms of weakening social stability. What Bauman's work suggests is that motility, through its notion of uncertain and unpredictable potential mobility, is a factor of danger and risk in the fluid and nomadic presence of "liquid modernity."

Also in the work of the social philosopher Virilio, we find reference to the notion of motility, in this case in relation to the human use of interactive technologies: "Having first been *mobile,* then *motorized,* man will thus become *motile,* deliberately limiting his body's area of influence to a few gestures, a few impulses like channel surfing" (1997, 17). Virilio points to a particular coexistence of movement and inertia, where the latter refers to a certain resistance to mobility (Beckmann 2004, 85; Virilio 1997).

In anthropology, motility has been applied analytically; not least in Holbraad's work on Afro-Cuban divination where he develops an "analytics of motility" to ontologically question the relations between concept and things (Holbraad 2007, 2008, 2012). Examining the premises of Ifá cosmology, Holbraad (2007) argues for instance that certain deities should not be thought of as individual entities or relations, but as motions. Such motile deities are however not detached from humans, Holbraad shows, but humans' relations with motile deities are not straightforward since "there is no guarantee that the deities' movement will be elicited in the right direction" (2007, 209). The human relation with motile deities is thus *potential*. Through Holbraad's work, we can trace motility and its notion of potentiality to other strands of anthropology. Holbraad clearly shows how his analytics of motility bears great resemblance to Viveiros de Castro and Goldman's arguments on the Deleuzian conceptions of "virtuality" and "becoming" (Holbraad 2007, 209; see also Deleuze and Guattari 1994). The idea of potentiality and what Holbraad (2007, 2008) terms "potential relations" is here located within the frames of what recently has come to be referred to as anthropology's ontological turn, and common to both the work of de Castro and Holbraad is their empirical interest in regional forms of cosmology.

In anthropology, we can find other examples of how a concept of motility has been applied in studies of human mobility. In a PhD dissertation on the post-forage Baka in Gabon, Weig (2013) approaches relational mobility by particularly discussing the term motility. Her dissertation shows how a motility concept opens up for a temporal dimension of mobility and argues through an extensive use of Kaufmann's (2002) framework that motility provides a specific link between social and spatial mobility. It is precisely in the work of sociologist Kaufmann (2002, 2004, 2008, and 2011) that motility is fully incorporated as a key concept for the interdisciplinary study of mobility, transport, and urban infrastructure, and from this very brief review of the application of motility in the social sciences, Kaufmann's work calls for a somewhat more exhaustive presentation.

## Kaufmann's Motility and Its Problems

The main purpose of Kaufmann's *Re-thinking Mobility* (2002) is to introduce the concept of motility, which he defines as the "capacity of a person to be mobile" or "the way in which an individual appropriates what is possible in the domain of mobility and puts this potential to use for his or her activities" (2002, 37). Kaufmann's aim is to clarify what he considers to be a blurred understanding of potential mobility and realized mobility, and his central argument is that every person has some kind of potential for mobility that, depending on aspirations and circumstances, can be realized in actual movement. Kaufmann defines mobility (in its realized form) as a phenomenon revolving around four main forms: migration, residential mobility, travel, and daily mobility, which are interconnected and linked to social temporalities (2002, 40). Whereas in his later work Kaufmann puts more emphasis on mobility as social change, the 2002 book still rests upon an understanding of mobility as crossing of geographical space.[2]

Kaufmann identifies three motility elements ("access," "skills," and "appropriation") that "together constitute a propensity to be mobile which is motility, and which is likely to vary in intensity from one person to another" (2002, 38–39). He furthermore states, quite vaguely, that while motility is defined on an individual level, it is not formed individually; it is a highly social concept that is "formatted by the life course of those involved and by their financial, social, and cultural capital, which together define the range of possible specific choices in terms of opportunities and projects" (2002, 40). The model of motility has been further developed in Kaufmann's more recent work and that of some of his colleagues (Flamm and Kaufmann 2006; Kaufmann 2011; Kaufmann et al. 2004; Kaufmann and Montulet 2008; Kesselring 2006).[3]

Motility, as introduced to the social sciences by Kaufmann, has been generally accepted as a key term in interdisciplinary mobility studies.[4] This has not least been a result of its inclusion in the "new mobilities paradigm," proposed by Hannam, Sheller, and Urry, where the authors argue that "an emphasis on the relation between human mobilities and immobilities, and the unequal power relations which unevenly distribute motility, the potential for mobility," is one crucial aspect of mobilities research (2006, 15; see also Sheller 2011; Sheller and Urry 2006; Urry 2007). Also in more recent discussions of the future of mobility studies and methodology (D'Andrea, Ciolfi, and Gray 2011), and in the anthropological take on mobility studies (Salazar and Smart 2011), we find motility referred to simply as potential mobility or the ability of humans to move. Recently, anthropologists have however directed sharp criticism against several aspects of the "new mobilities" research paradigm, not least for its dubious treatment of the complex relationship between mobility and stasis (Glick Schiller and Salazar 2013). In light of such criticism, we realize that Kaufmann and colleagues' application of the motility concept is not entirely unproblematic, and in the following, I try to point to some of the questionable connotations motility carry.

Kellerman (2012) has gone far in suggesting the need for an alternative concept, based on his explicit skepticism toward the use of biological terms to explain societal phenomena. He argues that extending this biological term to humans entails a blurring of the distinction between locomotion and motility: "It further implies, at least implicitly, that human potential moving through natural means, that is walking and running, is similar in its basic nature to the human ability to move through most powerful man-made technologies" (Kellerman 2012, 172). This criticism can be viewed as directed against the degree of social and cultural complexity embedded in a concept, as well as a collision between different regimes of science. We can illuminate Kellerman's criticism by recourse to Malinowski's (2001) study of Trobriand sexuality and his way of challenging the psychoanalytical theories prompted by Freud and his followers. Malinowski advances the point that Darwin's theories did not explicate the distinction between animal and human behavior, and hence Freud, in his reconstruction of Darwin's theories, brushed aside any possible distinction that lied implicit in the naturalist theory (2001, 127). It would be unfair though, to claim that Kaufmann's work involves a similar kind of blurring of biological and social phenomena.

Kellerman's (2012) own answer to the problems found in Kaufmann's use of motility is to avoid the biological connotations by employing the term "potential mobilities." However, by stressing the importance of mobility rather than potential, Kellerman's conceptual move reproduces one of the major problems of the motility term. What both Kaufmann and Kellerman to large degree neglect is that potential is not necessarily something that needs to be realized, as mobility is not always what people are after; it could well be a "potentiality that has as its object potentiality itself" (Agamben 1993, 36).

A reading of Kaufmann reveals that his conceptual modeling contains other dubious features of how the content of motility is enunciated. Despite the inclusion of migration in his understanding of realized mobility, it becomes clear, however, that in empirical terms, motility is mostly applied to settings of transport. Kaufmann's own attempt at empirically testing his motility model is based on a qualitative survey and twenty in-depth interviews with people living in the Swiss Lake Leman region about their travel habits and histories, which leads up to a lengthy consideration of private car ownership and daily transport (Flamm and Kaufmann 2006).

Though Kaufmann himself (2002) points at the fact that motility is socially constructed, his model nevertheless rests upon a visualized expression of the autonomous, individual agent. This is foremost the result of a theoretical basis in a particular form of sociology of action through Dubet's *Sociology of Experience* (Kaufmann 2002, 44–45). A more complex question is how such action-based sociology works when considering the relation between freedom and mobility (Sager 2006), a topic that clearly preoccupies Kaufmann, but where his own position remains debatable.[5] He considers that spatial mobility is interpreted too often through notions of power and constraints, such as the ideas found in Bauman's (2000) work, and argues that he does not consider people as "free a priori," but "simply as actors in a situation" (Kaufmann 2002, 43). The latter statement is highly questionable, as it involves a general take on mobility that gives primacy to the individual actor's strategic choices and to a large degree disregards the influence of societal structures.[6]

Doherty's (2015) use of Kaufmann's model in a study of Australian families' relocation in educational markets illustrates this problematic well, as she uses motility to explain individual action, but considers the concept unable to capture the actual institutional factors that trigger, channel, or constraint these families' mobility. Forming a model on the explicit statement that mobility is a choice made among various options furthermore implies that several processes of mobility, such as forced migration, would possibly fall outside the conceptualization of motility. Malkki's (1995) study of camp and town refugees in exile from the Hutu violence in Burundi points to the complex and internally conflicting potentiality between an imagined victorious homecoming and the strategies of ignoring it; showing how a potential mobility hardly can be seen as a choice among options. As Chu (2010) notes, the positioning of people and groups in relation to flows and movement is "uneven and unequal" (2010, 10).

We can link the previous criticism to a more general observation of the Eurocentric bias that Kaufmann's work communicates. Not only are Western Europe and its urban transport systems often used as examples in his writings, there is also a problem in how culturally specific expressions of, for instance, class and residential behavior are taken to be universal in the attempt at introducing a holistic view of mobility through the concept of motility. In Chu's (2010) study of an emigrant town in the Chinese province of Fuzhou, we see how mobility can be a disjunctive and tense "condition of everyday life" for unequally positioned people, many of whom in fact never leave China, but nevertheless aspire for a cosmopolitan ideal (2010, 11–12). In Chu's work, we find mobility both in its realized form, but also as a potential force; among people in a permanent state of departure or in the connections between remittances and the intensity of local ritual life. Chu's attentiveness to the way mobility potential is locally and temporally reshaped can help us question the usefulness of a motility framework so closely modeled on the highly advanced mobility infrastructure of Western Europe and one that is empirically tested mainly in settings of European, urban and daily commuting. Whereas Kaufmann's conceptualization of mobility at firsthand seems to encapsulate also migration and other forms of complex movement, his discussion on motility forefronts a focus on transport and short duration mobility (Kaufmann 2002, 41).

The troublesome relation to a Eurocentric model is further revealed in the market-based vocabulary these writings are prone to; a terminology that is most strongly visible in Kaufmann's *Re-Thinking Mobility* (2002) .[7] To explain the content of motility, Kaufmann makes extensive use of the following words: "access," "options," "conditions," "choice," "skills," "abilities," and "strategies" (2002, 35–47). One of Kaufmann's main aims for developing the concept of motility is the expressed need for a conceptual tool to "measure" mobility (2002, 35). What these words provoke is a linkage to certain forms of economic principles that are closely attached to ideas about the market. At the basis lies the rational agent making choices, and such framework renders little room for exploring how long-term historical, social, and cultural processes contribute to and structure the relation between motility and (im)mobility.

## Aspirations and the Not-Yet

Considering these apparent weaknesses identified in Kaufmann's modeling, how can a concept of motility help us approach, understand, and problematize the instances, gaps, and potential that lie in between mobility and immobility? If motility is stripped of the economized vocabulary, and simultaneously accepted as a term that refers to a general potential mobility applicable also on human beings, there are several reasons to consider this a concept "good to think with." One way to proceed is by looking closer at what Kaufmann (2002) refers to as "appropriation." If we look at motility's trajectory from a biological concept to one of explaining human potential mobility, the key to what is actually human in this approach lies in the notion of appropriation. Appropriation, as explained by Kaufmann, is shaped by aspirations and plans and is intrinsically linked to an individual's interiorization of values, perceptions, and habits (2002, 39).On that note, it is interesting to see how Kaufmann gives aspirations a central part in his motility framework.[8] In explaining the acquisition of motility (as a form of capital) and its transformation into mobility, Kaufmann argues that "motility is at the service of people's aspirations, their projects and their lifestyles, and constitutes a 'mobilisable' capital for their realization and their combination" (2002, 44).

Aspirations of mobility can however never be only individually constructed, nor isolated from various social and cultural processes. My suggestion is that aspirations—as referring to strong desires and hopes or ambitions to achieve something—should be key factors in understanding and framing motility. Appadurai has gone far in proposing an anthropology that puts "the future back in" to our understanding of culture. Appadurai distinguishes between what he terms (1) a "capacity to aspire," referring to a capability to navigate, and (2) "aspirations" as they "form parts of wider ethical and metaphysical ideas that derive from larger cultural norms" (Appadurai 2013, 187–89; Fischer 2014, 5–6). So, while aspirations are linked to individual "wants, preferences, choices and calculations," they are, as Appadurai puts it, "formed in interaction and in the thick of social life" (2013, 187). Aspirations can thus provide a link between the intimate hopes, plans, and desires of an individual in relation to mobility, and political, religious, and economic practices, processes, and transformations in broader society; as they are "tied up with more general norms, presumptions, and axioms about the good life, and life more generally" (Appadurai 2013, 188).[9] Aspirations in this sense come close to a concept of *imaginaries* as historically laden, socially shared, and transmitted (Salazar 2011), or to use Salazar's words, "imaginaries of the world and of oneself always go hand in hand" (Salazar 2013, 234).

In a different context, writing comparatively on Germany and Guatemala, the anthropologist Fischer (2014) teases out precisely aspirations as a key quality that defines "the good life." Fischer's argument is that to understand the good life, one needs to look not only to people's material conditions, but also "desires, aspirations and imaginations—the hopes, fears, and other subjective factors that drive their engagement with the world" (2014, 5). In studies of lifestyle migration on the other hand, we find how Westerners' ideas of the good life elsewhere come out as an aspirational self-realization project (Benson and O'Reilly 2009). Whereas Fischer is adding an important stance to studies of poverty that has tended to overlook the "nonmaterial" aspects of the good life and well-being, when seen in relation to the issue of motility, I am more cautious about framing aspirations as nonmaterial per se. Actually, aspirational qualities are not only related to, but intricately embedded in material forms, such as vehicles and larger mobility infrastructures, and are therefore a undistinguishable part of the material technologies of motility. That such mobile "technologies of the imagination" (Sneath, Holbraad, and Pedersen 2009) can have strong aspirational elements, is shown in Vigh's (2009) analysis of how mobile Western technologies such as cars, planes, and phones, trigger young Bissauans imaginations of the possibilities located elsewhere. Meshed with notions of forward-looking and aspects of hope, aspirations hold a potentiality of their own. A potential of setting something into movement that may be the route to some kind of social change.

The idea of the potential, or potentiality, in relation to religious forms and social change, is not new to anthropology or philosophy (see for instance Agamben 1999). One version of potentiality is found in Turner's (2011) work and his portrayal of the potential embedded in liminal immobility. Thomson (2013) shows how the notion of the *not yet*, as he reads the similarities in the work of Bloch (1970) and Badiou (2007), brings epis-

temology and ontology together in particular ways. In a humanist interpretation of Marx's historical materialism, and inspired by Aristotle and
Hegel's concept of *werden* or becoming, Bloch offers a processual "ontology
of not-yet-being" (Thomson 2013, 34). In Bloch's concrete utopia, the relationship between material realities and human intervention is filled with
potential, but the incompleteness of the material conditions yet prevents
its realization.

A detour to an example from migration literature can help illuminate the
relations between potential mobility, aspirations, and the not-yet. Based
on his experience from studying the Lebanese Diaspora, Hage (2005) questions the use of the concept of mobility, focusing on how it has been applied in studies of migration. Hage argues that the kind of mobility that
migrants become associated with is actually very limited in terms of time.
It is a mobility that shapes their lives significantly (2005, 469). Hage points
out that, as in the case of tourism, it is a mistake to believe that people's
crossing of national borders is necessarily significant for their lives (2005,
469). Where Hage's argument becomes most useful, is when he points out
that migration is connected to the feeling of being stuck and that we as
humans need to feel "we are going somewhere" (Hage 2005). Hage argues
that in the case of migrants, they prefer to be "going places" by staying in
familiar environments. Only when this environment causes one to be "going
nowhere" or "going too slowly" does the need for physical mobility crop up
(Hage 2005, 470). Hage introduces the term "existential mobility" to show
how "we move physically so we can feel we are existentially on the move
again or at least moving better" (2005, 470). Hage may help us think of
motility in a way where it is not directly employed as a form of capital, but
nevertheless converge aspects of both physical and social mobility.

Taking migrant homebuilding as another point of departure, Hage suggests that home building could be defined as "the building of the feeling of
'being at home'" (1997, 102). He considers the home to be constructed of
affective building blocks that provide four key feelings: security, familiarity,
community, and a sense of possibility. The latter is an element often for-
gotten in theorizations of the home, Hage argues, when he asserts that a
home is also a space of opportunities (1997, 103). Hage shows how such
a notion of possibility is crucial in understanding feelings of home, because
home building is after all about future possibilities "of more security, familiarity and so on" (1997, 104). What Hage's terminology does is to stress the
importance of the aspirational in relation to human mobility; a "sense of
possibility." We find similar ideas in the work of Bloch, but there in the form
of concrete utopia (Thomson 2013). The *Heimat,* the home, is to Bloch not
a return to an idyll, but one that is still in creation. This utopia, Thomson
shows, is "concrete in its abstract quality of not-yetness but also concrete in

that the preillumination of what it might be is always already present within the individual and collective invariant of direction" (Thomson 2013, 35).

In Hage's work, the sense of possibility is intimately linked to migratory (im)mobility and homemaking. We can, however, see the aspirational aspect as a central feature of the notion of motility more generally. The reasons for staying put or for moving physically are closely attached to aspirations of social mobility, or, put differently: how we imagine our future to be. The space of possibility, as framed by Hage (1997), implies an openness to receive opportunities for a better life, and, though placed within a different ontological setting, in its emphasis on potential it is not dissimilar to Bloch's concrete utopia (Thomson 2013). The rather abstract not-yetness and aspirational elements found in the work of Bloch and Hage, point to a more concrete challenge in where to locate motility in form of mobility aspirations and appropriations. As Kellerman points out: potential mobilities do not constitute separate entities, "rather they are a preparatory step towards practiced mobility and specific movements" (2012, 179). Therefore, whereas realized or practiced mobility most often is observable, mobility aspirations are found in situations or places that for the anthropologist can be hard to identify.

## An Anthropological Potential

Following Adey's (2006) point that "if mobility is everything, then it is nothing," the same warning could probably be raised against the use of the term motility. As a concept that is directed toward the intersections of mobility and immobility, motility's analytical potential may nevertheless well lie in its holistic take on social and spatial mobility. What could be dealt with more thoroughly is the proposal that motility should be understood as a form of capital in the Bourdieuan sense that forms links with, and can be exchanged for, other types of capital (Kaufmann et al. 2004). This implies that potential mobility needs to be understood as a commodity, exchangeable to other forms of capital (Adey 2010, 101; Kaufmann et al. 2004). Understanding motility as capital, however, is not unproblematic, as it presents complicated relations to other forms of capital, partly because, as Kellerman argues, "motility as exchangeable capital is not always a standalone element in one's decision to perform and/or exchange" (2012, 176).

Motility is located in processes of decision making, but also in the dreaming of, planning for, or fear of mobility. Motility needs to be treated then, to use Salazar and Smart's words on mobility, not as a "brute fact" (2011, v). An anthropological approach to motility needs to go beyond Kaufmann's measuring, into a sociocultural exploration of how mobilities are constructed, experienced, and imagined. Such widespread phenomena as the potential migrant organizing her departure or waiting in transit, brutally described in Khosravi's (2010) autoethnography of borders, the imaginations and anticipations embedded in various forms of tourism (Skinner and Theodossopoulos 2011), as well as the fear and anxieties of mobility that are involved in processes of displacement (see Jansen and Löfving 2009), all present complicated cases where motility is at stake. Nevertheless, motility has an important relational aspect and can be identified in different social and economic relationships that at firsthand might not seem to be about mobility at all.

Motility can avail our examination and understanding of these processes of not-yet-realized, not-yet-completed, or never-to-be-realized mobility, as we find them in for example situations of planning, transit, or being left behind. Motility thus allows us to approach the temporalities of mobilities in a particular way, as it directs our attention toward the processes where mobility not yet has taken place, not has been completed, or those where it actually is never going to be realized. However, the not-yet-realized or might-never-happen mobility provide the ethnographer with a methodological challenge, because there is no mobility, yet or never. Returning to Holbraad's (2007) work on motility and materiality, he implicitly points to an additional challenge that motility presents us with; since the potential mobility is not a realized form, the course and the outcome of it are still unknown. Taking these aspects of temporality into consideration, we can see motility as a form of methodological situating that helps us direct our analytical gaze toward the not-yet.[10]

In his analysis of a small Indonesian island's transformation into a large-scale development project, and the tourism and migration mobilities involved, Lindquist (2009) presents an illustrating example of the not-yet as a particular mode of temporality. The open-endedness of the not-yet characterizes life on Batam, Lindquist argues, showing how also modernist visions of urban development has resulted in unfinished buildings locally referred to as "not yet ready" (2009, 7). Particular futures are anticipated in this setting, Lindquist's ethnography shows, and such anticipated futures are found in the mobility of migrants and tourists, as well as in the planned—and not yet realized—transformation of space.

Another reason for considering motility a concept good to think with would be its analytical potential for revealing the material expressions of mobility-immobility intersections. This can be achieved through the examination of forms of material culture and infrastructure that enable, negotiate, or hinder mobility, and of how such materialities embed different forms of mobility imaginaries. "We all need moments and spaces of rests," Cresswell and Merriman argue, referring to the importance of materiality that structure mobility (2011, 7). Hannam, Sheller, and Urry refer to this in the form of complex systems of "immobile material worlds," exemplified with transmitters, roads, garages, airports, or what Urry also has termed "moorings" or "fixities," and Sheller refers to it as systems that "make and break connections between people and places" (Hannam et al. 2006, 3; Sheller 2013; Urry 2003, 2007).

Kleinman's (2014) analysis of the Paris Gare du Nord railway station offers a particularly interesting example of how a transportation system can feed mobility imaginaries and mold social practices. She describes how West African migrants transform the railway infrastructure into a particular node of communication and exchange. The position of Gare du Nord as a central social environment for the young migrant men is far from a co-incidence, Kleinman argues, showing that "the potentiality for movement suffused this social space, with trains constantly coming and going and humans pouring in and out of the station's doors" (2014, 292).

The growing research on borders provides a different view on the crucial importance of the material expressions of (im)mobility. Shapira (2013) brings forward an alternative version of the not-yet, here placed in a detailed ethnographic account of the American Minutemen's patrolling of the US-Mexican border. In this context, an "illegal" immigrant is imagined, feared, and patiently awaited, but his imagined border-crossing mobility is seldom completed, or at least not discovered. Andersson (2014) makes a similar point when describing the large-scale EU border regime targeting an imagined (but seldom existent) clandestine African migrant. What can be drawn from these examples is how the illegal immigrant is constructed through a complex and highly politicized evaluating of human motility understood as threatening potential mobility. In both cases, we see that a materialized border embody notions of the not-yet.

Material expressions are however not only visible in large-scale infrastructures, such as the border regimes described above. In my research on European caravan and motorhome dwelling (Leivestad 2015), I draw attention to other aspects of material culture—in this case the home on wheels—in producing specific tensions between mobility and immobility. A potential mobility, I argue, is at stake here; it might not be the case that the caravan wheels geographically take you anywhere, but the wheels' physical presence and the fact that they can take you away opens up for aspirations of mobility that embed important notions of social mobility. This rather undefined notion of potential mobility is also present in the ways the caravanning industry manufactures and markets leisure vehicles with reference to the freedom of taking your home "wherever you like."

The conceptual fruitfulness lies perhaps in the way motility bridges the sometimes-rigid understandings of the differences and oppositions between mobility and immobility. By employing a concept of motility that overlooks the work of Kaufmann (2002), Beckmann (2004) points to the crucial coexistence of mobilities and immobilities. Beckmann understands motility as "the ability to be mobile without necessarily performing movement," referring to the hybrid forms that lay in-between mobility and immobility (2004, 85). Though Beckmann's examples mainly relate to issues of transport and traffic, he makes an interesting remark on how motility holds the capacity "to both paralyze and mobilize" (2004, 85). I would suggest that this capacity to paralyze and mobilize is closely intertwined with imaginaries of mobility and the social aspirations with which they are tied up (Salazar 2011, 2013).

Yet, there lies a danger in framing motility only through a window of aspirations and possibilities that are positively valued (Glick Schiller and Salazar 2013). When attempting to reconceptualize motility, there might be a risk of reproducing exactly the forms of positive valuations of mobility that the "new mobilities" research has been criticized for (Glick Schiller and Salazar 2013, 186). Not least is there a danger in conceptualizing motility, like I have done in this chapter, through notions of aspiration, hope, and possibilities, terms that provoke similar tendencies toward the positively loaded. We need not to forget that aspirational engagement can hold "dystopian potentials" (Sneath et al. 2009, 10). Yet aspirations of mobility are also placed within constraints and complex power relations that need our sensitive attention. Motility is unevenly distributed and part of unequal power relations in a world where control over people's potential mobility has become an important asset for politics and governance (Glick Schiller and Salazar 2013; Hannam et al. 2006).

An anthropological approach to motility requires an attentive exploration of how people envision potential mobility, but also a questioning of under what circumstances and conditions this potential mobility is enacted, and when it is actually denied or constrained (Salazar and Smart 2011). As Salazar and Smart (2011) point out, the separations between choice and constraint are not clear-cut. Glick Schiller and Salazar (2013) underline the challenge of the murkiness of choice and constraint, when pointing to how ability and right to travel has become one of the criteria for how class is defined and class differences are maintained. Motility then might provide an important analytical tool for further conceptualizing and understanding social class.

Kaufmann's (2002) extension of motility to sociology and mobility studies has, probably unintentionally, brought in questionable notions of freedom and individualism, foremost through a use of what I have (perhaps a bit harshly) dubbed a market-based terminology. An anthropological approach to motility, I have argued in this chapter, may nevertheless have the potential to direct us toward those situations and positions of temporality where mobility is yet-to-be-realized, yet-to-be-completed, or not-intended-to-happen. Despite this conceptual potential, I believe that there is still an obstacle attached to the word motility and it can possibly be traced to many of my colleagues' blank expressions when being confronted with the term. While the other mobility keywords discussed in this volume all provoke ethnographic associations, histories, similarities, and analytical understanding, motility most often does none of this to the anthropologist. Motility's problem is its deep rootedness in an interdisciplinary mobility discourse that has partly suffered from its marriage to subdisciplines such as transport studies, where economized models and methodological individualism has come to set the agenda.

**Hege Høyer Leivestad** currently works as a researcher at the Department of Social Anthropology, Stockholm University, Sweden. In her doctoral dissertation from 2015 she examines caravan dwelling in Europe, focusing on issues of mobility and materiality.

## NOTES

1. *Oxford Dictionaries Online,* Online Etymology Dictionary. "Motility." Available at http://www.etymonline.com/index.php?search=motility. *Oxford Dictionaries Online.* "Motility." Available at http://oxforddictionaries.com/definition/english/motile?q=motility#motile__5.

2. In a 2004 article, however, Kaufmann et al. seeks to further develop what the 2002 book first initiated: the idea of motility as a form of capital, a discussion that Jayaram in chapter 1 engages with in-depth. The main argument is that motility constitutes a link between spatial and social mobility, and that it should be considered a form of capital that can be exchanged with other kinds of capital (Kaufmann et al. 2004, 751). In a later book, Kaufmann (2011) links motility more specifically to the urban sphere, stressing the importance of a holistic perspective that integrates both spatial and social mobility.

3. In a later article, Michael Flamm and Kaufmann attempt to demonstrate the operational capacity of motility in order to "explain the logic and rationales of the composition of an individual's motility" (2006, 169). Their basis is a qualitative survey and twenty in-depth interviews with people living in the Swiss Lake Leman region about their travel habits and histories, which leads up to a lengthy consideration of private car ownership and daily transport use.

4. Kaufmann's (2002) model of motility has been applied to a variety of case studies. See for instance Doherty (2015) on educational relocation and Penna and Kirby (2013) on crime and mobility.

5. The relation between freedom and mobility is extensively discussed elsewhere. See Sager (2006) and Sheller (2008) in Bergmann and Sager (2008).

6. Kaufmann claims that this is not the case when arguing the opposite: "this choice of methodology does not make any assumptions about the influence of social and spatial structures on the action that is precisely the object of the research" (2002, 43).
7. One side effect of neoliberal thinking is that mobility ideologically has come to be associated with notions of freedom, liberty, and universalism; ideas which have also slipped into the theoretical vocabulary surrounding the concept (see Adey 2010, 87).
8. In his 2011 book, Kaufmann gives aspirations a central role in explaining and measuring motility, but emphasizes that it cannot be treated separately from access and skills, as these three are "inextricably" linked (2011, 44).
9. Appadurai's treatment of aspirations nevertheless contains questionable arguments regarding the distribution of the capacity to aspire and its relation to poverty (2013, 188–89).
10. I am grateful to Johan Lindquist for pushing this point after reading an earlier version of this chapter.

## REFERENCES

Adey, Peter. 2006. "If Mobility Is Everything Then It Is Nothing: Towards a Relational Politics of (Im)mobilities." *Mobilities* 1(1): 75–94.
———. 2010. *Mobility.* Oxford: Routledge.
Agamben, Giorgio. 1993. *The Coming Community.* Translated by Michael Hardt. Minneapolis: University of Minnesota Press.
———. 1999. *Potentialities: Collected Essays in Philosophy.* Stanford, CA: Stanford University Press.
Andersson, Ruben. 2014. "Hunter and Prey: Patrolling Clandestine Migration in the EuroAfrican Borderlands." *Anthropological Quarterly* 87(1): 119–50.
Appadurai, Arjun. 2013. *The Future as Cultural Fact: Essays on the Global Condition.* London: Verso.
Badiou, Alain. 2007. *Being and Event.* London: Continuum.
Bauman, Zygmunt. 2000. *Liquid Modernity.* Cambridge: Polity Press.
Beckmann, Jörg. 2004. "Mobility and Safety." *Theory, Culture, Society* 21(4–5): 81–100.
Benson, Michaela, and Karen O'Reilly. 2009. *Lifestyle Migration: Expectations, Aspirations and Experiences.* Aldershot, England: Ashgate.
Bergmann, Sigurd, and Tore Sager, eds. 2008. *The Ethics of Mobilities. Rethinking Place, Exclusion, Freedom and Environment.* Aldershot, England: Ashgate.
Bloch, Ernst. 1970. *Tübinger Einleitung in die Philosophie.* Frankfurt: Suhrkamp.
Chu, Julie Y. 2010. *Cosmologies of Credit. Transnational Mobility and the Politics of Destination in China.* Durham, NC: Duke University Press.
Cresswell, Timothy. 1999. "Embodiment, Power and the Politics of Mobility: The Case of Female Tramps and Hobos." *Transactions of the Institute of British Geographers* 24(2): 175–92.

Cresswell, Timothy, and Peter Merriman. 2011. "Introduction." In *Geographies of Mobilities: Practices, Spaces, Subjects,* edited by Tim Cresswell and Peter Merriman, 1–18. Farnham: Ashgate.

D'Andrea, Anthony, Luicina Ciolfi, and Breda Gray. 2011. "Methodological Challenges and Innovations in Mobilities Research." *Mobilities* 6(2): 149–60.

Deleuze, Gilles, and Felix Guattari. 1994. *What Is Philosophy?* New York: Columbia University Press.

Doherty, Catherine. 2015. "Agentive Motility Meets Structural Viscosity: Australian Families Relocating in Educational Markets." *Mobilities* 10(2): 249–66.

Fischer, Edward F. 2014. *The Good Life. Aspiration, Dignity and the Anthropology of Well-Being.* Stanford, CA: Stanford University Press.

Flamm, Michael, and Vincent Kaufmann. 2006. "Operationalising the Concept of Motility: A Qualitative Study." *Mobilities* 1(2): 167–89.

Glick Schiller, Nina, and Noel B Salazar, eds. 2013. "Regimes of Mobility across the Globe." *Journal of Ethnic and Migration Studies* 39(2): 183–200.

Hage, Ghassan. 1997. "At Home in the Entrails of the West: Multiculturalism, 'Ethnic Food,' and Migrant Home building." In *Home/World: Space, Community and Marginality in Sydney's West,* edited by Helen Grace, Ghassan Hage, Leslie Johnson, Julie Langsworth, and Michael Symonds, 99–153. Annandale: Pluto Press.

———. 2005. "A Not so Multi Sited Ethnography of a Not so Imagined Community." *Anthropological Theory* 5(4): 463–75.

Hannam, Kevin, Mimi Sheller, and John Urry, eds. 2006. "Editorial: Mobilities, Immobilities and Moorings." *Mobilities* 1(1): 1–22.

Holbraad, Martin. 2007. "The Power of Powder: Multiplicity and Motion in the Divinatory Cosmology of Cuban Ifá (or Mana Again)." In *Thinking Through Things: Theorizing Artefacts Ethnographically,* edited by Amiria Henare, Martin Holbraad and Sari Wastell, 189–225. London: Routledge.

———. 2008. "Relationships in Motion: Oracular Recruitment in Cuban Ifá Cults." *Systèmes de Pensée en Afrique Noire* 18: 219–64.

———. 2012. *Truth in Motion. The Recursive Anthropology of Cuban Divination.* Chicago: University of Chicago Press.

Jansen, Stef, and Staffan Löfving, eds. 2009. *Struggles for Home. Violence, Hope and the Movement of People.* New York: Berghahn Books.

Kaufmann, Vincent. 2002. *Re-Thinking Mobility: Contemporary Sociology.* Aldershot, England: Ashgate.

———. 2011. *Re-Thinking the City. Urban Dynamics and Motility.* Oxford: Routledge.

Kaufmann, Vincent, Manfred Max Bergman, and Dominique Joyce. 2004. "Motility: Mobility as Capital." *International Journal of Urban and Regional Research* 28(4): 745–56.

Kaufmann, Vincent, and Bertrand Montulet. 2008. "Between Social and Spatial Mobilities: The Issue of Social Fluidity." In *Tracing Mobilities: Towards a Cosmopolitan Perspective,* edited by Weert Canzler, Vincent Kaufmann, and Sven Kesselring, 37–55. Aldershot, England: Ashgate.

Kellerman, Aharon. 2012. "Potential Mobilities." *Mobilities* 7(3): 171–83.

Kesselring, Sven. 2006. "Pioneering Mobilities: New Pattern of Movement and Motility in a Mobile World." *Environment and Planning A* 38(2): 269–79.

Khosravi, Shahram. 2010. *'Illegal' Traveller. An Auto-Ethnography of Borders.* Basingstoke: Palgrave.

Kleinman, Julie. 2014. "Adventures in Infrastructure: Making an African Hub in Paris." *City & Society* 26(3): 286–307.

Leivestad, Hege Høyer. 2015. "Lives on Wheels: Caravan Homes in Contemporary Europe." PhD dissertation, Stockholm University.

Lindquist, Johan A. 2009. *The Anxieties of Mobility. Migration and Tourism in the Indonesian Borderlands.* Honolulu: University of Hawai'i Press.

Malinowski, Bronislaw. 2001. *Sex and Repression in Savage Society.* London: Routledge. First published 1927.

Malkki, Liisa. 1995. *Purity and Exile: Violence, Memory, and National Cosmology amongst Hutu Refugees in Tanzania.* Chicago: Chicago University Press.

Merleau-Ponty, Maurice. 1996. *Phenomenology of Perception.* Dehli: Motilal Banarsidass Publisher. First published 1962.

Penna, Sue, and Stuart Kirby. 2013. "Bridge Over the River Crime: Mobility and the Policing of Organized Crime." *Mobilities* 8(4): 487–505.

Sager, Tore. 2006. "Freedom as Mobility: Implications of the Distinction between Actual and Potential Travelling." *Mobilities* 1(3): 465–88.

Salazar, Noel B. 2011. "The Power of Imagination in Transnational Mobilities." *Identities: Global Studies in Culture and Power* 18(6): 576–98.

———. 2013. "Imagining Mobility at the 'End of the World.'" *History and Anthropology* 24(2): 233–52.

Salazar, Noel B, and Alan Smart. 2011. "Anthropological Takes on (Im) Mobility." *Identities: Global Studies in Culture and Power* 18(6): i–ix

Shapira, Harel. 2013. *Waiting for José. The Minutemen's Pursuit of America.* Princeton, NJ: Princeton University Press.

Sheller, Mimi. 2008. "Mobility, Freedom and Public Space." In *The Ethics of Mobilities. Rethinking Place, Exclusion, Freedom and Environment,* edited by Sigurd Bergmann and Tore Sager, 25–38. Aldershot, England: Ashgate.

———. 2011. "Mobility." *Sociopedia.isa.*

———. 2013. "The Islanding Effect: Post-Disaster Mobility Systems and Humanitarian Logistics in Haiti." *Cultural Geographies* 20(2): 185–204.

Sheller, Mimi, and John Urry. 2006. "The New Mobilities Paradigm." *Environment and Planning A* 38(2): 207–26.

Skinner, Jonathan, and Dimitros Theodossopoulos, eds. 2011. *Great Expectations. Imagination and Anticipation in Tourism.* New York: Berghahn Books.

Sneath, David, Martin Holbraad, and Morten Axel Pedersen. 2009. "Technologies of the Imagination: An Introduction." *Ethnos: Journal of Anthropology* 74(1): 5–30.

Thomson, Peter. 2013. "Bloch, Badiou, Saint Paul, and the Ontology of the Not Yet." *New German Critique 119* 40(2): 31–52.

Turner, Victor. 2011. *The Ritual Process.* London: Aldine Transaction. First published 1969.

Urry, John. 2003. *Global Complexity.* Cambridge: Polity Press.

———. 2007. *Mobilities.* Cambridge: Polity Press.

Vigh, Henrik. 2009. "Wayward Migration: On Imagined Futures and Technological Voids." *Ethnos: Journal of Anthropology* 74(1): 91–109.

Virilio, Paul. 1997. *Open Sky.* London: Verso.

Weig, Doerte. 2013. "Motility and Relational Mobility of the Baka in North-Eastern Gabon." PhD dissertation, Universität zu Köln.

Young, Iris Marion. 1980. "Throwing Like a Girl: A Phenomenology of Feminine Body Comportment, Motility and Spatiality." *Human Studies* 3(2): 137–56.

CHAPTER
# 8

# Regime

*Beth Baker*

The term *regime* comes from the Latin *regimen,* meaning "rule, guidance, government, means of guidance, rudder," by way of the old French term *régime* (*Merriam Webster Dictionary*). Its meaning in current English usage usually invokes notions of national government or a supranational system of governmental regulation. The term regime was frequently used in the past to denote a regularized system of behavior or self-governance, a regimen, and continues to be used in this way in medical terminology (Zimmer 2009). In recent times, the word appeared in popular discourse as a pejorative label to suggest that a national government is illegitimate in some way. Taken together, these meanings suggest that modern usage of the term *regime* refers to both governance and self-governance, pointing to issues surrounding the legitimacy of governance as well as the relationship of the governed to governance and power. Current usage of the term regime in mobility studies encompasses elements of all these meanings—technologies of governance, systems for the self-regulation of behavior, and moral economies—and the ways these simultaneously produce and constrain action and thought. Anthropological perspectives on regimes in general, and on regimes of (im)mobility in particular, focus on the discursive constructions of personhood, rights, sovereignty, and society, and how these constructions can simultaneously mobilize and immobilize in diverse ways.

Following Salazar (2012), I use the term *regime of (im)mobility* because mobility only becomes possible in relation to immobility; the two are inextricably linked and any regime of mobility is at the same time a regime of immobility. Thinking in terms of mobility alone may evoke images of freedom, of the self-directed movement of an autonomous and self-determined individual. Dean (in chapter 3) points out the Occidental and bourgeois origins of this notion of freedom, while Leivestad (in chapter 7) critiques neoliberal models of motility and the potentiality for self-directed movement. Neoliberal models of mobility understand movement as a rational choice of the self-governing individual, and they privilege subjects who seem to embody entrepreneurialism, independence, and the generation of capital (Ong 2003). This model of movement suggests that immobility is, like mobility, a rational and individual choice, and that mobility and immobility are somehow opposites. To the contrary, I argue that mobility can only exist in relation to structured immobility, and the two emerge as products of the same regime. Freedom, then, emerges in dialectical tension with constraint and collusion; linking mobility to immobility highlights the fact that human movement in today's world is not, in fact, a product of some pure, presocial freedom, but is impelled and constrained by structural conditions and discourses. Indeed, as I argue below, it is in looking closely at the linkages between mobility and immobility that we can locate and begin to understand regimes of (im)mobility, where power is enacted, in part, through producing or limiting actors' mobilities. And in looking at these linkages, the inequalities embedded in regimes of (im)mobility, along with their contradictions and uneven and overlapping domains, become more clear.

If regimes are national and supranational governmental schema for the regulation of behavior, then regimes of (im)mobility are rationalized systems for the regulation of movement—of people, goods, capital, and certain forms of knowledge—that encompass both infrastructural and discursive technologies. They may be formal and governmental, corporate, or informal and outside of legal frameworks, and they produce the material conditions for mobility and immobility, as well as the values and ideas that justify and legitimize distinctions between classes of objects and kinds of people who are accorded differential rights to mobility. For example, academia is a regime of (im)mobility for scholars, staff, administrators, and students. For instructors, the tenure system provides a broad infrastructure for mobility within and between institutions, rationalizing who enjoys upward mobility and why, and justifying a certain (im)mobility for nontenure track faculty who are largely excluded from improvements in salary, benefits, and power in the institution, and who are, therefore, forced to be mobile in order to pursue opportunities where they may arise. For students, university often involves moving in order to access education, and the hope that a degree will bring upward class mobility. For staff and administrators, university employment provides opportunities for upward class mobility, and frequent movement between institutions implies geographic movement as well. While the infrastructures of academia are important to producing these outcomes, the discourses surrounding the value and purpose of education, the legitimacy of scholarly knowledge production, the credentialing of university instructors, and the ideas that validate who can be a student and what constitutes being a worthy student, all make the infrastructure seem rational, even moral, in the ways it operationalizes these distinctions. All regimes of (im)mobility are built upon these complex imbrications of infrastructure and moral discourse, and they all produce and legitimize differential access to forms of mobility, be they spatial, economic, institutional/structural, or other.

Currently, there are two main tendencies in mobilities studies for framing the concept of regimes (im)mobility—functionalist approaches that seek to identify the ways that systems for the regulation of mobility work in order to design more efficient and comprehensive regimes, and discursive approaches that parse out the ways institutions, technologies, ideas, and identities are constructed in relation to mobility, and how this might produce, shape, and prevent different kinds of mobilities. Scholarship in political science (e.g., Hollifield 2011; Koslowski 2011; Krasner 1982) and sociology (e.g., Vannini et al. 2012) tends to highlight the first approach while work in anthropology and cultural studies is disposed toward the latter, though some works include aspects of both approaches. Functionalist analyses of regimes of (im)mobility are concerned with assessing and improving the efficiency, and even the morality, of these systems. In contrast, discursive approaches to regimes build on the work of Foucault (1977; 1990; 1991)—particularly his concepts of governmentality, biopower, regimes of truth, and discipline—situating regimes as local and historically specific, and seeing the regulation of populations as proceeding through knowledge production, technologies of governance, and discourses of personhood and rights. In the context of neoliberalism, discursive approaches highlight the affective self-regulation these produce, as well as how people may subvert, and in the process, transform them (Karakayali and Rigo 2010). In sum, discursive approaches to regimes of (im)mobility seek to understand different forms of power, how they are established and justified in relation to mobilities, how they both produce and constrain thought and action, and how they change over time.

While these two tendencies are markedly different in some respects, they share many of the same concerns—to understand the structuring of mobility in the modern world and its implications, and to examine the ways that mobility is linked to ideas about sovereignty, rights, freedom, and sociality. These concerns often translate into a focus on the nation-state and international forms of governances. Furthermore, both approaches tend to fixate on certain forms of mobility—the physical movement of people and capital, and social mobility.[1] This chapter focuses on the application of these approaches to the mobility of people, both physical and social, and on the methodological and epistemological complexities of studying regimes of (im)mobility. I suggest that both approaches—the discursive and the functionalist—would benefit from examining the experiences of people whose movement is constricted, those who are the objects of technologies of immobilization, as much as they scrutinize the experiences of the more privileged whose movement is facilitated by technologies of (im)mobility. My concern with current approaches in mobilities studies is that they too often fetishize movement. Like research in globalization and transnationalism that preceded mobilities studies, scholars often assume movement, connectivity, and flow, and therefore neglect to document the immobilities at the heart of the global nation-state system. This may be due, in part, to the fact that scholars enjoy and depend upon a high degree of both geographic and social mobility; they tend not to experience the everyday immobilities that so often afflict working class people, migrants, and those who are criminalized.

## Functionalist Accounts of (Im)mobility

Functionalist approaches to understanding regimes predominate in international relations, where scholars began debating the concept and developing definitions of it in the 1980s. Krasner argued that "regimes can be defined as sets of implicit or explicit principles, norms, rules, and decision-making procedures around which actors' expectations converge in a given area of international relations" (1982, 186). In addition, "the basic causal variables that lead to the creation of regimes are power and interest. The basic actors are states" (1982, 186). Under this definition, an international regime is a set of agreed-upon values and practices between national states that regulates behavior between, and sometimes within, them. This definition has, for the most part, prevailed in political science.

Much of the functionalist focus on regimes of (im)mobility centers on analyses of infrastructure—physical and institutional systems and services. Koslowski distinguishes between three overlapping mobility regimes—an international travel regime, an international labor migration regime, and a refugee regime. He argues for analyzing them as "a set of interacting global mobility regimes" (2011, 5) and develops recommendations so that older and more established protocols for regulating international travel might develop into a more systematized global labor migration regime, the absence of which he finds troubling. Martin (2011), in the same volume, echoes Koslowski in calling for a more rational and formal international regime to regulate human mobility with greater international cooperation. Rudolph points to the World Trade Organization as a model for future institutionalization of a global mobility regime, arguing that "it is appealing to consider the orderly management of human mobility to be something of a global public good" (2011, 182) and concluding that "achieving a comprehensive global mobility regime may not be outside the realm of possibility (2011, 197). And Hollifield writes, "in at least one crucial respect a migration regime can approximate a global public good—achieving orderly, legal movements of people across national boundaries, movements that can be beneficial and highly profitable to both the sending and receiving societies requires a *degree of international cooperation*" (2011, 230; italics in original). These authors—all political scientists—express alarm at the poor institutionalization of nation-state cooperation on measures to regulate mobility. Of course, international institutions such as the International Organization for Migration (an arm of the United Nations) share the same concerns and goals—efficient regime formation.

Some sociologists reflect these same concerns in their work on mobility. For instance, Vannini et al. write, "the study of mobilities rightly encompasses sociotechnical processes that focus on the material, imaginative and/or virtual movement of people, signs, and objects" (2012, 5). This techno-social definition of mobilities seems to assume mobility as a force that is unlimited, equally accessible by all, and politically neutral in its flow. They go on to write, "Each sovereign nation within the Americas had developed a transport and mobility system to suit its own needs and exhibits very diverse manifestations of mobility. However, in addition to facilitating the mobility of people, goods, and information around the world, transport technologies also enable the transnational mobility of smugglers, migrants, infectious diseases, narcotics, criminals, and terrorists" (Vannini et al. 2012, 9). This lumping of migrants into the same category as infectious diseases, criminals, and terrorists is reflective of a technocratic logic that seeks to rationalize, celebrate, or control mobilities rather than understand them in their complex social totality as a reflection of global and local inequalities and forms of population control. Urry takes a more critical stance toward (im)mobilities regimes, incorporating a concern for "ideology" into his discussion of systems and institutions. However, he concludes with a functionalist model, writing "Overall travel would need to be rationed on the basis of need, reducing the frequency for many travelers while enhancing the copresence of many others" (2007, 209). These scholars invoke a powerful desire to create rational, institutionalized, and comprehensive mobility regimes that would regulate all human movement to maximize what they see as the common good—orderliness, efficient utilization of economic resources, and protection from dangerous mobile persons and organizations.

Humans are subjects who demand tight regulation within a mobility regime to ensure that their mobility is rationalized and contained. In this calculus, some people are fetishized as fleshy materializations of economic resources (labor, migrant remittances) or dangerous vulnerabilities (crime, environmental degradation, disease, and chaos). These qualities come to exceed the humanity of excluded individuals, who are to be regulated as economic resources or threats, not as people embodying "rights." Citizens, on the other hand, have rights to mobility and to an orderly system that assures their ability to move as well as their ability to stay put. Controlling human mobility, for these scholars, is more than a question of governance; it is a moral question guided by distinctions between those who deserve mobility and those who do not, and between kinds of mobility that are sanctioned and socially healthy and those that are not. Furthermore, functionalist scholars tend to reify the state and its power to define mobility (e.g., Vannini et al. 2012), rather than developing a critical perspective on the origins, functioning, and implications of regimes of (im)mobility and their relation to power.

## Discursive Approaches to Regimes of (Im)mobility

From a functionalist perspective, the *lack* of institutions and norms that would provide for the rational and orderly governance of international human mobility is alarming, a condition requiring intervention. However, discursive approaches to the study of regimes of (im)mobility point to an accretion of technologies and tactics aimed at controlling human mobility—state surveillance, criminalization, detention, and control of mobile populations. Where functionalist analyses see the institutionalization of a global mobility regime as an important public good, discursive work focuses on the systems of power and inequality underlying regimes of mobility—how they function, reproduce themselves, or change. The notion of *regime of mobility* takes on a very different meaning here—a system of state-based discourses and technologies that reproduce the inequalities and exclusions that produce and drive mobility and immobility in the first place.

Glick Schiller and Salazar use the term "regime of mobility" to refer to "the relationships between the privileged movements of some and the codependent but stigmatized and forbidden movement, migration, and interconnection of the poor, powerless, and exploited" (2013, 188). They note that, "the term 'regime' calls attention to the role both of individual states and of changing international regulatory and surveillance administrations that effect individual mobility. At the same time, the term reflects a notion of governmentality and hegemony in which there are constant struggles to understand, query, embody, celebrate and transform categories of similarity, difference, belonging and strangeness" (Glick Schiller and Salazar 2013, 189). From this perspective, regimes of mobility emerge as an excess of unevenly applied regulation, rather than the absence of efficient regulatory institutions.

Furthermore, from a discursive perspective, regimes of (im)mobility are effective, but not because of their technocratic design so much as the power they have to frame discourses on belong, exclusion, rights, and freedom. As De Genova (2006) argues, the vulnerability of undocumented Mexican immigrants in the United States arises from the racialized spatialization of rights that results in their categorization as deportable, not their inability to navigate an otherwise efficient mobility regime. Their categorization as deportable preceded the development of the institutions and infrastructure for deporting them. Therefore, the underlying discourses are just as important, if not more important, to understand than their manifestation in technocratic systems.

Much of the discursive scholarship on regimes of (im)mobility focuses on migration. For historian Ngai (2005), state control of mobility is partial and contradictory; it creates the very subject that it wishes to eradicate—the undocumented migrant—and then naturalizes the very differential distribution of rights to movement that it creates. Calavita and Suárez-Navaz examine African immigration to Spain, framing the nation-state and citizenship as "moral and cultural projects, not entities" (2003, 103; italics in original). They find that the creation of what was to be more rational and efficient regulatory systems in Spain and the European Community recast the identities and relations between African immigrants and Andalusian peasants, creating new solidarities and antipathies, reconstituting the rights of some in relation to the abjection of others. Similarly, Inda's book on migration regimes in the United States, "is concerned with how assorted forms of knowledge, modes of calculation, kinds of governing authorities, and technical means intertwine to construct particular objects—in this case 'illegal' immigrants—as objects of government." (2006, 8). Citizens, he argues, are managed and controlled through market forces while criminals, migrants, and the poor are subject to ever more penalizing institutional control. Karakayali and Rigo call for a "regime theory of migration" that links "knowledge, discourses, and practices of migration" to understand the emergent regime that produces and constrains human mobility (2010, 132).

My own work with undocumented youth also points to the excess of technocratic regulation, not its absence or failure (Baker and Marchevsky 2014). State regulation of migrant mobility is effective, in large part, because of its spectacular, public, violent, and destructive nature as well as its arbitrary and inconsistent application. In other words, its power comes precisely from the fact that it defies efficiency and orderliness. In all these cases, inequality, both economic and in one's ability to initiate and sustain movement, are a *product* of regimes of (im)mobility, not a condition they can ameliorate. As Salazar and Smart (2011: iv) remind us, "... global-ization dynamics produce significant forms of immobility for the political regulation of persons." Along with the production of mobility, society gen-erates immobilities.

Discursive approaches to regimes of (im)mobility also diverge from func-tionalist ones in locating power in a more diverse and diffuse field of social interaction, not simply in formal institutions of governance. Ong examined at how Cambodian refugees in the United States learned to become "Amer-ican," and the interactions, institutions, and discourses that shaped their emergent identities. She writes, "instead of considering citizenship solely in terms of the state's power to give or deny citizenship, I look at social poli-cies and practices beyond the state that in myriad mundane ways suggest, define, and direct adherence to democratic, racial, and market norms of belonging" (Ong 2003, 15). From this perspective, mobility is not move-ment through neutral or unconstructed space, but what Cresswell calls "so-cially produced motion," constrained by political-economic conditions and social discourses (2006, 3). Regimes of (im)mobility emerge, in part, in and through what Salazar (2012) refers to as "imaginaries of (im)mobility," closely linked to national imaginaries and the distinct ways particular na-tions are thought to embody both sedentarism and movement.

For example, mobility is expressed in images of freedom and autonomy that form the bedrock of the "American," and other, national imaginaries (Cresswell 2006). Citizenship is thought to embody a right to movement, both juridically and in the popular imagination (Cresswell 2006). But citi-zen mobility relies on an unspoken acceptance of forms of immobility, the dark side of a regime of (im)mobility. Those who transgress the nation, by crossing borders outside of official channels or by committing material or imagined crimes against society, do not qualify for freedom of movement—they are incarcerated, institutionalized, detained, deported. Indeed, for a country so obsessed with motion, it is notable that the United States im-mobilizes more of its citizens than any other country in the world in prisons, jails, and juvenile detention centers. As Cresswell argues, mobility depends upon a "moral geography," in which rights and identities are spatialized (2006, 186).

Discursive approaches to mobilities situate capitalism and the mobility of capital as dependent upon local, socially-produced meanings, and there-fore part of broader discourses of value and rights, not simply productive of them. While popular discourse tends to envision capital as "free," that is unconstrained by the limitations of nation-state boundaries, it is highly constrained by discursive formations itself (Maurer 2003). "Free trade," for example, is anything but "free"; free trade agreements are highly constrained and technocratic documents that spell out the exact conditions under which capital and commodities can move. But in accepting the putative "freedom" of capital at the same time as we tightly limit human mobility, we subordinate human freedom to capital and the state, and this constellation of forces—capital, the nation-state, and human movement, define the global regime of (im)mobility.

In sum, discursive approaches to studying regimes of (im)mobility problematize both the nation-state and capitalism, and situate these in the broader discourses that define mobility and rights. Shamir describes a mobility regime based on "processes of closure, entrapment, and containment" (2005, 199) and the disjunctures between social distance (inequality and the danger it represents) and the physical proximity that mobility creates—"the global mobility regime is predicated, first, on the classification of individuals and groups according to principles of perceived threats and risks, and second, on an emergent technology of intervention that provides the technical/statistical means for creating elaborate forms of such social distinctions" (2005, 200). Shamir tries to understand the construction of walls and physical barriers to movement, as well as gated communities and ghettos. The nation-state is but the gated community writ large, invoking a classificatory system that distinguishes between insiders and dangerous outsiders and erecting physical and symbolic barriers to their intermingling. Peutz and De Genova point to the nation-state as a particularly important institution in defining the limits of mobility, and the logics of exclusion, in particular in the "deportation regime" in which "nation-state sovereignty and citizenship has become the conventional determinant of an individual's liberty to move into, out of, or across various national, international, and sometimes even subnational spaces" (2010, 7). In contrast, functionalist approaches tend to take the nation-state or supranational institutions for granted as the de facto infrastructure regimes of mobility, the natural and taken granted arbiter of rights.

Finally, discursive approaches to regimes of (im)mobility interrogate the meanings of freedom and constraint, and in a variety of ways. Korpela (in chapter 6) explores how "soft" infrastructures of mobility, such as passports and other documentation, may make immobility impossible for those unable to procure authorization or those who fail to achieve full social and economic incorporation in the social spaces where they seek to settle. Likewise, De Genova points out how "free" and mobile labor, produced by the evolution of capitalism, is "a distinctly circumscribed" form of freedom (2010, 56)—the "freedom" to move about and sell one's labor is produced by the lack of freedom to withhold one's labor. Migration is, then, a contradictory form of freedom, produced by the needs and effects of global capital, yet resistant to total control by capital or the state. Outside of migration studies, Lakoff and Collier characterize regimes as ethical systems with their concept of "regimes of living," or "ethical configurations formed in relationship to technology and biopolitics" (2004, 420). They write, "we should understand technological reason and biopolitics not only as sources of loss but also as sites of dynamism. Those modern forms provoke uncertain situations in which the very terms of ethical activity—the subject in the name of whom action takes place, the values that guide ethics, and the relevant forms of ethical reason and practice—are in question" (2004, 427). In this context, regimes of (im)mobility emerge as ethical configurations, which offer up specific modalities of "politics and the practice of living" (2004, 431).

As ethical and technocratic systems, regimes are inherently unstable. Regulatory regimes are vulnerable to change—moments where the technologies of regulation falter or produce unexpected outcomes—or where their legitimacy crumbles. Collective movement can also produce regime shifts. Alan Smart looks at illegal housing settlements in Hong Kong that continue to exist amid government attempts to eradicate them. He suggests that we look closely at "places and populations that succeed in resisting or subverting regulation" (2001, 40). Similarly, Nugent documents a crisis of rule in the Amazonas region of Peru in the 1950s where the coherence of complete government control suddenly seemed a chimera, even to government authorities. Nugent describes how state power is "produced" through everyday acts and performance that reaffirm boundaries of interiority and exteriority, writing, "Much can be learned about state formation by examining moments in which political rule falters or fails, for it is then that the lineaments of power and control that otherwise remain masked become visible" (2010, 681). As I discuss below, regulatory and penal tactics aimed at undocumented migrants produce clear barriers to migrant mobility, both spatial and social, but also produce spaces of nonregulation, or where regulation fails, and therefore produce the possibility of change—of forms of movement that transcend the tight regulation of a regime (see also Heyman 2014).

## Undocumented Mobility in Regimes of (Im)mobility

Agreeing that regimes of (im)mobility are discursive systems (which include technocratic arrangements), my work looks, in part, at how undocumented youth in the United States understand this regime and subvert it, in both individual and collective ways. While I cannot provide a full treatment of the subject here, it is significant to mention because undocumented youth are able to apprehend aspects of the (im)mobility regime that appear to be less visible to more privileged subjects—citizens. In part, this is because citizens are not subject to some of the more oppressive features of the (im)mobility infrastructure that, as Korpela (in chapter 6) argues, enable as well as control and prevent mobility—roadside checkpoints in immigrant neighborhoods, workplace raids, lack of access to identity documents, or limitations in access to higher education. Interestingly, undocumented youth movements critique the regime of (im)mobility—the discourses of belonging, freedom, and ethical values that they entail—not simply the technocratic features of the regime. For activists like undocumented youth leader Laura Lopez, immigration is a moral issue, not simply a question of regulatory efficiency. She writes, "immigration reform is not just about changing the regulations about who can cross what border; it's about allowing families to stay together and live in dignity" (Lopez 2012, 77). The morality of family and affect transcend the importance of orderliness, efficiency, and predictability—qualities so important in the functionalist approach to regimes of (im)mobility.

Like the United States, most countries in Europe have moved toward a more exclusionary and disciplinary migration regime, increasingly recurring to deportation and the criminalization of "irregular" migrants (Chimienti 2011; Hall 2012). In European countries where undocumented migrants have organized protest movements, they have often adopted similar tactics and claims as migrants in the United States, though these are limited in scope and locality (Chimienti 2011). Hall (2012) describes how detainees in an English immigration removal center enacted resistance to their subjection to bodily discipline, but these moments appear fragmentary and are aimed at resistance/rejection rather than transformation of the "detention regime."

Wherever it occurs, undocumented migration points to the inequality at the heart of regimes of (im)mobility (Hannam, Sheller, and Urry 2006). It emerges from exclusionary classificatory schemes (nation, race, ethnicity, class) and is enforced through violently excessive regulation that nonetheless fails to establish a seamless and coherent space free of illicit presence; being undocumented stigmatizes immigrant youth and limits their spatial and social mobility, but the mobility regime produces undocumented migration in the first place. Although undocumented youth are part of society, educated and raised alongside their papered peers, they are marked as different, as having fewer rights to mobility. At the same time, these restrictions on their mobility open up unexpected routes of movement and the possibility of strategic resistance to immobilization.

Undocumented migrants often move of necessity, yet their inability to not move, to stay home, is equaled by the limitations on their movement once they cross national boundaries. Leivestad (this volume) employs "motility" as a useful concept to understand the conceptual space between mobility and immobility; motility reflects the potential for movement and aspirations to mobility as well as the inequalities that produce different forms of mobility and immobility. In the case of undocumented migrants, motility can represent many aspirations—to stay put, to move geographically, and for upward class mobility, yet it reflects their lack of control over the economic and political conditions for mobility.

The most obvious and often first limitation to migrant mobility is the international border itself. Once inside the country of destination, undocumented immigrants face a somewhat different, though intermingled, set of institutional barriers and limitations on their mobility, including border patrol forces, and militarization of the border. In the United States, undocumented migrants grapple with citizenship requirements for driver's licenses, ID requirements for interstate travel, Immigration and Customs Enforcement (ICE) searches of buses and trains, roadside checkpoints, workplace raids, detention centers, immigration courts, citizenship requirements for college enrollment and financial aid, and the very same prison system that citizens face. This leads to what Coutin calls the "space of nonexistence," where "immobility, which is also a sign of death, prevents full social personhood" (2010, 178).

While some of these barriers to immigrant mobility may be visible, many of them are largely invisible to citizens. This is not coincidental. These systems of (im)mobility—the prison system and the detention and deportation machines—benefit from their partial invisibility, which hides from citizens the (im)mobility entailed in their citizenship. The justification for these institutions is to protect the citizen, though in both cases such claims seem unwarranted.[2] Again, Cresswell is insightful, "the kind of mobility attached to the citizen is produced through the simultaneous production of the noncitizen" (2006, 151). In Europe, official discourses differentiate between "mobile citizens" with EU citizenship and "migrants," or those from other countries (Karakayali and Rigo 2010). The inequalities associated with this system reflect regional and racialized distinctions as well as national boundaries. The (im)mobility imposed on undocumented migrants is a strong illustration of the relationship of mobility to privilege, in this case, the privilege of citizenship and the access to security and mobility that it promises to provide. While most citizens appear to believe the immigrant system protects their interests as citizens, migrants subjected to systems of (im)mobility are often able to see this regime as a carceral system meant to reproduce inequality.

In response, undocumented youth in the United States are creating organized movements that employs radical strategies of protest in order to question and transform their immobilization, both exploiting and revealing the potential fragility of regimes of (im)mobility—their contingency and incompleteness. These forms of activism openly critique the system that would make them invisible and are a rejection of the implicit morality of citizenship. Nonviolent civil disobedience including mass street protests and sit-ins, bus tours, hunger strikes, blocking buses leaving detention centers, and self-deportation have been successful at galvanizing a movement and drawing more media and public attention to the question of immigration reform. These movements are having concrete successes at the local level, pushing for state-level legislation throughout the United States that would allow undocumented college students to pay in-state tuition and receive financial aid, undocumented immigrants to receive drivers' licenses, and an end to local police forces handing immigrants who have been arrested or cited for minor infractions to ICE or impounding the cars of undocumented drivers without licenses. These movements of those who are denied movement are a bold effort to draw attention to and transform a system that was meant to remain invisible and to make its victims invisible. Regimes of (im)mobility create heterodoxy and movement precisely by seeking to contain them.

The myth of the "American Dream" is built on this idea of mobility—the geographic mobility of the immigrant coming to a nation of immigrants and the social mobility that education and employment are supposed to bring. But this myth is increasingly fragile, eroded by the militarization of the interior of the country through policing, incarceration, and the deportation system, and strained by the collapse of the housing market, the sustained high rates of unemployment, and the increasing costs of higher education. Motility is aspirational. These assumptions are mirrored in popular Latin American discourses on migration, expressed in terms like *seguir adelante* (continue *moving* forward, succeeding) and *superarse* (to overcome, excel, surpass oneself) that mirror neoliberal discourses of economic progress and freedom. Migration is supposed to lead to success, but in the case of undocumented migrants, there are conspicuous and inconspicuous barriers to their physical and social mobility. This leads to a system of legally justified inequalities (mobility inequalities) that are enforced through violent policing, racial profiling, and mass detention and deportation.

From the perspective of the undocumented, the carceral nature of the regime of (im)mobility is impossible to ignore. This is more than just an ethnographic or a political point. Methodologically, some of the mobilities literature focuses almost exclusively on mobilities at the expense of a true understanding of the interdependence of mobilities and immobilities (e.g., Urry 2007; Vannini et al. 2012). This may reflect the privileged positions of these scholars, and of academics in general, who tend to enjoy relatively high levels of sanctioned mobility. Looking at the system of mobilities from the perspective of people who face the real and grave consequences of technologies and rationalities that seek to immobilize them, one can see the complex connections between mobility, immobility, and inequality, and how these depend upon the violent reproduction of social distinctions such as nationality, race, ethnicity, and gender. It is here, at the intersection of infrastructures, social structures, and regimes of truth that a mobility regime emerges.

## Mobilities and Movement

Glick Schiller and Salazar (2013) have pointed out the liabilities of methodological nationalism, which leads us to fetishize national borders and their integrity. Such a stance would require that we see the national state not as arbiter of rights but enforcer of inequalities. Shamir aptly writes, "thus, paraphrasing Foucault, we may argue that a dense web of nonegalitarian distinctions establishing a system of highly differential movement licenses—underwrites the universal declarations of human rights that are so strongly associated with globalization" (2005, 213). Echoing Shamir, I find that regimes of (im)mobility do not exist to facilitate freedom of movement (a neoliberal fantasy); they are regimes of inequality in which the morality of the state predominates, and the logic of statecraft and capital overrides the needs or supposed "rights" of people. Undocumented migrants are, whether they have a legal status or not, members of society. Their lack of a stable legal status marks them as members of society who do not have rights to free movement, employment, political representation, protection from extreme exploitation, stability, and many other privileges that other members of their society enjoy. The regime that justifies, structures, and polices these rights and their denial cloaks inequality in claims to representative democracy—the morality of the state. In this system, some people deserve physical and economic mobility, security, and much more; some do not. The inequalities that a regime of (im)mobility secures are linked to capital accumulation and to the exercise of political power, with differential access to mobility as a marker of one's ability to produce or command capital.

Thus, the regime of (im)mobility is not simply meant to stop people from moving (i.e., entering the country) or stop them from integrating into society (Heyman 2014), it is meant to "render individuals docile and useful" (Foucault 1977, 231). Migrant mobilities, marked by the imposition of restrictive regulation, are entirely consistent with neoliberal labor regimes and their need for flexible, docile, and expendable labor (Karakayali and Rigo

2010). Not surprisingly, those with state-sanctioned rights to mobility have been rendered the most docile and useful, while subjects whose mobility is unsanctioned or punished are the first to question the logic of the regime. As Amit (2007) points out, global (im)mobility regimes are meant precisely to produce avenues of sanctioned movement for privileged travelers, whose movement is usually considered legitimate in whatever form it takes. For example, she describes how "an increasingly important segment of 'guest' workers, a status once identified with relatively disadvantaged migrants, is thus now ironically composed of middle-class Western youths who can at once and the same time be wooed as tourists and serve as a cheap, compliant, and temporary labor" (Amit 2007, 5). In other words, privileged travelers, and this includes academics, are situated to enjoy whatever benefits a global (im)mobility regime can provide and are therefore less likely to contemplate the interdependence of others' immobility and their mobility, and therefore less likely to be able to fully apprehend how regimes of (im)mobility work.

Undocumented movement sheds light on the carceral nature of regimes of (im)mobility and how they depend upon and reproduce different forms of inequality. Undocumented immigrant tactics for moving through geographic space, into particular social spaces, and achieving social mobility are common individual and family strategies for navigating regimes of (im)mobility. The organized movement for undocumented immigrant rights, which questions the discursive foundations of the (im)mobility regime that seeks to allow some people movement while denying it to others, is a collective critique of the very construction of regimes of (im)mobility. Strange is correct to point out that "the study of regimes" is "rooted in a state-centric paradigm that limits visions of a wider reality" (1982, 479). She suggests we ask other questions about regimes: "what is the net result and for whom, in terms of order and stability, wealth and efficiency, justice and freedom; and in terms of all the opposite qualities—insecurity and risk, poverty and waste, inequity and constraint?" (1982, 496). The movements of undocumented immigrants to question their exclusion and (im)mobilization and to draw attention to the carceral nature of citizenship are an important contribution to our understanding of regimes of (im)mobility, but we can only grasp that contribution if we can listen to the (im)mobilized rather than fetishize mobility. Further, paying attention to migrant resistance to and negotiation within regimes of (im)mobility reframes our understanding of migrant consciousness, decentering the familiar dichotomization of migrants as criminals or victims (Karakayali and Rigo 2010), and allowing us to understand illicit migrants not as the abject but at the very center of regimes of (im)mobility.

Functionalist perspectives on regimes of (im)mobility exist alongside of discursive ones, rather than in conversation with them. Seeing regimes as discursive formations—constellations of technologies, infrastructure, and discourses of meaning—allows scholars of mobilities to develop a more critical, and I suggest, comprehensive, understanding of regimes of (im)mobility as more than simply arrangements between states for the regulation of human movement; they are moral systems that depend upon and seek to reproduce inequality as they define legitimacy and illegitimacy. I suggest that as mobilities studies develops, scholars continue to employ the concept of regime of (im)mobility as a way to highlight the discursive nature of technologies and systems of movement and their dependence upon the simultaneous production of immobility and inequality.

**Beth Baker** is Professor of Anthropology at the California State University, Los Angeles. She is author of *Salvadoran Migration to Southern California: Redefining El Hermano Lejano* as well as many articles on migration and transnationalism. Her current research is focused on immigration detention and deportation and the impacts of deportation on local communities. In addition, she is reexamining citizenship as a system for the structuring of inequalities, like race, gender, and other distinguishing social markers.

## NOTES

1. The majority of inmates in the US prison system are nonviolent offenders who do not pose a threat to society, and the majority of detained immigrants also do not have a criminal record, although most people in the United States have been led to believe that immigrant detentions and deportations have targeted criminal immigrants.
2. In anthropology, the concept of *regime of truth* is often applied in studies of science and technology, though usually outside of a mobilities perspective.

## REFERENCES

Amit, Vered. 2007. "Structures and Dispositions of Travel and Movement." In *Going First Class? New Approaches to Privileged Travel and Movement,* edited by Vered Amit, 1–14. New York: Berghahn Books.

Baker, Beth, and Alejandra Marchevsky. 2014. "Freedom's Movement: Spatial Regulation of Immigrants and Resistance by Undocumented Youth." Paper presented at the Annual Meeting of the Latin American Studies Association, Chicago, IL, 21–24 May.

Calavita, Kitty, and Liliana Suárez-Navaz. 2003. "Spanish Immigration Law and the Construction of Difference: Citizens and 'Illegals' on Europe's Southern Border." In *Globalization Under Construction: Governmentality, Law, and Identity*, edited by Richard Warren Perry and Bill Maurer, 99–127. Minneapolis: University of Minnesota Press.

Chimienti, Milena. 2011. "Mobilization of Irregular Migrants in Europe: A Comparative Analysis." *Ethnic and Racial Studies* 34(8): 1338–56.

Coutin, Susan Bibler. 2010 "Confined Within: National Territories as Zones of Confinement." *Political Geography* 29(4): 200–208.

Cresswell, Tim. 2006. *On the Move: Mobility in the Modern Western World*. New York: Routledge.

De Genova, Nicholas. 2006. "The Legal Production of Mexican/Migrant 'Illegality.'" In *Latinos and Citizenship: The Dilemma of Belonging*, edited by Suzanne Oboler, 61–90. New York: Palmgrave.

———. 2010. "The Deportation Regime: Sovereignty, Space, and the Freedom of Movement." In *The Deportation Regime: Sovereignty, Space, and the Freedom of Movement*, edited by Nicholas De Genova and Nathalie Peutz, 33–65. Durham, NC: Duke University Press.

Foucault, Michel. 1977. *Discipline and Punish: The Birth of the Prison System*. Translated by Alan Sheridan. New York: Vintage Books.

———. 1990. *The History of Sexuality: An Introduction*. Vol. 1. New York: Vintage Books. First published 1978 by Lane.

———. 1991. "Governmentality." In *The Foucault Effect: Studies in Governmentality*, edited by Graham Burchell, Colin Gordon, and Peter Miller, 87–104. Chicago: University of Chicago Press.

Glick Schiller, Nina, and Noel B Salazar. 2013. "Regimes of Mobility across the Globe." *Journal of Ethnic and Migration Studies* 39(2): 183–200.

Hall, Alexandra. 2012. *Border Watch: Cultures of Immigration, Detention, and Control*. London: Pluto Press.

Hannam, Kevin, Mimi Sheller, and John Urry. 2006. "Mobilities, Immobilities, and Moorings." *Mobilities* 1(1): 1–22.

Heyman, Josiah. 2014. "'Illegality' and the U.S.-Mexico Border: How It Is Produced and Resisted." In *Constructing Immigrant 'Illegality': Critiques, Experiences, and Responses*, edited by Cecilia Menjiver and Daniel Kanstroom, 111–135. New York: Cambridge University Press.

Hollifield, James. 2011. "Migration and Global Mobility of Labor: A Public Goods Approach." In *Global Mobility Regimes*, edited by Rey Koslowski, 219–40. New York: Palgrave MacMillan.

Inda, Jonathan Xavier. 2006. *Targeting Immigrants: Government, Technology, and Ethics*. Malden, MA: Blackwell.

Karakayali, Serhat, and Enrica Rigo. 2010. "Mapping the European Space of Circulation." In *The Deportation Regime: Sovereignty, Space, and the Freedom of Movement*, edited by Nicholas De Genova and Nathalie Peutz, 123–44. Durham, NC: Duke University Press.

Koslowski, Rey. 2011. "The International Travel Regime." In *Global Mobility Regimes,* edited by Rey Koslowski, 51–72. New York: Palgrave MacMillan.

Krasner, Stephen. 1982. "Structural Causes and Regime Consequences: Regimes as Intervening Variables." *International Organization* 36(2): 185–205.

Lakoff, Andrew, and Stephen Collier. 2004. "Ethics and the Anthropology of Modern Reason." *Anthropological Theory* 4(4): 419–34.

Lopez, Laura. 2011. "Civil Disobedience in Washington, D.C." In *Undocumented and Unafraid: Tam Tran, Cinthya Felix, and the Immigrant Youth Movement,* edited by Kent Wong, Janna Shadduck-Hernandez, Fabiola Inzunza, Julie Monroe, Victor Narro, and Abel Valenzuela Jr., 76–77. Los Angeles: UCLA Center for Labor Research and Education.

Martin, Susan. 2011. "International Cooperation on Migration and the UN System." In *Global Mobility Regimes,* edited by Rey Koslowski, 29–50. New York: Palgrave MacMillan.

Maurer, Bill. 2003. "International Political Economy as a Cultural Practice: The Metaphysics of Capital Mobility." In *Globalization Under Construction: Governmentality, Law, and Identity,* edited by Richard Warren Perry and Bill Maurer, 71–97. Minneapolis: University of Minnesota Press.

*Merriam Webster Dictionary.* 2014. "Regime." Available at http://www.merriam-webster .com/dictionary/regime.

Ngai, May. 2005. *Impossible Subjects: Illegal Aliens and the Making of Modern America.* Princeton, NJ: Princeton University Press.

Nugent, David. 2010. "States, Secrecy, Subversives: APRA and Political Fantasy in the Mid-20th-Century Peru." *American Ethnologist* 37(4): 681–702.

Ong, Aihwa. 2003. *Buddha Is Hiding: Refugees, Citizenship, and the New America.* Los Angeles: University of California Press.

Peutz, Nathalie, and Nicholas De Genova. 2010. "Introduction." In *The Deportation Regime: Sovereignty, Space, and the Freedom of Movement,* edited Nicholas De Genova and Nathalie Peutz, 1–29. Durham, NC: Duke University Press.

Rudolph, Cristopher. 2011. "Prospects and Prescriptions for a Global Mobility Regime: Five Lessons from the WTO." In *Global Mobility Regimes,* edited by Rey Koslowski, 181–200. New York: Palgrave MacMillan.

Salazar, Noel B. 2012. "Imaginative Technologies of (Im)mobility at the 'End of the World.'" In *Technologies of Mobility in the Americas,* edited by Phillip Vannini, Lucy Budd, Ole Jensen, Christian Fisker, and Paola Jiron, 237–54. New York: Peter Lange Publishers.

Salazar, Noel B, and Alan Smart. 2011. "Anthropological Takes on (Im)Mobility." *Identities: Global Studies in Culture and Power* 18(6): i–ix.

Shamir, Ronen. 2005. "Without Borders? Notes on Globalization as a Mobility Regime." *Sociological Theory* 23(2): 197–217.

Smart, Alan. 2001. "Unruly Places: Urban Governance and the Persistence of Illegality in Hong Kong's Urban Squatter Areas." *American Anthropologist* 103(1): 30–44.

Strange, Susan. 1982. "Cave! Hic Dragones: A Critique of Regime Analysis." *International Organization* 36(2): 479–96.

Urry, John. 2007. *Mobilities*. Malden, MA: Polity Press.

Vannini, Phillip, Lucy Budd, Ole Jensen, Christian Fisker, and Paola Jiron, eds. 2012. *Technologies of Mobility in the Americas*. New York: Peter Lange.

Zimmer, Ben. 2009. "Mailbag Friday: 'Regime' or 'Regimen'?" Available at http://www .visualthesaurus.com/cm/wordroutes/mailbag-friday-regime-or-regimen.

# Multiple Mobilities and the Ethnographic Engagement of Keywords

*Brenda Chalfin*

The collective return to Raymond Williams's *Keywords: A Vocabulary for Culture and Society* demonstrated by this volume is not for lack of originality. The reworking of Williams's approach four decades after its inauguration is both a test of relevance in a new cultural and intellectual era and an indication of uncharted potentials within a well-known mode of epistemological stock-taking. As Salazar notes in his introduction, well-acknowledged by Williams, *keywords* by definition call for updating given that they constantly accumulate new meanings and are situated within a constellation of concepts and events marking historical turns and preoccupations.

Among other leading terms of the current social-scientific lexicon, the exploration of mobility through its conceptual correlates and codependents is a timely effort to map a multifaceted intellectual commons. If mobility is the paradigmatic signifier of the twenty-first century, then it is crucial to take stock of its array of meanings, uses, limits, and interlocutors before it becomes so normalized and naturalized that it is no longer visible or morphs into another experiential and explanatory order altogether. The need for a self-administered dose of historical reflection, however, is insufficient explanation of the contents of this book. Moving from the retrospective to the prospective, the entries contained within go beyond agenda tracking to agenda setting. Each chapter expands upon William's method to chart a course for further exploration, tracing potential paths for sustained comparative inquiry as well as theory-building.

They do so through a distinctively anthropological engagement with keywords that does not stop at words but delves headlong into practice. Revealed via the methods, findings, and subjects of ethnographic inquiry, mobility occupies a much larger conceptual space than is at first evident. In turn, the sort of resonances and resemblances of interest to Williams emerge outside the realm of literature and text to instead take form in empirical example and lived experience. Anthropology, in short, "does" keywords differently, repurposing Williams's etymological approach through a sustained encounter with ethnographic evidence. The outcome redeems anthropology in its own right and demonstrates the distinct value of anthropological practice to seeding conversations across social science and humanities disciplines. Namely, the complexity, diversity, and depth of ethnographic example brings something distinct to the table, destabilizing consensus and changing the course of consideration, ultimately enriching interdisciplinary exchange.

These reconsiderations also entail a remapping of anthropology, by which I mean not only the spatial orientations of anthropological analysis, but a broader consideration of the causes and effects of anthropology's baseline territorial assumptions, something analysts have come to call "methodological nationalism" (Salazar and Glick Schiller 2014). Each entry in this volume reminds us that making ethnographic sense of the current world order involves more than flipping a paradigmatic switch from the study of boundaries to flows, enclosures to networks, localities to circuitries. Rather, it is about contending with a complex mix of emergent and residual forms, some of which are intensely policed and territorialized to restrict mobility at the same time human survival in the current moment requires flexibility, dis- and relocation, and insertion in multiple registers of movement. It is essential to maintain this disciplinary double consciousness and avoid treating mobility as the new, truer, point of entry compared with the colonizing lens of anthropological conventions of analytical emplacement. The larger forces driving such analytic emplacements have very real effects. What is more, if classic conflations of persons and place were the implicit by-product of twentieth-century conventions of state-building (see Gupta and Ferguson 1997), we cannot forget that twenty-first century preoccupation with mobility has much to do with the ascendance of global markets relations, which depend on the movement of goods, capital, labor, livelihoods, media, and raw materials (Appadurai 1990). The outcome of these historical shifts is never an unfettered transition but always partial and unfinished forms.

With this in mind, how does anthropology speak to, with, and through understandings of mobility? How does mobility speak to and through anthropology? What does this mean for a broader transdisciplinary conversation in search of common reference points but not always shared meanings? What are the implications for conventions and new directions of anthropological method? When considering the entries on infrastructure, gender, regime, and immobility, these conjunctures of the ethnographic, the etymological, the disciplinary, and the historical, around definitions and directions of mobility and mobility studies play out in different ways.

Korpela's investigation of mobility through the keyword *infrastructure* demonstrates the value of systematically attending to ethnographic complexities for gaining insight into the nexus of infrastructure and motion. Moving beyond the formal, official, and prescriptive, Korpela uses ethnographic examples to reveal how individuals as well as institutions experience and improvise upon lived contradictions and ambiguities. Further, her comprehensive evaluation of what at first glance appears to be one-off cases and idiosyncrasies captures trends that are otherwise difficult to recognize.

For Korpela, the most pressing infrastructures are those related to passage between state systems. Korpela begins with a standard distinction between hard and soft infrastructures, yet soon turns to the ethnographic record to trouble any categorical division between them. Considering current conditions of border crossing, she reveals the how movement across the hard divide of the border landscape is ever more dependent on soft infrastructure of passports, permits, documents, and increasingly, the critical infrastructures of biometry: a form of hard and soft infrastructure combined. Korpela's detailed inventory of infrastructures of mobility makes it clear that mobility today is infrastructure intensive, involving ongoing inventions and interventions to coordinate and suture their intersections and gaps.

Whether hard or soft, the ethnographic record demonstrates that infrastructures of mobility have edges, and edges engender ever larger infrastructures to manage them. Korpela interrogation of mobility through the ethnographic optic of infrastructure ultimately moves infrastructure studies beyond older definitional dichotomies of hard and soft, visible and invisible, to an altogether different consideration of the question of infrastructure's own mobility in sync with the movements of persons and goods along with the many other objects and agents that now traverse state boundaries.

While Korpela's probing of mobility puts the anthropology of infrastructure in a new light, Elliot's anthropologically informed consideration of gender as both form and process, schema and practice, brings the investigation of mobility back to the first principles of sociocultural inquiry. Treating gender as an actively embodied state, Elliot alerts us to the two defining features of movement: the figure of movement and the ground of movement. Taking gender seriously thus reveals the deep encoding of the most basic features of our social world. With space fundamentally gendered, mobility, we realize, is never unmarked or free-flowing. Yet, if with Elliot, we consider the locomoting body in space an agentive force, a gender perspective on mobility alerts us to the transformative possibilities of motion.

Spanning the gamut of the anthropological corpus, from phenomenological studies of bodily routines to works on the political economy of transnational trafficking, Elliot uses ethnographically inspired theorizations of gender to reconceive the gender/mobility nexus. Taking a cue from Strathern's ground breaking work, she notes that beyond the usual consideration of gender relations in the context of mobility, one needs to investigate the manner and extent mobility affects the genders related and hence the very nature of personhood and agency. Conceived in relational terms, as Elliot sees it, careful attention to gender can open up conceptions of mobility at the same time the consideration of mobility helps us to unseat preconceived understandings of gender.

The insights derived from the anthropological examination of the keywords of mobility also come from putting the ethnographic perspective in a cross-disciplinary dialog, juxtaposing the anthropological with other disciplinary approaches to take stock of their impasses, overlap and interchange. This is the strategy employed by Baker in her discussion of mobility via the keyword *regimes*.

Juxtaposing the perspectives of anthropology, sociology, political science, and geography, Baker traces how these different approaches reflect on one another as a way to address the blind spots and assumptions of any single intellectual or political position. Baker's most productive exchange involves the perspectives of political science. Challenging older anthropological notions of boundedness as well as the more recent infatuation with concepts of unfettered flow, Baker draws on political science to highlight the highly structured, rule-, and law-bound conditions of mobility and immobility in the contemporary moment. Yet, she goes on to point out that political science tends to treat mobility as a global public good and favors the codification of the terms of movement on a global scale. Countering the abstracted idealism of this proposition with a dose of ethnographic realism, Baker suggests that a political science perspective, by focusing on mobility regimes as guarantors of the "freedom to move," overlooks the right to "freedom from" the predations and unevenness of mobility regimes in practice.

Privileging the experience-near ethnographic perspective, Baker looks to the operational nuances of legal mandates in order to understand how they are lived. She does this not through a broad-based ethnographic survey like Korpela and Elliot, but through the close-reading of a select subject: the predicament and insights of undocumented youth. These are individuals tremendously constrained by the regulatory regimes of mobility but also extremely adept navigators of their excesses and interstices. Theorizing from within by recognizing the ethnographic subject to be actor, object, and theorist, Baker's poses undocumented youth as example and analytic authority. Deeply mired in the migration apparatus, they are uniquely positioned to know its nuances, structural interconnections, and contradictions. From this multiplex vantage point, Baker derives the terms of a broader conceptual and sociopolitical category she labels "regimes of (im)mobility."

The keyword of *immobility* and its correlate, *(im)mobility,* are systematically addressed in the entry of Kahn. A form of permanent transition or arrested flow, Khan casts (im)mobility in historical terms. (Im)mobility as Kahn sees it is symptomatic of the late-modern condition: a kind of "post-mobility" that follows upon the unfulfilled promises of advanced modernity. Built upon the false hope of unimpeded flow, it is different from both the immobilities and emplacements of other eras and the multilocalities of transnationalism. Khan calls (im)mobility "politically enforced liminality." Using a Bergsonian construct of relational mobility and immobility, it occupies what might be described as a third space, increasingly characteristic of late-modern life.

To convey this construct, Khan moves beyond broad historical claims and speaks to more fine-grained notions of temporality, and temporality in conjunction with spatiality. The time of (im)mobility is marked by an "endless present" merging aspiration and resignation. Illustrated in Khan's own research on Afghan men working and residing in the United Kingdom, it is a mode of being on the cusp of motion and stasis. Often imposed, it can also be deliberately routinized, as when Khan's migrant subjects claim a time and place to rest amid their thwarted mobilities.

Khan's consideration of (im)mobility interweaves a deep-reading of affect with the frame of political economy. Like her coauthors in the volume, the cultivation of such a vantage point raises questions about disciplinary boundaries and borrowings. Does anthropology stand alone as the master of the "ethnographic approach," or is it already implicitly tied to conversation with other disciplines? If so, where does our work stop and theirs begin? In her quest to understand the affective dimensions of human experience, Khan is pushing the limits of anthropology. Mining other fields for ethnographic insight, she reads the ethnographic record, including Turner's classic work, against the grain for glimpses of human psyche. In this regard, in addition to philosophy and psychology, Khan gains important traction and inspiration from Williams's much rendered notion, "structures of feeling." Coming full circle, in a departure from Williams's original work in terms of era as well as evidence, she probes diverse manifestations of structure and feeling as a definitive diagnostic of (im)mobility—her own key term. From here, a distinctive research agenda takes shape, for if (im)mobility produces a distinct affective register, as Khan suggests, our next move is to consider how the manifest affects are linked to political, economic, and historical conditions.

Working through manifold styles, uses, and examples of ethnography, each of these entries raise considerable insight as well as questions about the nature of what we have come to call "mobility" in all its variety and dynamism. These works demonstrate the very timeliness (see Rabinow and Marcus 2008) of this inquiry. They are certainly timely in their urgency and systematic analysis of the current era, when mobility looms as force and specter, at once promise and imperative. They are also timely in their innovation. For each paper offers a highly original interpretive stance, working through the vagaries of mobility through the concise analytic of their chosen keyword. Beyond such synthesis, each offers a well-developed agenda for further research, whether mobile infrastructures, mobility-made genders, or the types, affects, and resistances to (im)mobility.

In the course of unpacking the meanings and modalities of mobility, these works reframe Williams's method, and with it, endow ethnography with new momentum. Taken together, the essays utilize the many faces of the ethnographic: from its encyclopedic comparative possibilities, classic works, and first-principles, to intensive person-centered case studies, along with ethnography beyond the discipline of anthropology. In these statements, we see ethnography as a powerful record for bearing witness to the contemporary condition; ethnography as a means of inspiring cross-disciplinary borrowing, debate, and self-reflection; and ethnography as a mode of critically theorizing complex social processes and problems.

The insights and injunctions that follow from these musings and investigations are several. There is the baseline recognition that a move to supplant wholesale older paradigms of localism and boundedness with newer notions of motion and flow is both historically mistaken and analytically untenable. For those older paradigms have very real and enduring effects. Moreover, as interpreters of the present or the past, we must be wary of pure forms (pace Latour 1993). Likewise, complicating frameworks that overlook lived historical conditions, processes of mobility are always full of friction and require effort to organize, sustain, and institute. Human mobility is no more "natural" than human emplacement. Sustaining this insight is the enduring relevance of ethnographic engagement and the quest for intersubjective copresence even amid flow. Thus, the challenge for anthropology is to maintain an analytic and phenomenological intimacy and immediacy despite the increasingly scale and spatiotemporal fluidity of the very conditions and experiences of mobility we seek to study. A rejoinder to the late-twentieth century move toward multilocalism (Marcus and Fischer 1986), pursuing this ideal requires attention to the contradictions and intersections of multiple regimes of mobility. Far from abstract systems, these shifts and contentions are most vividly engaged and instantiated in the midst of human lives.

**Brenda Chalfin** is professor of anthropology at the University of Florida. Her areas of expertise are political and economic anthropology with a focus on West Africa, state-processes, maritime mobilities, and the governance of global commodity flows. She is the author of two monographs, *Shea Butter Republic: State Power, Global Markets and the Making of an Indigenous Commodity* (Routledge, 2004) and *Neoliberal Frontiers: An Ethnography of Sovereignty in West Africa* (University of Chicago, 2010). She is currently engaged in two major research projects: one on infrastructure and public life in Ghana's city of Tema and another on off-shore governance and oil prospecting in the Gulf of Guinea.

### REFERENCES

Appadurai, Arjun. 1990. "Disjuncture and Difference in the Global Cultural Economy." *Theory, Culture & Society* 7(2): 295–310.

Gupta, Akhil, and James Ferguson. 1997. *Anthropological Locations: Boundaries and Grounds of a Field Science.* Berkeley: University of California Press.

Latour, Bruno. 1993. *We Have Never Been Modern.* Translated by Catherine Porter. Cambridge, MA: Harvard University Press.

Marcus, George, and Michael Fischer. 1986. *Anthropology as Cultural Critique: An Experimental Moment in the Human Sciences.* Chicago: University of Chicago Press.

Rabinow, Paul, and George Marcus. 2008. *Designs for an Anthropology of the Contemporary.* Durham, NC: Duke University Press.

Salazar, Noel B, and Nina Glick Schiller, eds. 2014. *Regimes of Mobility: Imaginaries and Relationalities of Power.* London: Routledge.

# Emergent and Potential Mobilities

*Ellen R. Judd*

It has been a pleasure to read the chapters that form this superb collection and to add an afterword on issues they address in contemporary anthropology. The depth and breadth of these essays underline the importance of mobility as a perduring feature of human life, and one with distinctive importance in the present. One is especially struck by the wisdom of the editors in eschewing the demarcation of a separate terrain or vocabulary for mobility and instead firmly situating mobility—together with immobility and motility—as intrinsic to the discipline as a whole.

The choice of *keywords* as an organizing heuristic has proven exceptionally productive. Language and significant words or phrases selected from some other departure point might also have proven very useful, but keywords brought with it a methodology and record of engagement with anthropology that has been unusually illuminating. Keywords, associated since its threshold use by Raymond Williams in the first edition of his book of the same title, *Keywords: A Vocabulary of Culture and Society* (1976), has provided a point of entry to a literary and linguistic toolkit drawing upon social formalism and honed by Williams in close formal analysis of English literary and dramatic texts. This analysis was consistently combined with equally exacting situating of the written or performed work in its social and cultural milieu, always viewed as historical or processual. This approach was early recognized as converging in some respects with anthropology and with ethnography. The points of convergence are multiple, and the essays here are marked by a substantial recognition of this in their methodological and ethnographic components.

This is most explicit in the treatment of each keyword itself, and the authors have been consistent and rigorous in this undertaking. Among the chapters which I have the privilege of addressing at greater length—those on motility, capital, cosmopolitanism, and freedom—Acharya's contribution is especially extensive in this regard, tracing the meanings and contexts of cosmopolitanism in a historical and cross-cultural exploration of the ambiguities that enrich the term through time and space. The result is a historically deep account of diverse and shifting meanings, with fruitful attention to vernacular cosmopolitanisms and their decentering trajectories in a field of contested constructions of mobility. This methodology furthers debate by generating contrasting and processual clarity on ambiguous and contested usages of the same (and cognate) keyword(s).

This is further evident in Dean's chapter on freedom, where the weight of this politically charged term makes its excavation exceptionally challenging. Parallel in part with Acharya's attention to vernacular cosmopolitanisms, he has taken inspiration from a nonromanticized engagement with understandings of freedom that are held beyond Occidental self-representations. These emerge in his chapter from extensive Amazonian ethnography with indigenous peoples conducted by himself and by others. He has concurrently also engaged with Occidental interpretations of this freedom represented as sovereignty, both as intrinsic to Bataille's imagining of the primeval human condition, and as the localized practice of peoples who are confronting the disruption of massive population movements and the free movement of capital (freer than the movement of people). Words, textual reference, and ethnography are deployed to sharpen contrasting threads and potentially intrinsic connections between sovereignty as human nonalienation and as destructive excess. Possibilities of autonomy and fulfillment coexist in his chapter with prospects of violence and devastation.

Linked with the explication of these keywords as language is their situating in social and cultural process. This is addressed in relation to modern and contemporary structures in the chapters by Baker on regime, Korpela on infrastructure, Khan on immobility, and Jayaram on the inescapable concept of capital. In addition to situating capital as a term, Jayaram makes a number of observations that resonate with the volume as a whole. He rejects the concept of a particular "mobility capital" and instead underlines the intrinsic character of capital as able to exist and grow only through the process of circulation by which capital is converted into a distinctive commodity (labor power) that is deployed to create surplus value. The labor power may itself be significantly in spatial movement, as in times of massive labor migration, although this is not necessarily the case. Jayaram gives particular attention to the issue of exchange in its mobile dimensions, whether spatial or conceptual. Although exchange does happen without capital as well as with it, the interesting issue and one given attention by Dean and Leivestad as well, is Bourdieu's argument (1977) that various forms of capital—most obviously economic capital and symbolic capital—are intrinsically and reversibly exchangeable. This raises provocative questions about the reach of capital and of capital-based exchangeability.

As these chapters indicate, questions about the meaning of keywords extend beyond language, narrowly construed, and require connecting with a world that is arguably outside text. This raises issues about the material and the ideal that have been the subject of recurrent explorations and debates and that have long figured prominently in American anthropology. To limit this discussion to a relatively recent period, one need only consider the attention given to ethnography conceptualized as a practice of writing culture and as both poetics and politics. This turn, which has been highly influential since the early 1980s, drew heavily upon social formalism as exemplified by Bakhtin and Williams, both in conceptualization and in analytical execution. As it unfolded within American anthropology, the direction was primarily oriented toward issues of form, genre, and voice, as marked by the School of American Research seminar volume, *Writing Culture* (Clifford and Marcus 1986). The School of American Research seminar that followed a decade later to assess and respond to that collection resulted in a quite different volume, *Recapturing Anthropology* (Fox 1991), that argued for the historicizing of ethnography and for situating it in the present. This approach is in deep continuity with Williams's historical approach to cultural analysis as realized in his series of studies of the underlying structures of cultural change (Williams 1961) and his later expansions of the concepts and methodology involved in this work (Williams 1977, 1980). While not rejecting the political in other senses, his scholarly legacy in this respect is in the concepts and example he has provided for analyzing meaning, expression, structure, and process in a range of cultural studies akin to critical ethnography. The convergence is evident throughout this volume in each of the ethnographic components.

A current revisiting and deepening of this cluster of concerns can be found now in the ontological turn and in its critiques. This is a matter of mining philosophy rather than literature for new insights into meaningfulness and possibilities in the human condition. As with the other issues raised, it is not specific or limited to mobility, but the connections and relevance are very clear. In one formulation concurrent with this collection, ontology in anthropology is the "comparative ethnographically-grounded transcendental deduction of Being ... as that which differs from itself ... —being-as-other as immanent to being-as-such" (Holbraad, Pedersen, and Viveiros de Castro 2013, 10). It is immediately apparent that spatial mobility entails changes to oneself and changes in relations with others, as does mobility in any other sense. At the same time, this is not unique to mobility, although mobility implies specific dimensions of change within the larger encounter with otherness that is pervasive in all of anthropology.

The ontological turn is also committed to the priority of potentiality over actuality in the human condition, such that we can always become (or not) different from ourselves (and necessarily others) at every moment, refiguring the more familiar ontology in which actuality has priority over potentiality. Potentiality appears in this frame as a commitment to the viability of being otherwise oneself and to sustaining the potentiality of others by not precluding anything for others in the terms of (imputed) actuality (Agamben 1998; Holbraad, Pedersen, and Viveiros de Castro 2013; Povinelli 2011, 2012; Rethmann 2013). This is a departure from the mainstream of ethnography characterized by modernist methodologies for evidence-based investigations that prioritize actuality, including actuality envisaged or yet to be (such as Bourdieu et al. 1993, Fassin 2012). Such an ethnography may insist on the importance of evidence and actuality in critique of the ontological turn (Fassin 2013, 2014).

The most sustained engagement here with this debate is in Leivestad's chapter on motility, a recent term referring to capacities to move. This term has not yet made its way into everyday usage, unlike the other keywords examined in this volume, but has rapidly become important in anthropological and interdisciplinary studies. In the first instance, it pushes forward the issues raised by contrasting mobilities and immobilities and thereby adds a more explicit perspective on possibility. In so doing, it opens the door toward theoretical engagement with the ontological turn and its prioritization of potentiality. Leivestad further notes the gendered nature of motility, as of all features of the human condition, placing this also within the broad frame of potentiality and linking her paper with Elliot's keyword chapter on gender that so productively expands on this dimension.

Among the many ways in which Leivestad demonstrates that motility is a concept "good to think with" is the manner in which she draws upon ethnography and brings materiality into view. Here she evokes class difference and related divisions particularly addressed in this volume through the concepts of capital, infrastructure, regime, and sovereignty. This constructively brings materiality and its constraints and conditions into the discourse of motility and potentiality. This is not a new departure, as the ontological turn has not failed to observe potentiality stretched to its most extreme limits, but it is essential to the project of placing mobility, immobility, and motility within this framework. This step provides essential linkages between key elements of the field and the issues with which it is presently occupied.

If we attempt to project where discovery and discourse might lead, we could usefully consider Williams's (1977) methodological observations on the emergent. While he wrote of this in epochal terms together with dominant and residual cultural features, there are some readily transferable elements of his method to a smaller time scale and more accessible historical frame. One of these elements is the attention given to selective processes of domination, exclusion, and conflict. These processes are evident in current (im)mobilities, and the essays in this collection reflect those processes, although the attention given is in some cases muted. One senses and respects a tone of troubled scholarly care here, consistent with Williams's cautions about the challenge of identifying the complex and uneven alignments of new cultural elements, and the difficulty of recognition even when evidence is abundant.

The times we live in are turbulent, and the movement (or not) of people and populations is part of the turbulence. At least since 1989, we have also been in a time of heightened recognition of the uncertainty of our knowledge of the world, whether we remain committed to or question Enlightenment models of knowing the world as a goal. Acharya's chapter is a strong reminder of the decentering of movement and of wider social and cultural processes. This entails multiple contesting and conflicting directions and conceptualizing how to think this fragmentation may be one of the scholastic (Bourdieu 1998) research issues most clearly confronting anthropology at present.

A further resource for this may be found in the key concept of "structure of feeling" (Williams 1977), also valuably identified by Khan in her chapter on immobility. This is especially challenging, as it requires that we attempt to reach beyond the structurally formed and empirically observable to discern social consciousness while it remains on either side of a process of becoming. This modernist or, as Williams (1980) later termed it, cultural materialist approach, has very much in common with directions as varied as practice theory's emphasis on practical strategies and the ontological turn's move toward potentiality. It may affirm the depth of a recent methodological convergence and add subtlety to the exploration.

Demanding and partially new structures of feeling may be heard in Dean's excavation of the darker dimensions of freedom, a space where he evokes counterpossibilities of mutuality and responsibility. This might seem unduly optimistic, were the suggestion not emerging from the dangers lurking in a sovereignty found in both mobility and immobility on the frontier of capitalist expansion. But practices of mutuality and responsibility are not new—they can be found throughout ethnographic and literary accounts of kinship, religion, economy, and polity. They provide the lived human responses to a vision of "the joys, eternally denied to social man, of a world in which one might *keep to oneself*" (Lévi-Strauss 1969, 497, emphasis in the original). These practices are widely realized in the daily demands through which people fashion lives together and strive to make them as secure and meaningful as they can. Recently, we hear echoes of these in the discourse on hospitality (Lynch et al. 2011) as it explores modes of sociality through which strangers may be transmuted into neighbors. An alert may occasionally flash in times of danger—"Each of us is responsible for everything and to every human being" (Dostoyevsky quoted in de Beauvoir 1964)—but we are not accustomed to hearing mutuality and responsibility in the manifestos and ringing declarations of our time. If a new structure of feeling is to be detected, it may be where embedded, implicit strategies and practices of mutuality and responsibility whisper and stir to emerge more openly in our social consciousness—actual and potential.

**Ellen R. Judd** is an anthropologist who is a distinguished professor at the University of Manitoba and a senior visiting fellow at the London School of Economics. She is an ethnographer of contemporary China and the author of *Gender and Power in Rural North China* and the *Chinese Women's Movement between State and Market*. Her recent ethnography has examined mobilities and immobilities in rural west and urban coastal China, especially in the context of health and health care. She is presently working on comparative questions of exclusion/inclusion, cooperation, and mutuality.

## REFERENCES

Agamben, Giorgio. 1998. *Homo Sacer: Sovereign Power and Bare Life.* Stanford, CA: Stanford University Press.

Bourdieu, Pierre. 1977. *Outline of a Theory of Practice.* Cambridge: Cambridge University Press.

———. 1998. *Practical Reason.* Stanford, CA: Stanford University Press.

Bourdieu, Pierre et al. 1993. *The Weight of the World: Social Suffering in Contemporary Society.* Stanford CA: Stanford University Press.

Clifford, James, and George E Marcus, eds. 1986. *Writing Culture: The Poetics and Politics of Ethnography.* Berkeley CA: University of California Press.

de Beauvoir, Simone. 1964. *The Blood of Others.* Harmondsworth: Penguin Books.

Fassin, Didier. 2012. *Humanitarian Reason: A Moral Economy of the Present.* Berkeley CA: University of California Press.

———. 2013. "AE Interviews Didier Fassin." *American Ethnologist.* Available at http://ameri canethnologist.org/2014/ae-interviews-didier-fassin-institute-for-advanced-study-princeton-nj/

———. 2014. "The Uncertain Promise of Ethnography." Keynote address at the Annual Meeting of the Canadian Anthropology Society, Toronto ON.

Fox, Richard G. 1991. *Recapturing Anthropology: Working in the Present.* Santa Fe, NM: School of American Research Press.

Holbraad, Martin, Morten Axel Pedersen, and Eduardo Viveiros de Castro. 2013. "The Politics of Ontology: Anthropological Positions." Position paper for roundtable discussion at the 112th AAA Meeting, Chicago, IL.

Lévi-Strauss, Claude. 1969. *The Elementary Structures of Kinship.* Boston MA: Beacon Press.

Lynch, Paul, Jennie Germann Molz, Alison McIntoch, Peter Lugusi, and Conrad Lashley. 2011. "Theorizing Hospitality." *Hospitality and Society* 1(1): 3–24.

Povinelli, Elizabeth A. 2011. *Economies of Abandonment: Social Belonging and Endurance in Late Capitalism.* Durham, NC: Duke University Press.

———. 2012. "The Will to Be Otherwise/The Effort of Endurance." *The South Atlantic Quarterly* 111(3): 453–75.

Rethmann, Petra. 2013. "Imagining Political Possibility in an Age of Cynical Reason." *Reviews in Anthropology* 42: 227–42.

Williams, Raymond. 1961. *The Long Revolution,* rev. ed. New York: Harper and Row.

———. 1976. *Keywords: A Vocabulary of Culture and Society.* London: Fontana.

———. 1977. *Marxism and Literature.* Oxford: Oxford University Press.

———. 1980. *Problems in Materialism and Culture.* London: Verso Editions.

# Index

CPSIA information can be obtained
at www.ICGtesting.com
Printed in the USA
LVHW02s2308190618
581245LV00017B/1788/P